PARLIAMENTARY HISTORY: TEXT & STUDIES

13

Pressure and Parliament

T0366591

Pressure and Parliament

From Civil War to Civil Society

Edited by
Richard Huzzey

WILEY
for
THE PARLIAMENTARY HISTORY YEARBOOK TRUST

© 2018 The Parliamentary History Yearbook Trust

John Wiley & Sons

Registered Office
John Wiley & Sons Ltd, The Atrium, Southern Gate, Chichester, West Sussex, PO19 8SQ, UK

Editorial Offices
101 Station Landing, Medford, MA 02155, USA
9600 Garsington Road, Oxford, OX4 2DQ, UK
The Atrium, Southern Gate, Chichester, West Sussex, PO19 8SQ, UK

For details of our global editorial offices, for customer services, and for information about how to apply for permission to reuse the copyright material in this book please see our website at www.wiley.com/wiley-blackwell.

The rights of Richard Huzzey to be identified as the editor of the editorial material in this work has been asserted in accordance with the Copyright, Designs and Patents Act 1988.

Wiley also publishes its books in a variety of electronic formats. Some content that appears in print may not be available in electronic books.

Library of Congress Cataloging-in-Publication Data
Library of Congress Cataloging-in-Publication data is available for this book
A catalogue record for this title is available from the British Library
Set in 10/12pt Bembo
by Aptara Inc., India
Printed and bound in Singapore
by Markono print Media Pte Ltd

1   2018

For the graduate students, faculty, and participants of the
British Historical Studies Colloquium at Yale University.

Parliamentary History: Texts & Studies

Editorial Board

CLYVE JONES (Editor)
Institute of Historical Research, University of London

RICHARD GAUNT
University of Nottingham

DAVID HAYTON
Queen's University, Belfast

HANNES KLEINEKE
History of Parliament

CONTENTS

LIST OF ILLUSTRATIONS

NOTES ON CONTRIBUTORS

Lawrence Goldman is research professor in the Institute for Historical Research, University of London. Editor of the *Oxford Dictionary of National Biography* from 2004–14, he is also the author of *Science, Reform, and Politics in Victorian Britain* (2002) and *The Life of R.H. Tawney* (2013).

Julian Hoppit is the Astor professor of British history at University College London and a fellow of the British Academy. In addition to many articles, he has published *Risk and Failure in English Business, 1700–1800* (1987); *Failed Legislation, 1660–1800* (1987); and *A Land of Liberty? England, 1689–1727* (2000). His latest book, *Parliament and Britain's Political Economies, 1660–1800*, was published in 2017.

Richard Huzzey is a reader in history at Durham University. He has published *Freedom Burning: Anti-Slavery and Empire in Victorian Britain* (2012), and co-edited, with Robert Burroughs, a volume entitled *The Suppression of the Atlantic Slave Trade* (2015). Alongside Henry Miller, he leads the Leverhulme Trust research project 'Re-thinking Petitions, Parliament, and People, 1780–1918'.

Mark Knights is professor of history at the University of Warwick. He has published *Politics and Opinion in Crisis, 1678–1681* (1994); *Representation and Misrepresentation in Later Stuart Britain: Partisanship and Political Culture* (2005); and *The Devil in Disguise: Deception, Delusion and Fanaticism in the Early English Enlightenment* (2011); as well as editing a volume of *The Entring Book of Roger Morrice* (2007), and contributing to *The History of Parliament: The House of Commons 1690–1715* (2002). He is currently writing a history of corruption in Britain and its empire from the Reformation to Reform.

Amanda Moniz is the David M. Rubenstein curator of philanthropy at the National Museum of American History. She received her PhD in history from the University of Michigan and then held a Cassius Marcellus Clay postdoctoral fellowship at Yale University. Her book *From Empire to Humanity: The American Revolution and the Origins of Humanitarianism* was published in 2016.

Sarah Richardson is associate professor of history at the University of Warwick and has published extensively on women and politics in the 19th century. Her latest book is *The Political Worlds of Women: Gender and Political Culture in Nineteenth-Century Britain* (2013).

Stephen Taylor is director of the Institute for Medieval and Early Modern Studies and professor of early modern British history at Durham University. He was co-director of the Clergy of the Church of England project and is one of the investigators for the British State Prayers project. He is a former editor of the *Parliamentary History* Texts & Studies series.

William Whyte is professor of social and architectural history at the University of Oxford and a fellow of St John's College. His latest book is *Redbrick: A Social and Architectural History of Britain's Civic Universities* (2015), and he is currently completing a material history of universities for Harvard University Press.

ACKNOWLEDGEMENTS

All collaborative volumes are the work of many hands, but this one is indebted to scholars beyond those listed as contributing essays. This project was funded by my postdoctoral fellowship in British historical studies at the Macmillan Center for International and Area Studies, Yale University. Steven Pincus and Keith Wrightson, who selected me and the 'pressure' project for a revolutionary opportunity, advised me on the approaches this edited volume should pursue and which individuals I should approach to participate. I am, then, foremost grateful to them and those who subsequently shaped the collection.

A conference in New Haven, in 2010, offered the first opportunity for authors to present their research and discuss the value in rethinking the dynamics of 'pressure and parliament'. We are deeply grateful to all conference attendees for their contributions, but especially to Julia Adams, Becky Conekin, Beverly Gage, Steven Pincus, Frank Prochaska, Brendan Kane, Susan Stokes, Miles Taylor, Adam Tooze, Heather Welland, Alice Wolfram, and Keith Wrightson, all of whom chaired panels or gave papers. The interdisciplinary and comparative presentations were especially helpful in framing histories of pressure and Britain's parliament in a wider context. Marianne Lyden and Katherine Rowe, from the European Studies Council, provided unrivalled support for the event.

The development of contributors' essays has followed me to Plymouth University and then the University of Liverpool, and I appreciate the encouragement and collegiality I have enjoyed in departments of history at both. Likewise, I am grateful to the contributors for their collegiality at every stage of the publication process, and the exceptional generosity of Clyve Jones, for the *Parliamentary History* Texts & Studies series, in shepherding us through a dilatory delivery of the final manuscript.

To end, I must return to the inception of this project at Yale and the intellectual agenda sustained by collaboration with a wide network of scholars since. When early career paths between the doctorate and secure employment are rare and precarious for historians, I am well aware how fortunate I was to enjoy such a generous postdoctoral experience. My time at Yale was transformative, in intellectual and career terms, and I am deeply grateful to Steve, Keith, and the community of the British Historical Studies Colloquium, alongside all of whom I worked in New Haven. The volume is therefore dedicated to them.

Richard Huzzey

Contesting Interests: Rethinking Pressure, Parliament, Nation, and Empire*

RICHARD HUZZEY

This introduction argues for the need to study 'pressure' and the Westminster parliament across three centuries, from roughly 1660 to 1914. While no definition will satisfy all researchers, this essay suggests that the category of 'representative pressure' is useful in highlighting those claims for special consideration by parliament which fell outside either the electoral system of representation or outright defiance of parliamentary sovereignty. By considering the historiography of 'pressure' and the influence of social science models of 'interest groups', the essay argues for a more fluid understanding of pressure as a dynamic rather than a force on parliament from without. A further section examines ways in which those pressuring parliament often championed their interests as national, not selfish or sectional, through examples of imperial pressures and particularly the West India lobby and its enemies. Assaying the contributions of other essays in this volume, the introduction concludes by pointing to the multiplication and institutionalisation of avenues of pressure across this period, rather than a teleological rise of popular sovereignty over parliamentary deliberation.

Keywords: empire; interest groups; lobby; lobbyists; nation; parliament; pressure; representation; slavery; West India interest

1

The essays in this volume seek to broaden and revisit the history of pressure on parliament. Grouped into three thematic sections, the essays range from the 17th to the early 20th centuries. In doing so, these studies link research on older studies of the politics of court and country to contemporary histories of pressure groups. We focus in Part I on methods, in Part II on causes, and in Part III on (very different) constituencies of pressure. The authors of these essays play with 'pressure' as a concept straddling the representative functions of legislators and the broader social constraints in which they operate. In doing so, we are able to examine the ways in which Britons claimed parliament's attention, crystallised in contests over 'interest'.

As generative as this approach may be, it is necessarily selective and our treatment can only be episodic. This introduction offers a conceptualisation of 'pressure' across the varied essays which follow, beginning with a definition of the term and an explanation of our focus on parliament, rather than government. We then consider the pivotal role of 'interest' in our period, separate from the recent category of 'interest group' to describe a particular

*Many thanks to Anna Bocking-Welch, Justin DuRivage, Mark Towsey, and Henry Miller for their comments on this essay, though they bear no responsibility for any calumny or error the author may have included.

kind of political pressure. A third part traces these issues into questions of empire and nation, which recur throughout the volume but otherwise lack consolidated reflection. Finally, we review how these themes of pressure and interest emerge from the essays which follow. Rather than reach for comprehensive coverage, these essays offer future researchers a provocative synthesis on particular forms of pressure on parliament and suggest new ways of understanding them.

2. *Conceptualising Pressure and Parliament*

Since this is a volume about pressure on parliament, it really ought to begin by explaining what that means. We might colloquially speak of all political considerations – the existential threats of war, revolt, or economic ruin, for example – as pressures on legislators' decisions. This certainly fits with the traditional meaning of the English word 'pressure', which mutated from being a medieval bodily ailment to become a 17th-century burden more often imposed by parliament than placed on it. However, the concept of pressure is only useful when disentangled from broader political considerations by defining it in terms of the intention rather than effect. Hence, one of the earliest examples of metaphorical pressure as a 'coercive, persuasive, or dissuasive force' comes from the earl of Monmouth in 1656, describing rebels under 'the pressure of Forrein Princes'. In particular, we should note the 19th-century innovation of putting pressure *on* or bringing pressure *to bear* 'to exert influence to a specific end' especially '*on* a person or thing'.[1]

Political pressure might then be defined by attention to the body causing pressure and the 'specific end' to which it is applied, rather than by attention to the target or effect. Such terminology would undoubtedly include many uses of violence – or threats and fears of violence – deployed outside of a representative system. Over nearly a century, social historians have challenged the historical characterisation of protesters, rioters and rebels as apolitical, cathartic, or impulsive, even if elites in parliament historically failed to recognize this.[2] In particular, the early modernist, Andy Wood, has sought to collapse traditional distinctions between high political history and gritty social history, focusing on the constant negotiation between national potentates and their localities. A generation of scholars' insistence on the 'social depth' of politics encourages us to think about the parliament as a permeable site of reaction rather than the exclusive drama of patricians.[3]

Far from reifying elite parliamentary distinctions, by excluding these unruly pressures on parliament, this volume focuses on the utilisation and subversion of the representative system to pressure the legislature. Essays on the mutability of petitioning – and its close relationship with public assembly – take us into the local politics of constituencies. However, the following essays miss much of the pressure of direct action or violent resistance which clearly overlaps with pressure on parliamentary representatives. We sacrifice scope for

[1] 'pressure, n. 1', *Oxford English Dictionary* online, available at *http://www.oed.com/view/Entry/150823* (accessed 14 Dec. 2015); Graham Wootton, *Pressure Groups in Britain, 1720–1970* (1975), 6, 10.

[2] For recent discussions, see John Bohstedt, *The Politics of Provisions: Food Riots, Moral Economy, and Market Transition in England, c. 1550–1850* (Farnham, 2010), 80–90; David Rollison, *A Commonwealth of the People: Popular Politics and England's Long Social Revolution, 1066–1649* (Cambridge, 2010), 236–91.

[3] Andy Wood, *Riot, Rebellion and Popular Politics in Early Modern England* (Basingstoke, 2002), 8–18 (quotation at p. 8).

coherence, signposting a literature on revolutionary upheaval rather than ignoring it or doing it scant justice.[4] Similarly, the most obvious form of representative pressure, from elections, are already served by a thriving literature, much of it pointing to the ways in which non-electors pressured candidates and voters to represent the whole community even in an age dominated by patronage.[5]

We seek to explore something different, which is the question of which, and whose, representations should be heard alongside, not inside, the electoral process. In doing so, we unearth, historically, the political theorist Michael Saward's observation that we should place extra-electoral links in 'a chain of factors that provide us with a context in which representative claims are made and received'.[6] Hence, we want to explore the space between literatures on electoral contests within the representative system and work on the revolutionary threat of overthrowing parliament. For ease of reference, that space and the action within it might be termed representative pressure – or, simply, pressure.

One clear avenue of representative pressure was the ancient right to petition. As our first essay highlights, this right would be challenged at moments of conflict throughout our period. MPs in the 18th century had proven undecided on whether they were obliged to present all petitions from their constituents, or only those they personally supported.[7] This hesitation did little to abate the popularity of petitioning – in both volume of signatures and petitions – and so led to Peel's creation of a Commons' public petitions committee in 1833, marginalising them from the floor of the lower chamber. Even so, petitions remained an important avenue through which the pressure of public opinion could be constructed, as well as the informed, weighty concerns of a particular interest.[8]

Those exerting pressure implicitly acknowledged parliament's legitimacy or, at the very least, wished to draw attention to ways in which its perceived failures undermined its legitimacy. As such, representative pressures offered formal supplication alongside contention. Indeed, one anonymous author of 1792, reviewing the technical debates over whether the Westminster parliament could reverse its historic support for the slave trade to the West Indies, noted that 'the colonies, either by themselves, their agents, or some of the most respectable individuals among them, have consented or requested to be examined' and hence showed '*acquiescence*, in the power of our legislature, on this subject'.[9] Engagement with

---

[4]See, e.g., discussion of contemporary issues in Wyn Grant and Michael Rush, 'Pressure Politics: The Challenges for Democracy', *Parliamentary Affairs*, lvi (2003), 54–68.

[5]John A. Phillips, *Electoral Behavior in Unreformed England: Plumpers, Splitters, and Straights* (Princeton, NJ, 1982); Francis O'Gorman, *Voters, Patrons, and Parties: The Unreformed Electoral System of Hanoverian England 1734–1832* (Oxford, 1989); James Vernon, *Politics and the People: A Study in English Political Culture, c. 1815–1867* (Cambridge, 1993). See also the constituency entries for *The History of Parliament: The House of Commons, 1820–1832*, ed. D.R. Fisher (7 vols, Cambridge, 2009).

[6]Michael Saward, *The Representative Claim* (Oxford, 2010), 83–5, 92–101 (quotation at p. 108).

[7]See Julian Hoppit's essay in this volume, esp. note 47.

[8]Henry Miller, 'Popular Petitioning and the Corn Laws, 1833–1846', *English Historical Review*, cxxvii (2012), 882–919, see esp. 887–8, 893; David Lemmings, *Law and Government in England During the Long Eighteenth Century: From Consent to Command* (Basingstoke, 2011), 162–4; David Judge, 'Public Petitions and the House of Commons', *Parliamentary Affairs*, xxxi (1978), 391–405; Peter Fraser, 'Public Petitioning and Parliament before 1832', *History*, xlvi (1961), 195–211; Colin Leys, 'Petitioning in the Nineteenth and Twentieth Centuries', *Political Studies*, iii (1955), 45–64; see also forthcoming work by Miles Taylor, *The Sovereign People: Parliament and Representation in Britain since 1750*, and Henry Miller, 'Petitioning and Demonstrating', in *The Oxford Handbook of Modern British Political History, 1800–2000*, ed. David Brown, Robert Crowcroft and Gordon Pentland (Oxford, 2017).

[9]*Remarks on the new sugar-bill, and on the national compacts respecting the sugar-trade and slave-trade* (1792).

the houses of parliament, through individual or corporate addresses, committee evidence, or other forms of pressure, necessarily acknowledged the authority of the target of pressure. This sets pressure on representative institutions apart from the subversive pressures of revolution, disobedience, or violence.

Even so, the technologies of pressure did not rely on procedures established by tradition (or invented tradition) such as petitioning. Long before websites such as 38 Degrees filled parliamentarians' inboxes, legislators known to support – or oppose – a measure might be inundated with correspondence or visits from those seeking to change or ameliorate their view. For example, enormous bundles of Viscount Goderich's papers from the early 1830s attest to the volume and range of representations which he received on issues where he had shown an interest. These included the wages of the poor and the wool tax, quite distant from his cabinet post as colonial secretary, in the form of letters from individuals, addresses from lobbies, or unsolicited pamphlets.[10] In regard to the latter, the practice of dedicating or addressing published tracts to unsuspecting politicians should be seen as a concerted act of pressure. Less speculatively, lobbyists began paying 18th-century doorkeepers to hand out printed material to those entering parliament.[11]

Analysing parliamentary legislation across the 18th century, Joanna Innes and Julian Hoppit conclude that the fact that growing 'positive pressure … was not associated with a general increase in the proportion of abortive initiatives suggests the relative sophistication of many of the interactions involved'; at the same time 'negative pressure' against bills may well have secured amendments rather than the actual failure of legislation. A symbiotic relationship was probably truest of established local or economic interests than of general reformist causes. As Innes and Hoppit suggest, the proliferation of organised pressure followed the annual meetings of parliament introduced in 1688.[12] The creation of corporate lobbies, 'interests', or pressure groups, is clearly a significant trend, exemplified by growing the parliamentary activism of London's livery companies since the Elizabethan period.[13] In an old, but rather good, synthesis of historical research on pressure groups, Graham Wootton emphasized the middle years of the 18th century as a period of formalisation; Lord Rockingham relied on mercantile support to such a degree that he seems to have encouraged public meetings to support commercial measures in parliament. At the same time, the established charter companies lived or died by the preservation of their monopolies, charters or privileges in parliament.[14] Notable here were imperial lobbies, discussed below.

The economic models of pressure groups probably influenced religious and political movements of the 18th century. The Religious Society of Friends, or quakers, developed an elaborate committee structure with members dedicated to persuading parliamentarians of their concerns, thanks to a network of local correspondence. This approach would be

---

[10] West Sussex Record Office, Goodwood MSS, 655–9: Viscount Goderich's parliamentary letters and papers, 1833.

[11] Joanna Innes and Julian Hoppit, 'Introduction', in *Failed Legislation, 1660–1800: Extracted from the Commons and Lords Journals*, ed. Julian Hoppit (1997), 21.

[12] Innes and Hoppit, 'Introduction', 18–22 (quotation at p. 22).

[13] See, e.g., Ian Archer, 'The London Lobbies in the Later Sixteenth Century', *Historical Journal*, xxxi (1988), 17–44; David Dean, 'London Lobbies and Parliament: The Case of the Brewers and Coopers in the Parliament of 1593', *Parliamentary History*, viii (1989), 341–65. On the American roots of later 'lobbyists', see Wootton, *Pressure Groups in Britain*, 4–5.

[14] Wootton, *Pressure Groups in Britain*, 3, 4, 6, 10, 22–4, 38.

copied by other dissenters and Roman catholics in the later 18th century.[15] Meanwhile, radical organisations in support of the political programmes of John Wilkes, Christopher Wyvill, or John Cartwright, walked a fine line between pressure on parliament, demands for admission to the franchise, the exploitation of more inclusive franchises where they existed, and intimidation. The famous Gordon riots, where the presentation of an anti-catholic petition prompted widespread destruction of property in the capital, shows how fragile the borders of representative pressure and violent disobedience could be.[16]

A key inspiration for our volume is the collection *Pressure from Without*, published in 1974 and edited by Patricia Hollis (now Baroness Hollis of Heigham). More than 40 years later, our essays revisit some of the themes from her collection, while expanding beyond the period of early Victorian Britain and also the model of constituted groups or individuals. Her dynamic of 'pressure' at the heart of the changing representative role of parliament still frames our essays, since it is such a fluid and contested space; pressures lies somewhere between the representative functions of elected trustee and corporatist delegate, on the one hand, and the social stability required to avoid revolution, on the other.[17] It is striking that Hollis's essayists stuck to pressure groups as middle class, or at the very least middle-class-led organisations, reflecting a strict division of political history from Chartist and working-class studies in work of the 1970s.[18] Rather than updating entries on well-known Victorian pressure groups or adding essays on earlier movements, our authors were asked to approach pressure by method, broad typology, or unexpected collectivities, rather than through particular groups or issues.

A conceptualisation of pressure through groups probably owes something to research in political science where, during the second half of the 20th century, anxieties about 'pressure groups' in liberal democratic societies became a key focus. As late as 1958, Oxford University Press puffed J.D. Stewart's monograph on the topic with the observation that while 'the influence of pressure groups on government in our country is now very considerable, it is a surprising fact that there has been, hitherto, no serious book about them; the field has been left to American writers, who have naturally been much more interested in their own "lobbyists"'.[19] The 'group' framework of subsequent political studies is reflected in the definition of pressure used by scholars such as Stewart, W.J.M. Mackenzie, and others who remedied this absence of research. They agreed that their subject was 'organized groups possessing both formal structure and real common interests' which 'seek to influence the

[15] Jordan Landes, *London Quakers in the Trans-Atlantic World: The Creation of an Early Modern Community* (Basingstoke, 2015), 30–6, 67–76; Wootton, *Pressure Groups in Britain*, 19–20; see also the special issue on 'Parliament and Dissent', *Parliamentary History*, xxiv (2005).

[16] Eugene Charlton Black, *The Association: British Extraparliamentary Political Organization, 1769–1793* (Cambridge, MA, 1963); Arthur Cash, *John Wilkes: The Scandalous Father of Civil Liberty* (New Haven, CT, 2006); *The Gordon Riots: Politics, Culture and Insurrection in Late Eighteenth-Century Britain*, ed. Ian Haywood and John Seed (Cambridge, 2012); Wootton, *Pressure Groups in Britain*, 47–9, 51.

[17] On the trustee/delegate debate, see, e.g., Andrew Rehfeld, 'Representation Rethought: on Trustees, Delegates, and Gyroscopes in the Study of Political Representation and Democracy', *American Political Science Review*, ciii (2009), 214–30.

[18] *Pressure from Without in Early Victorian England*, ed. Patricia Hollis (1974). Note, however, the different emphasis of case studies assembled in *Popular Movements, c. 1830–1850*, ed. J.T. Ward (1970), where the focus was on the 'popular' not the concept of 'pressure'.

[19] J.D. Stewart, *British Pressure Groups: Their Role in Relation to the House of Commons* (Oxford, 1959), dust jacket.

process of government'.[20] This conceptualisation of political pressure reflected post-war anxieties over the corporatist balance between the interests of capital and labour. Pressure groups could categorise together trades unions, employers' organisations, and those many civil society organisations which did not map neatly onto a Manichean cold war struggle.[21]

In the literature of British political studies, the 'pressure group' remains an ideal type of non-party organisations seeking to influence representative government outside of the electoral process.[22] However, as Jeremy Richardson notes, the conceptualisation of pressure groups has evolved to reflect the societies in which each generation of political scientists live. The decline of unionised labour and the 1980s Conservative ministries' hostility to interest groups shook 1970s models of 'policy communities' between government and groups, while new technology – especially e-petitioning – continues to change the dynamics of pressure. Notwithstanding revision and caveat, however, research from political science departments has been strongly shaped by two sets of binaries.[23] On the one hand, Wyn Grant offers a distinction between insider and outsider groups. The former groups seek to influence politicians and win acceptance as legitimate consultees in their area; the latter groups appeal to the electorate in the hopes of influencing representatives.[24] On the other hand, scholars have tended to draw distinctions between interest groups and cause groups. The former represent a defined social or economic membership, while the latter seek to impose their values on policy makers. If they existed neatly in real life, we could happily categorise the business and labour groups of our period as 'interests' and the religious and political organisations as 'causes'. However, as researchers are well aware, the distinctions tend to collapse in practice.[25]

Such debates amongst political scientists remain provocative for historical research. Most problematic for the purposes of this volume is the shift away from the study of legislators in favour of understanding the executive and, most especially, the civil service as 'the state'. Such a change in research, as well as reality, is reflected by a 1979 work, *Governing Under Pressure*, bearing the subtitle 'The Policy Process in a Post-Parliamentary Democracy'. The main title reflects an emphasis on pluralist pressures beyond corporatism, very much in sympathy with the varied approaches of the essays in the present work.[26] However, our focus on parliament as the object under pressure reflects a conscious desire to explore the

[20] Stewart, *British Pressure Groups*, 1.

[21] Wyn Grant, 'The Changing Pattern of Group Politics in Britain', *British Politics*, iii (2008), 204–22; Leo Panitch, 'Recent Theorizations of Corporatism: Reflections on a Growth Industry', *British Journal of Sociology*, xxxi (1980), 159–87; see also Francis Castles, *Pressure Groups and Political Culture: A Comparative Study* (1967), 1–5.

[22] W.N. Coxall, *Pressure Groups in British Politics* (2001), 2–3.

[23] See Jeremy Richardson, 'Pressure Groups and Parties: A "Haze of Common Knowledge" or Empirical Advance of the Discipline?', in *British Study of Politics in the Twentieth Century*, ed. Jack Hayward, Brian Barry and Archie Brown (Oxford, 1999), 189–94; Jeremy Richardson, 'Government, Interest Groups and Policy Change', *Political Studies*, xlviii (2000), 1006–25; Wyn Grant, 'Pressure Politics: The Changing World of Pressure Groups', *Parliamentary Affairs*, lvii (2004), 408–19.

[24] William Maloney, Grant Jordan and Andrew McLaughlin, 'Interest Groups and Public Policy: The Insider/Outsider Model Revisited', *Journal of Public Policy*, xiv (1994), 17–38.

[25] Rob Baggott, *Pressure Groups Today* (Manchester, 1995), 12–16; Laura Baroni, Brendan J. Carroll, Adam Chalmers, Luz Maria Munoz Marquez and Anne Rasmussen, 'Defining and Classifying Interest Groups', *Interest Groups & Advocacy*, iii (2014), 141–59.

[26] J.J. Richardson and A.G. Jordan, *Governing under Pressure: The Policy Process in a Post-Parliamentary Democracy* (Oxford, 1979); Richardson, 'Pressure Groups and Parties', 192–6.

relationship between interest groups and representative institutions. Hence, our concept of pressure extends beyond 'pressure groups' organised along the lines expected by many political scientists, but focuses on parliament, not government *per se*.

The choice of parliament, of course, reflects the greater salience of parliamentary sovereignty, as a concept, and parliamentary management, as a practice, in the government of the 17th, 18th, and 19th centuries. The particular importance of private legislation, well into the 19th century, anchored a role for parliament as a focus of political pressure, quite aside from ministerial initiative.[27] The rise of partisanship and, consequently, whipped votes, did not eliminate legislators' role as targets for pressure, even if a trend towards executive power was real and is easily detected in our essays.[28] In 1852, W.R. Greg admitted that 'Parliament is no longer the only, nor the chief arena for political debate', but this was not because of greater discipline amongst its members. Rather, he thought organised pressure through campaigns and the press 'takes precedence of the Legislature'.[29] Our focus on parliament rather than government, then, should not be mourned more than the omission of an essay on pressure from the press – though William Whyte's essay explores the latter in terms of intellectual popularisation of parliament's role. Thankfully, there is a strong literature on the importance of the reporting and discussion of parliamentary deliberation in print.[30] Likewise, it is beyond the scope of our volume to consider the pressures of patronage, whether from borough mongers or an interventionist monarch, but these have been discussed in recent issues of *Parliamentary History*.[31] Ultimately, the consistent importance of passing acts – at least until the 20th-century explosion of delegated legislation and ministerial fiat – made parliament a fulcrum of pressure even as other institutions developed.[32]

Our focus on a particular form of pressure allows the authors to consider, in very different ways, contests over the proper representation of interests, which sat at the heart of parliament in this period. It bears emphasizing, though, that a focus on representative pressures on the legislature does not confine our study to pressure on the house of commons. The upper chamber, though not elected, still sought to discriminate a national interest amidst competing pressures on policy. The division of the Houses into commoners and peers represented a medieval schema of corporatism. However, magnates continued to claim legitimacy from their roles as paternalist landlords and disinterested plutocrats.[33] Indeed, the lack of elections

[27] Joanna Innes, 'The Local Acts of a National Parliament: Parliament's Role in Sanctioning Local Action in the Eighteenth Century', in *Parliament and Locality, 1660–1939*, ed. David Dean and Clyve Jones (Edinburgh, 1998), 23–47.

[28] Philip Laundy, *Parliament and the People: The Reality and Public Perception* (Aldershot, 1997), 11–23, 45–50, 53–60; Harry Eckstein, *Pressure Group Politics: The Case of the British Medical Association* (Stanford, CA, 1960), 17–19; Jonathan Parry, 'Patriotism', in *Languages of Politics in Nineteenth-Century Britain*, ed. David Craig and James Thompson (Basingstoke, 2013), 69–92, esp. 81–2; Wootton, *Pressure Groups in Britain*, 6.

[29] As quoted by Patricia Hollis, 'Pressure from Without: An Introduction', in *Pressure from Without in Early Victorian England*, ed. Hollis, 25–6.

[30] Bob Harris, 'Parliamentary Legislation, Lobbying and the Press in Eighteenth-Century Scotland', *Parliamentary History*, xxvi (2007), 76–95.

[31] See, e.g., M.W. McCahill, *The House of Lords in the Age of George III, 1760–1811* (Oxford, 2009), 371.

[32] Harold Laski, 'The Growth of Administrative Discretion', *Public Administration*, i (1923), 92–100; Michael Taggart, 'From "Parliamentary Powers" to Privatization: The Chequered History of Delegated Legislation in the Twentieth Century', *University of Toronto Law Journal*, lv (2005), 575–627.

[33] McCahill, *The House of Lords in the Age of George III*, quotation at p. 363; see also Paul Langford, *Public Life and the Propertied Englishman, 1689–1798* (Oxford, 1990), 191–6.

for members of the house of lords makes their relationship with other pressures of representation all the more clear. In this vein, one of our essays explores the role of the lords spiritual who held a unique position as representatives of, but also conduits for pressure from, the established Church and, eventually, other churches. Our focus on parliament is not a quixotic reassertion of parliamentary government but a choice to study representatives rather than the executive.

3. *Contesting Interests*

Indeed, this choice allows us to explore the idea of interest over the structures of interest groups by studying the changing understandings of legitimate 'interests' and pejorative 'pressure' taken into consideration. British politics remained bound up with the representation, virtually or electorally, of all manner of interests in the houses of parliament, throughout this period; by studying the contests over whose and which interests should be represented, 'pressure' is a serviceable concept to trace the legitimisation of particular methods or particular causes in parliamentary decision making. It also helps us depart from the 'group' emphasis of much political science literature. An excellent recent study of 20th-century non-governmental organizations (NGOs) took the opposite tack, decentring Westminster to focus on groups as communities themselves.[34] The essays which follow focus on the process of pressure and the political ideas contested by different forms of it, rather than the organisation of particular bodies.

The uses of 'interest' within our period of study are particularly helpful in navigating the distinctions between interests and causes which have plagued political scientists.[35] In the 20th century, a body such as the British Medical Association – part union and part lobby – straddled the boundaries between cause groups and interest groups dictated by many typologies.[36] The definition of 'interest' as sectional, and especially economic, clearly encompasses the groups petitioning based on occupation and location, as much historical research on earlier 'lobbying' has emphasized.[37] The second essay of the present volume ably demonstrates the continuing importance of local pressure for economic legislation in the 18th century, re-emphasizing the importance of locality. More generally, the distinction between material self-interest and principled belief is muddied by their constitutive interpretation of each other.[38]

However, claims to special consideration as national, or common, interests cut across all pressures for special consideration by a legislature. The early modern research group led by Mark Knights has shown how the conceptual and political uses of 'commonwealth' mutated from earlier notions of a 'common weal' and then became subsumed in part of a chang-

---

[34] Matthew Hilton, James McKay, Nicholas Crowson and Jean-François Mouhot, *The Politics of Expertise: How NGOs Shaped Modern Britain* (Oxford, 2013).

[35] On which problems, see Baggott, *Pressure Groups Today*, 16; Hilton, McKay, Crowson and Mouhot, *The Politics of Expertise*, 11–12.

[36] Eckstein, *Pressure Group Politics*, 17–19.

[37] David Dean, 'Pressure Groups and Lobbies in the Elizabethan and Early Jacobean Parliaments', *Parliaments, Estates and Representation*, xi (1991), 139–52; Alison Gilbert Olson, *Making the Empire Work: London and American Interest Groups, 1690–1790* (Cambridge, MA, 1992), 2–4.

[38] Note especially Charles Wilson, *Economic History and the Historian: Collected Essays* (1969), 141–5.

ing cosmology of 'public good' and 'public interest'.[39] J.A.W. Gunn long ago argued that 17th-century conflict saw a 'public interest' of aggregated individualism emerge in contradiction to a 'common good' of traditional collectivities.[40] Peter Miller has suggested that 18th-century thinkers drove this shift, and he makes important correctives to the individualistic direction of Gunn's story.[41] Indeed, Paul Langford long ago drew attention to the way 18th-century complainants presented 'a conflict as one which affected the national interest', such as when those transporting coal by sea claimed that inland canals would damage the nation's preparedness for future naval conflict – and not just their own profits.[42] As Rosemary Sweet argues, claims to represent 'public interest' offered even more flexibility than 'the language of nation or kingdom' for local legislation initiated by petition.[43] If the Anti-Corn Law League had, by the 1840s, mastered the art of presenting sectoral concerns as national interests, they were perfecting an old practice.[44] Hence, one of the primary roles for parliament was to resolve competing pressures of interests and construct some sense of the nation's interests.

Indeed, this question of the representation of interests lies at the heart of a dialogue which forms one of the urtexts of the theory of political representation. Though punctuated by the passage of a few centuries, the debate between 18th-century MP, Edmund Burke, and 20th-century theorist, Hanna Pitkin, highlights the crucial question of how interests are properly represented. Burke famously insisted that:

Parliament is not a congress of ambassadors from different and hostile interests, which interests each must maintain, as an agent and advocate, against other agents and advocates; but Parliament is a deliberative assembly of one nation, with one interest, that of the whole.[45]

Pitkin critiques his faith that 'interests are not only broad and objective but additive' alongside his dangerous premise that the best representatives know their constituents' interests better than they might know their own. A distinction between real 'interest' and subjective 'opinion' marks this oligarchic approach, where the opinion of electors or those represented are judged alongside evidence and opinions represented by other sources.[46] However, a

[39] Early modern research group [Mark Knights *et al.*], 'Commonwealth: The Social, Cultural, and Conceptual Contexts of an Early Modern Keyword', *Historical Journal*, liv (2011), 659–87.

[40] J.A.W. Gunn, *Politics and the Public Interest in the Seventeenth Century* (1969), 1–54. On the earlier tradition, see M.S. Kempshall, *The Common Good in Late Medieval Political Thought* (Oxford, 1999).

[41] Peter N. Miller, *Defining the Common Good: Empire, Religion and Philosophy in Eighteenth-Century Britain* (Cambridge, 2004). On the broader literature on interests and economic thought, see, e.g., Albert O. Hirschman, *The Passions and the Interests: Political Arguments for Capitalism before its Triumph* (Princeton, NJ, 1977); Stephen Engelman, *Imagining Interest in Political Thought: Origins of Economic Rationality* (Durham, NC, 2003). For reservations on a shift to individualisation of interests, see Jon Lawrence, 'Paternalism, Class, and the British Path to Modernity', in *The Peculiarities of Liberal Modernity in Imperial Britain*, ed. Simon Gunn and James Vernon (Berkeley, CA, 2011), 147–64.

[42] Langford, *Public Life and the Propertied Englishman*, 204.

[43] Rosemary Sweet, 'Local Identities and a National Parliament, c. 1688–1835', in *Parliaments, Nations and Identities in Britain and Ireland, 1660–1850*, ed. Julian Hoppit (Manchester, 2003), 48–63.

[44] For a superb consideration of this question, see Cheryl Schonhardt-Bailey, *From the Corn Laws to Free Trade: Interests, Ideas and Institutions in Historical Perspective* (Cambridge, MA, 2006), 75–8.

[45] As quoted, appropriately enough, by Hanna Pitkin, *The Concept of Representation* (Berkeley, CA, 1967), 171.

[46] Pitkin, *The Concept of Representation*, 176–87 (quotation at p. 187).

historicist reading, paying attention to the context of Burke's views, has, instead, emphasized that 'the role of Parliament as a legislature was just becoming more important than its role as an overseer of the ministries'. Hence, Burke advocated a *'defensive trusteeship'* against the initiatives of the crown, with representatives judged by electors for their ability rather than their responsiveness to particularly vocal 'instructions' on how to vote. Moreover, Burke offered a polemical, not representative, view of 18th-century parliamentary practices, which was at odds even with his fellow MP returned for Bristol at the 1774 election.[47]

Historians studying early modern and modern Britain have focused on concepts of 'interest' because they dominated the discourse and practice of parliamentary representation. However, the surprisingly slow development of calls to expand the franchise or redraw constituencies, so that MPs could be more representative of economic and demographic changes, suggests that non-electoral pressure on parliament relieved some of the pressure for parliamentary reform.[48] Whether parliament is seen as legislature or scrutineer of executive power, representatives' claims to represent others depended on the extent to which they could discriminate between the proper balance of interests and the weight of sectional concerns. In 1857, the barrister, George Harris, could still argue that the 'numerical theory of representation' should be resisted by placing 'popular interest' in balance with 'interest of virtue', 'interest of intelligence', 'interest of order', 'interest of property', and 'professional interest'.[49] However, the slow expansion of a political community, and with it the electoral franchise, signalled a greater trust in Britons to determine their own best interests and hence their representatives.[50] Consistently, until universal suffrage (in 1918 or 1928 or 1948, depending on how we judge it), parliament relied on claims of 'virtual representation', a phrase of Burke's, to transcend competing interests and discern a common good.[51] In the upper chamber, the lack of electoral mandate made all representation virtual. This only rendered more transparent the two chambers' shared expectations that interests would be represented, not persons, and that the contest of pressure determined whose interests should weigh heaviest in determining legislation.

One of the principal justifications for entertaining pressures beyond the electoral process was the promise of better or broader information than parliamentarians might otherwise possess. Therefore, authentic petitions, expert evidence, and simple lobbying offered some of the principle avenues through which pressure might be accepted. It is in cases where the legitimacy of particular pressures was called into dispute that we can hear parliamentarians debating this conceptual space most clearly. Hence, in 1819, when discussing petitions from anglicans against the relief of Roman catholics, Lord Normanby insisted that 'this is precisely

---

[47] James Conniff, 'Burke, Bristol, and the Concept of Representation', *Western Political Quarterly*, xxx (1977), 329–41, esp. 332, 340; Richard Bourke, *Empire and Revolution: The Political Life of Edmund Burke* (Princeton, NJ, 2015), 379–87; David Eastwood, 'Parliament and Locality: Representation and Responsibility in Late-Hanoverian England', *Parliamentary History*, xvii (1998), 68–81.

[48] Paul Langford, 'Property and "Virtual Representation" in Eighteenth-Century England', *Historical Journal*, xxxi (1988), 83–115.

[49] Pitkin, *The Concept of Representation*, 189.

[50] For the broader concepts of democracy, besides expansion of the franchise, see Robert Saunders, 'Democracy', in *Languages of Politics in Nineteenth-Century Britain*, ed. David Craig and James Thompson (Basingstoke, 2013), 142–67; John Garrard, *Democratisation in Britain: Elites, Civil Society and Reform since 1800* (Basingstoke, 2002); Pitkin, *The Concept of Representation*, 190, 198–208.

[51] On these issues, see also J.A.W. Gunn, 'Jeremy Bentham and the Public Interest', *Canadian Journal of Political Science*, i (1968), 398–413; Langford, 'Property and "Virtual Representation"'.

the subject where these petitions ought constitutionally, to have the least effect in pre-judging the fair examination of the case' because they 'can here afford no local information' or 'affect no separate interest' not possessed by parliamentarians, who were all adherents of the Church of England themselves.[52]

While Normanby sought to marginalise pressure when it did not correct for under-representation of interests or concerns amongst peers or MPs, his point raises a broader issue. Pressure was rarely truly from without, since those proposing private legislation or opposing ministerial initiatives would often have allies within one or both chambers. Michael McCahill's recent study of the Lords during the reign of George III, for example, shows how various religious, economic, or philosophical groupings acted as reliable champions of particular causes in the upper chamber. Individuals with a personal or family connection to a concern would act as a bridge to extra-parliamentary pressure, whether in the Commons or the Lords.[53] Peers 'devoted substantial time and resources to forwarding in parliament the projects of dependants, neighbours, and more remote connections'.[54] Indeed, members of both Houses remained integrated with local political structures through which pressure could be applied by a respectable body, such as justices of the peace or a borough corpora-tion.[55] As a previous volume from *Parliamentary History* showed, the early medieval function of parliament as the forum for local representation to crown government continued, despite the evolution from periodic assemblies to standing, legislative sessions.[56]

4. *Empire, Nation, and the Pressure of Interests*

In determining whose interests are being represented to parliamentarians in a calculation of common interests, our authors all consider the importance of a national or imperial imagi-nary. However, without an essay of its own, this aspect might be overlooked, since it features rather than frames the essays which follow. Certainly, Julian Hoppit's essay foregrounds the balancing role of the Westminster parliament with the same attention to the interactions of four nations and national institutions as he has highlighted in his earlier work.[57] He demon-strates the dominant role of English petitioners to parliament, but this does not mean that the other three 'home' nations or the colonies overseas are neglected. Hoppit's case study of duties imposed on Irish yarn shows how English trade groups, especially in the south-west, lobbied for their sectional interests while promoting a particular economic development of Ireland to complement, rather than compete with, their industries. Such tensions were well known enough that Sarah Richardson, in her essay, finds the Victorian author, Anna Jameson, using the Westminster parliament's legislation on Ireland as a simile for male legis-lation governing women. The complex interplay of locality and sectoral interests is further

[52] Hansard, *Parl. Debs*, 1st ser., xl, col. 67: 3 May 1819.

[53] McCahill, *The House of Lords in the Age of George III*, 337–62.

[54] McCahill, *The House of Lords in the Age of George III*, quotation at p. 363; see also Langford, *Public Life and the Propertied Englishman*, 191–6.

[55] Sweet, 'Local Identities and a National Parliament', 48–63.

[56] David Dean, 'Introduction: Parliament and Locality from the Middle Ages to the Twentieth Century', in *Parliament and Locality*, ed. Dean and Jones, 1–11.

[57] Julian Hoppit, 'Introduction', in *Parliaments, Nations and Identities in Britain and Ireland, 1660–1850*, ed. Julian Hoppit (Manchester, 2003), 1–14.

illustrated by the influence of financiers over the City of London's common council and other local institutions, which made their views felt in pushing Walpole's ministry towards war with Spain in 1739. In the final decades of the 18th century, the emergence of manufacturers' organisations marked a shift away from associations explicitly representing particular cities, though regional specialisation still encouraged geographical affinities.[58]

Beyond the British archipelago, the following chapters find plenty of evidence of pressure on parliament from colonists and imperial interests. Amanda Moniz's examination of moral reform and humanitarian movements traces an enlarged frame of reference to Atlantic, and later global, concerns in which parliamentarians might be pressured to operate. Where baser concerns prevailed in business lobbies, strong work already exists on the role of colonial agents and merchants in demanding virtual representation in Westminster. Recent work by Heather Welland considers how Britain's most northerly American colonies were shaped by commercial lobbyists in the 17th and 18th centuries, while Andrew Smith shows how finance and business created the terms of their confederation as Canada in 1867.[59]

The American revolution offers one ideal example of the politics of pressure. Conflict over the extent to which the interests and rights of colonists had been defended, despite their lack of electoral representation, lay at the core of their grievances. Jack Greene sees the doctrine of virtual representation first articulated to justify the Stamp Act during 1764–5.[60] Intriguingly, given his Conservative views on the independence of MPs from their constituents, Burke sympathised with the need for representative institutions in the colonies, given their size and remoteness in comparison with other communities represented virtually, rather than actually.[61] However, American disenchantment with parliament lay at the core of the movement towards independence. The most odious impositions on American Britons came in the form of laws and taxes passed by parliament under pressure from other interests, such as the Molasses Act. As Alison Olson expertly traces, the failure of interest-group politics in the second half of the 18th century was a harbinger for the popular crisis of the 1780s.[62] In that context, James Bradley's path-breaking work on popular politics back in Britain revealed the complex interplay of business groups, pamphleteers, and local petitioning amongst the colonists' sympathisers. In particular, he notes how friends of the Americans turned to petitions to the monarch only once parliament had rejected their entreaties.[63] In both the politics of colonial policy which sparked the revolutionary crisis and the popular appeals during the crisis, the war of independence illustrates a labyrinth of pressures on parliament.[64]

---

[58] Wootton, *Pressure Groups in Britain*, 28–9, 42; Francis G. James, 'The Irish Lobby in the Early Eighteenth Century', *English Historical Review*, lxxxi (1966), 543–57.

[59] Heather Welland, 'Interest Politics and the Shaping of the British Empire, 1688–1839', University of Chicago PhD, 2011; Andrew Smith, *British Businessmen and Canadian Confederation: Constitution-Making in an Era of Anglo-Globalization* (Montreal, QC, 2008).

[60] Jack P. Greene, *The Constitutional Origins of the American Revolution* (Cambridge, 2011), 68–9.

[61] Bourke, *Empire and Revolution*, 297–8.

[62] Olson, *Making the Empire Work*.

[63] James Bradley, *Popular Politics and the American Revolution in England: Petitions, the Crown, and Public Opinion* (Macon, GA, 1986), 38–40, 91–120, ch. 4.

[64] See in particular, Justin duRivage, *Revolution against Empire: Taxes, Politics, and the Origins of American Independence* (New Haven, CT, 2017).

A sidelight on this transition lies in the politics of Britain's West Indian colonies in the long 18th century. Slave-owning proprietors in the sugar colonies relied on both familial parliamentary representation, and sophisticated paid lobbyists. As Perry Gauci has shown, the planting interest defended 'their supposed public spiritedness and right to special consideration'.[65] While the Royal Africa Company had failed to defend its monopoly on slave trading against West Indians' desire for cheaper captives, the proprietors themselves had a very good run shaping the legislation of the imperial parliament to reflect their interests.[66] The sugar barons succeeded in preventing free trade in sugar into North America, with the 1733 Molasses Act. They also won their own liberty to sell to Europe, with the Sugar Act of 1739. That year, William Beckford, scion of a planter family, made his first appearance in parliament, pressing for the West Indian cause; his career would see him elected lord mayor of London and become exemplar of Caribbean power over parliament (as well as within it). At the conclusion of the Seven Years' War, the sugar magnates succeeded in pushing for the annexation of Quebec rather than French sugar islands which might compete with their own estates.[67]

Their talents in fighting rival imperial lobbies, such as those of the East Indies, did not extend to the cultivation of wider support through popular print since, as one planter noted in the mid 18th century, 'doing thereof would be an appeal to the public in a matter wherein they are not judges or concerned'.[68] This reluctance is echoed in the confused disgust of the MP, Colonel Phipps, who, faced with hundreds of petitions for slave-trade abolition in 1792, insisted that 'the right of the subject to petition' was 'restrained to those who had an interest in the thing which was the subject matter of petition'.[69] That complaint cuts to the heart of the campaign which ultimately defeated the sugar interest, since anti-slavery activists made a virtue of their disinterest.

The abolitionists' success in pressing for an expansion in the understanding of the right to petition was just one of the innovations where they catalysed an expansion in the causes and methods of parliamentary pressure.[70] In making use of synchronised local petitions, Thomas Clarkson and his colleagues borrowed from traditions of municipal petitioning and the reform organisations of the past three decades. In theory and in practice, abolitionists borrowed from the corresponding campaigns of the quakers. And a commercial man, such as Josiah Wedgwood, who designed the 'Am I Not a Man and Brother?' cameo, brought consumerist tactics alongside his experience in founding the General Chamber of

[65] Perry Gauci, 'Learning the Ropes of Sand: The West India Lobby, 1714–60', in *Regulating the British Economy, 1660–1850*, ed. Perry Gauci (Farnham, 2011), 107–21 (quotation at p. 113).

[66] William A. Pettigrew, *Freedom's Debt: The Royal African Company and the Politics of the Atlantic Slave Trade, 1672–1752* (Chapel Hill, NC, 2013), 112–3.

[67] Richard Sheridan, *Sugar and Slavery: An Economic History of the British West Indies, 1623–1775* (Baltimore, MD, 1974), 68–71, 426–33; Wootton, *Pressure Groups in Britain*, 27, 40; Perry Gauci, *William Beckford: First Prime Minister of the London Empire* (New Haven, CT, 2013), 37–8; Perry Gauci, 'The Attack of the Creolian Powers: West Indians at the Parliamentary Elections of Mid-Georgian Britain, 1754–74', *Parliamentary History*, xxxiii (2014), 201–22.

[68] Rose Fuller, as quoted by Gauci, 'Learning the Ropes of Sand', 116.

[69] *The Parliamentary History of England from the Earliest Period to the Year 1803*, ed. William Cobbett (36 vols, 1805–20), xxix, 1241.

[70] See also *The Correspondence of Stephen Fuller, 1788–1795: Jamaica, the West India Interest at Westminster and the Campaign to Preserve the Slave Trade*, ed. Michael McCahill (Oxford, 2014).

Manufacturers just a few years earlier.[71] The sum total of these efforts was a sustained campaign of pressure from 1787 to 1792. However, fear of revolution spreading from France
led to Pitt the Younger's repression of civil liberties from 1793 onwards. Efforts to suppress
British revolutionaries also affected the respectable pressure of abolitionist petitioners. Yet,
if fear of revolution could disrupt representative pressures, it might also act as an acceler-
ant for them. The popular mobilisation of anti-slavery campaigners would be remembered
long after the war-time repression of public assembly.[72] Popular agitation in favour of the
abolition of the slave trade, repeatedly backed by the Commons and killed by the Lords,
triumphed in 1807 and indicated a new precedent for 'the Lords' relations with the broader
public', in the judgment of Michael McCahill.[73]

In many ways, the defeat of the West India interest by a new cause, forged from diverse 18th-century technologies of pressure, mirrors a narrative of political 'modernization'
favoured by some authors.[74] Certainly, the case study illustrates the broadening of political
debate and the mobilisation of public pressure on parliament rather than simply lobbying
parliamentarians. However, the success of West Indian proprietors in securing generous
compensation for the abolition of slavery in the 1830s, together with the continuing power
of business groups, makes a neat narrative of succession somewhat misleading.[75] Rather,
new opportunities for pressure could be accepted alongside old ones. This is particularly
true when we consider not only the well-known expansion of the political community, and
hence the franchise, within the British Isles, but also in the adaptation of pressure tactics
by colonized peoples across the empire. In the 1830s, 'native' residents of India petitioned
Westminster over issues including the expansion of anglophone courts and the exclusion
of Indians from civil offices.[76] As the following essays suggest, our period does not mark a
linear development of particular kinds of pressure.

5. *Methods, Objectives and Constituencies of Pressure*

Having apologised for the omissions, sleights and lacunae necessarily involved in our enterprise, we may turn, suitably chastened, to review the actual arguments advanced in these
essays. To begin the collection, Mark Knights, in his examination of the right to petition,
explores contests over the groups and causes which might be permitted to use this avenue
of pressure. As he shows, 17th-century conflicts over popular and parliamentary sovereignty
resurfaced in historically-informed subsequent battles. The right of petition was seen by its

---

[71] John Oldfield, *Popular Politics and British Anti-Slavery: The Mobilisation of Public Opinion against the Slave Trade*
(Manchester, 1995), 155–9; Judith Jennings, *The Business of Abolishing the British Slave Trade, 1783–1807* (1997),
39; Wootton, *Pressure Groups in Britain*, 42.

[72] Seymour Drescher, 'Whose Abolition? Popular Pressure and the Ending of the British Slave Trade', *Past &
Present*, No. 143 (1994), 136–66.

[73] McCahill, *The House of Lords in the Age of George III*, 255.

[74] E.g., Wootton, *Pressure Groups in British Politics*, 11–13.

[75] Nicholas Draper, *The Price of Emancipation: Slave-Ownership, Compensation and British Society at the End of
Slavery* (Cambridge, 2009).

[76] C.A. Bayly, *Recovering Liberties: Indian Thought in the Age of Liberalism and Empire* (Cambridge, 2012), 33, 64.
Note also the kind of impersonation of Indian petitioners discussed by Robert Travers, 'Contested Despotism:
Problems of Liberty in British India', in *Exclusionary Empire: English Liberty Overseas, 1600–1900*, ed. Jack Greene
(Cambridge, 2010), 191–219.

supporters as a guarantee of redress and a right to appeal, without which violent resistance would be justified. Detractors – from the English revolution to the French revolution – associated the absolute right to petition with seditious insubordination. It is striking to find 17th-century history at the heart of 1790s debates between figures such as Pitt the Younger and Charles James Fox, where they contested whether the restriction or encouragement of petitioning guaranteed parliamentary legitimacy. Beyond the right to petition in the abstract, Knights shows that the conduct and tenor of petitioning was also a matter for regular dispute. The peaceable, orderly organisation of petitions in their communities was clearly one such requirement. Reformers such as Christopher Wyvill, in the 1780s, sought to yoke the right to petition alongside the rights to assemble and speak freely in formulating these prayers to parliament. The 1795 Seditious Acts helped fuse this conception of interlinked political rights, since the tories lumped these popular disturbances together. The balance between appeal and demand was a question of language which concealed crucial political calculations about sovereignty.

Sarah Richardson continues this theme into the 19th century, when she examines the female majority of Britons whose formal and informal pressure on parliamentary deliberations expanded over our period. Petitions, alongside commissions and committees, offered women a voice in parliamentary deliberations long before they could offer their voices in either chamber of parliament. Richardson's argument is intimately tied to evolutions in parliamentary practice and hence avenues for pressure beyond those within the male pale of the constitution. Like other essays in this volume, she decentres the struggle for the franchise in order to explore the broader context in which women's expertise and opinions could shape parliamentary action. As such, Richardson's essay looks at a constituency of women who did find ways to pressure parliament across a variety of different issues, before campaigns for women's suffrage crystallised at the end of the century.

Contests, of whose interests should properly be pursued by parliament as national interests, sit at the heart of Julian Hoppit's essay on economic petitioning. He cites the commercial author Malachy Postlethwayt's dictum that 'opposite and contradictory petitions to parliament from traders … often tend to mislead, and even confound the legislature itself'.[77] However, as Hoppit suggests, historians have been too ready to presume economic policy is led by Westminster and shaped or resisted by the pressures of outsiders. Rather, the conception and initiative of measures originated outside parliament; the pressures were often original, not reactive or distortive of some *a priori* legislative agenda. Indeed, Hoppit's sample of petitions in the period 1660–1800 reveals that one of the most active groups of petitioners was local governments, mostly urban corporations: hence, many parliamentary petitions rested upon the prior mediation of civic institutions to assess interests worthy of corporate representation to Westminster. The second of Hoppit's two case studies, on petitions from the landowning proponents and borough opponents of improved navigation on the river Nene, in Northamptonshire, ably illustrates this. Readers of his essay will soon see that 'pressure' is most helpfully understood in the interplay of local institutions and parliament, rather than merely as a competition between different sectional interests.

Two essays in this volume examine reform in terms of broad objectives. These studies of moral reform and social reform movements, respectively, synthesise new and existing

---

[77] Malachy Postlethwayt, *The Universal Dictionary of Trade and Commerce* (2 vols, 1751–5), i, p. vi.

research on these families of reformist movements. Necessarily overlapping in scope, the interpretations by Amanda Moniz and Lawrence Goldman make sense of the wide range of campaigns which increasingly looked to parliament as the machine for realizing the moral regeneration or social 'progress' they wished to see. In both cases, they show how calls for parliamentary action are only comprehensible as part of broader movements in society; moreover, overt requests for parliamentary action tended to be married to insider championship of causes by parliamentarians or well-connected elites themselves. Hence, for these two authors 'pressure' is just part of a wider connectivity of society and parliament, which makes most sense when understood as a mode of action for reform ideals also promoted in, or beyond, legislative circles.

At the end of our second part, Goldman explores pressures for social reform by examining the creation of this topic as a political and historiographical objective. Here, a changing notion of historical progress forged growing expectations of parliamentary leadership in social reform, which he traces through the development of ideas. Goldman shows how histories of social reform, offering more or less credit to bureaucrats, structural pressures, or ideas, have reflected historians' contemporary experiences of politics. He examines how successive generations have understood pressure for social reform in light of 'pressure' in their own time. Hence, he notes how a 'tory interpretation' of the internalised growth of 19th-century bureaucracy gave way, by the 1970s, to a 'pressure group' model. Influenced by the vigour of the Campaign for Nuclear Disarmament (CND) and other civil society groups in contemporary political culture, such models gradually gave way to a focus on technocratic expertise in the final decades of the 20th century. In place of these approaches, Goldman proposes a high-level interpretation of how ideas and the political context of reform have formed a tempo – or mood – of wavering ambition, within which specific, contingent movements have prospered or faltered. Arising from his own research on the Social Science Association, he suggests an interpermeability of external pressure, expert opinion, and parliamentary initiative is often lost without an intellectual history of this topic. In this sense, his essay reaffirms our collection's emphasis on pressure as a dynamic spanning methods, causes, and constituencies for pressure.

In our third part, Moniz instructively delineates three periods of moral reform broadly focused on European, Atlantic, and global frames of reference; she not only examines imperial but also transnational influences on the targets of philanthrophy for those pressuring parliament from the 17th to the 20th centuries. Indeed, she finds the shifting focus on moral reformers helped establish parliament as the proper *locus* of action and pressure. In the early 18th century, many projects still adopted voluntarist evangelisation of particular causes to fellow Britons (or others oversees). By the end of that century, Moniz notes a tendency to focus on parliamentary redress of moral ills more readily, but still as components only of broader programmes of social suasion and voluntary association. In particular, she highlights the important role of humanitarians in stimulating early parliamentary involvement in medical affairs before public health become a developed focus on government action.

Two other essays re-examine concepts of pressure in relation to broad social groups, but they escape the economic or class dimensions of much literature on pressure. Richard Huzzey and Stephen Taylor's chapter shows how the bishops in the house of lords evolved a mediating role for religious pressure on parliament, after being an early target for critical pressure from without. As parliamentarians themselves, the lords spiritual held a unique role as representatives of the state Church and avenues for pressing its corporate interests.

However, as the essay shows, the bishops developed a far more innovative role as champions of pressure groups outside parliament, including other christian sects who did not benefit from this privileged role. This essay, then, shows both the hollowing out of new avenues for pressure within established institutions and also the important role of interested parliamentarians as bridgeheads for pressure.

William Whyte's essay considers the pressure exerted by intellectuals – a necessarily amorphous and inchoate category. Britain's universities rarely played the part of 'core of rebellion', accorded to them by Thomas Hobbes in the 17th century. However, Whyte identifies a growing public role for 'men of letters' in both universities and the burgeoning public prints from the 18th century onwards. In some formations, such as the mid-Victorian Social Science Association, intellectuals consciously sought to impose their academic rigour on a programme of legislation. By contrast, elected dons as MPs, for university or other seats, found themselves poor instruments for any programmatic initiative. Persuasively, Whyte points our attention away from tracing the influence or pressure of particular thinkers or schools and, instead, towards the crucial role intellectuals played in acting as interpreters of parliamentary government to parliamentarians and their wider public.

Taken together, these essays suggest a proliferation and concentration of pressures on parliament, as more Britons took advantage of existing avenues, for more reasons, and expanded the boundaries to create new forms of representative pressure. This remains, however, a thickening of pressure rather than a change in absolute types, except for very specific cases such as the decline of private legislation. In order to construct a model of political modernisation in Britain, Samuel Beer famously suggested in his 1965 study that Britain had developed from (i) a 'functional' 18th-century 'parliamentarism', into (ii) an 'associationist' Victorian pluralism, back to (iii) a 'functional' post-war collectivism. The essays in this volume suggest very long tails and overlaps for these modes, and Beer surely misjudged the degree to which individualism and 'strong moralism' of Victorians distinguished the reformed from unreformed parliaments.[78] Rather than seeing coherent ages, we might, instead, see mutating forms of pressure, expanding or contracting in the space available alongside forms of electoral participation and fears of revolution. Hence, between 1660 and 1900 we can see a striking shift in parliament's relationship to the country – the trite 'from civil war to civil society' periodising our volume's title – through a host of salutatory innovations rather than whiggish gradualism or stadial depatures. A very real growth in the number and permeability of channels for pressure on parliament should not distract from the instability within that general trend. This may seem a rather weak conclusion, but these essays suggest pressure is an imagined dynamic in a representative system rather than some fixed element. Crucially, the borders between formal interests, of economic sectors or groups, and general causes, of belief, were far more porous than is often recognized. We, therefore, have more to gain by exploring the dynamics of pressures on parliament through methods, concerns, and constituencies than stretching the metaphorical concept of pressure into a teleology.

---

[78]Samuel Beer, *Modern British Politics: Parties and Pressure Groups in the Collectivist Age* (1982), 16–48, 398 (quotation at p. 46).

'The Lowest Degree of Freedom': The Right to Petition Parliament, 1640–1800

MARK KNIGHTS

The essay examines the right to petition from the revolutions of the 17th century to the start of the age of reform. It shows that, by legislating for a right to petition the monarch, the revolution of 1688 appeared to resolve some of the uncertainty about the right to petition that had been apparent since the 1640s, but failed to confirm a right to petition parliament and left considerable ambiguities about the legitimacy of popular pressure exerted in this way. Throughout the 18th century, the right to petition parliament, and hence to exert popular pressure on it, thus remained contested. Indeed, a history of the points of conflict in Georgian Britain could be written through a study of petitioning controversies. Government supporters asserted the supremacy of formal parliamentary representation over informal representation of the popular voice through petitions and frequently sought to curtail, limit and emasculate any right to petition, and even, in 1795, to ban public petitioning altogether. Such attacks, nevertheless, provoked strong responses: claims to popular sovereignty over parliament, to natural rights, and to the notion that the right to petition was part of a set of interlinking rights of free speech and assembly. The 18th-century arguments were also played out with explicit reference to 17th-century ones, with the 1689 settlement in particular, providing a key reference point.

Keywords: delegates; instructions; petition(ing); popular sovereignty; popular voice; redress of grievances; representation; rhetoric; rights

1

Petitioning was a routine and ubiquitous way of lobbying, influencing and pressurising parliament. It was an activity undertaken by all social groups, from the lowest to the highest, and was used in the local, national and imperial arenas. The range of subjects that could be treated by petition was vast, ranging from the personal and individual to the grievances of a nation, from religion, trade, politics and war to social and moral issues.[1] Yet attention has more often been paid to individual petitioning campaigns than to the broader culture and genre of petitioning. David Zaret has gone some way to correct this by suggesting that

---

[1] This essay focuses on the national political culture, but petitioning was, of course, important at the local level as a means of communication of grievances and of doing business. The contest over the right to petition at the national level thus had important implications for the conduct of local governance and the economy. I consider some of these issues in 'Regulation and Rival Interests in the 1690s', in *Regulating the British Economy, 1660–1850*, ed. Perry Gauci (Farnham, 2011) but there is scope for a much larger treatment of petitions focused on local issues, many of which were economic and social in nature. See also Rab Houston, *Peasant Petitions: Social Relations and Economic Life on Landed Estates, 1600–1850* (Basingstoke, 2014).

17th-century petitioning constituted the 'origins of democratic culture'.[2] Until the collapse of censorship in 1641, he argues, mass petitions had normally been manuscript productions arising from local grievances, but thereafter were routinely published and engaged with national affairs. This change had, he argues, a series of unforeseen consequences. One was to create a process of dialogue – or more often, vituperative exchange – between petitioner and counter-petitioner that proved very difficult to end; another was that petitions came to address the public as much as their ostensible recipient and thus to stimulate the development of public opinion. Petitioning thus underwent, but also produced, Zaret suggests, major innovation.

This essay will explore, for a longer time span than Zaret attempted, a paradox that his work nicely highlights: petitioning adopted innovative practices that constituted and invoked the power of public opinion, but petitioners and their critics were often reluctant to embrace such pressure as a legitimate political force.[3] Petitioning thus exposed ambivalence about the legality, appropriateness, authenticity and acceptability of popular pressure on parliament. But whereas Zaret sees the triumph of a 'liberal-democratic model of the political order' by the end of the 17th century, I argue that this process continued to be a vigorously-contested one throughout the 18th century.[4] This is demonstrable through a study of the right to petition, which Zaret does not discuss at any length but which remained controversial long after the period covered by his study. Indeed, for much of the second half of the 18th century the right to petition parliament was the subject of major dispute.

The ambivalence and contest about petitioning can be highlighted by examining the disputed right to petition, since that raised interesting questions about how far popular pressure could legitimately be brought to bear on parliament. The disputed right to petition the legislature (as opposed to the monarch) remained a rather ill-defined area of the law and provoked a number of intersecting controversies. One arose over whether, if there was a right to petition, it had any limitations (especially if it could be used improperly) and whether it applied equally to petitioning the crown and parliament. Controversy also revolved around the relationship between a popular right to petition and the right of representatives to act on behalf of petitioners. The right to petition was frequently stated in ways that threatened the monopoly of the house of commons, or parliament more generally, to act as the voice of the people. Intrinsic to this debate was a question about whether petitions were a better gauge of public opinion than MPs (especially when parliament was perceived as corrupt). It was also debated whether petitions could be used to instruct or mandate representatives how to act. Arguments raged over whether a right to petition bound either parliament or the monarch to act on the grievances raised by petitioners; in other words, what *duties* the right implied. Some claimed that, if there was a right to petition, those in authority *had* to listen to and redress the grievances of the petitioners, otherwise the right was meaningless, and even suggested a right to resist when petitions were repeatedly ignored;

---

[2]David Zaret, 'Petitions and the "Invention" of Public Opinion in the English Revolution', *American Journal of Sociology*, ci (1996), 1497–555; David Zaret, *Origins of Democratic Culture. Printing, Petitions and the Public Sphere in Early-Modern England* (2000). For earlier petitioning, see R.W. Hoyle, 'Petitioning as Popular Politics in Sixteenth-Century England', *Historical Research*, lxxv (2002), 365–89.

[3]Zaret, *Origins*, 257.

[4]Zaret, *Origins*, 265.

but others denied every element of this stance, rejecting the idea that petitions were in any sense binding or could ever justify rebellion. Finally, there was a set of issues concerning what type of right was at stake. Some saw it as a customary and historical right; others as a right established by statute law; others, as a natural right (and some all of these). It was also disputed whether it was a right enjoyed in isolation from other rights or whether it was intrinsically linked to the right to assembly and free speech.

Before tackling these questions, however, it is worth trying to set out some of the contours of petitioning activity in 1640–1800, to provide the context for such a discussion. I have, elsewhere, made an initial attempt to map the national waves of subscriptional activity to crown and parliament on controversial 'public' issues.[5] Despite the problems in compiling the data, it is clear that mass petitioning – by which I mean petitions signed by thousands of subscribers or which came in mass numbers – was most prolific in the period 1640–1720 and, again, after 1780. The quantity of petitions and addresses in the first of these periods is impressive, and many, especially during the mid-17th-century revolution, at the Restoration and during the succession crisis in Charles II's reign, sought to put pressure directly on parliament. Even so, a good deal of the subscriptional activity was less direct: the flood of addresses in this period was often aimed (ostensibly at least) at the crown, even though there is a close correlation between the addressing activity and electioneering. Four factors towards the end of the 18th and early 19th centuries – anti-slavery, parliamentary reform, repression in the wake of the French revolution, and contentious religious legislation (catholic emancipation, the repeal of the Test and Corporation Acts) served to expand petitioning campaigns into mass movements that aimed to represent extra-parliamentary views and exert political pressure on parliament.[6] By the early 19th century, and arguably far earlier, petitioning was 'an integral part of the system of political representation'.[7] Indeed, it was a key means of 'informal representation', as opposed to formal representation in parliament. It was not until the 20th century, once mass democracy had been established, that petitioning faded as a means of representation, though arguably e-petitioning has recently rehabilitated the genre.

2

Although petitioning had long been a feature of English governance, establishing a right to petition was largely the work of the 17th century. But that was an uncertain and incomplete process that left many key issues unresolved and open to challenge. The first section of this

---

[5] Mark Knights, 'Participation and Representations before Democracy: Petitions and Addresses in Pre-Modern Britain', in *Political Representation*, ed. Ian Shapiro, Susan C. Stokes, Elizabeth Jean Wood and Alexander S. Kirshner (Cambridge, 2009); Mark Knights, *Representation and Misrepresentation in Later Stuart Britain: Partisanship and Political Culture* (Oxford, 2005), ch. 3. Except where they impinged on national events, my analysis tends to downplay the importance of local, economic petitioning, though this is discussed in Julian Hoppit's contribution to this volume. I have also interpreted 'petition' broadly to include multiple forms of subscriptional activity.

[6] Peter Fraser, 'Public Petitioning and Parliament before 1832', *History*, xlvi (1961), 195–6. The 1842 Chartist 'Grand Petition' had 3,317,702 signatures, was more than six miles in length, and was accompanied by a crowd of 50,000 people when it was carted to Westminster. The chartists gained 1.2 million signatures in 1839; 1.4 million in 1841; and 2 million in 1848, more than twice the size of the electorate.

[7] Paul Pickering, 'And your Petitioners &C: Chartist Petitioning in Popular Politics 1838–48', *English Historical Review*, cxvi (2001), 368–88 (quotation at p. 374).

essay lays out this rather piecemeal process, in order to highlight moments when a debate over the right to petition raged in, and outside, parliament. Charting these controversies also serves to show how the contest over the right to petition was part of a wider debate about the proper relationship between parliament and people, and show how petitioning frequently became an intrinsic part of political division. The second section of the essay will then consider the arguments used to deny, limit, or undermine, a right to petition, and the responses these provoked.

Although petitioning was a central feature of the conflicts of 1640–60, establishing a right proved much more difficult.[8] The value of public petitioning was recognized by both sides during the mid-century revolution but so, too, was the need to delegitimise rivals' petitioning activity, either by attempting to proscribe it or to categorise it as seditious or defective in some way. The ambiguity was all too obvious, for example, in 1647 when the conflict between parliament and army was played out through petitions, and led to the army coup. In March 1647, fears that parliament wanted to disband troops without giving them indemnity and paying arrears provoked the army's 'Large Petition'. This, in turn, prompted parliament's so-called 'declaration of dislike' of the petition and imprisonment of some of its promoters, a move that ruined already strained relations between parliament and the army. The army duly remonstrated that parliament's action represented an infringement of 'the liberty of the subject to petition' and asserted that 'sure there is a right of petitioning for us'.[9] A petition drawn up by army officers in April (quoting a parliamentary declaration of 2 November 1642) asserted that it was 'the liberty and privilege of the people to petition [parliament] for the ease and redresse of their grievances and oppressions'. It added that the liberty of petitioning was 'the lowest degree of freedom'.[10] In June 1647, a further army representation requested that the right to petition parliament should be 'cleared and vindicated'.[11] But parliament failed to come up with this clarification and pushed on with trying to disband the army, provoking the latter to seize the king.

Indeed, far from ceding the right to petition, parliament sought to curb it. On 20 May 1648, in the wake of a wave of royalist-inspired petitions urging accommodation with the king and the Kentish rising, MPs issued a declaration 'For the suppressing of all Tumultuous Assemblies, under pretence of framing and presenting petitions to Parliament', thereby linking the issues of petitioning and assembly in ways that were to become very significant. The

[8] For the role of petitioning, see Anthony Fletcher, *The Outbreak of the English Civil War* (1981), 91–3, 192; Judith Maltby, *Prayer Book and People in Elizabethan and Early Stuart England* (Cambridge, 1998), appendix 1; Judith Maltby, 'Petitions for Episcopacy and the Book of Common Prayer on the Eve of the Civil War, 1641–1642', in *From Cranmer to Davidson: A Church of England Miscellany*, ed. Stephen Taylor (Church of England Record Society, 7, Woodbridge, 1999), 103–67; Patricia Higgins, 'The Reactions of Women, with Special Reference to Women Petitioners', in *Politics, Religion and the English Civil War*, ed. B. Manning (1973); R. Ashton, *Counter-Revolution: The Second Civil War and its Origins 1646–8* (New Haven, CT, 1994), ch. 4; K. Lindley, *Popular Politics and Religion in Civil War London* (Aldershot, 1997); J. Walter, 'Confessional Politics in Pre-Civil War Essex: Prayer Books, Profanations and Petitions', *Historical Journal*, xliv (2001), 677–701; Peter Lake, 'Puritans, Popularity and Petitions', in *Politics, Religion and Popularity in Early Stuart Britain: Essays in Honour of Conrad Russell*, ed. Thomas Cogswell, Richard Cust and Peter Lake (Cambridge, 2002); David Cressy, 'Revolutionary England 1640–42', *Past & Present*, No. 181 (2003), 35–71; David Cressy, *England on Edge: Crisis and Authority, 1640–1642* (New York, 2006).

[9] *Letters from Saffron Waldon* (1647), 4, 7.

[10] *The Petition and Vindication of the Officers of the Armie under His Excellencie Sir Thomas Fairfax* (1647), unpaginated.

[11] *A Representation from his Excellencie Sr. Thomas Fairfax* (1647), 12, also issued as *A Declaration from Sir Thomas Fairfax and the Army under his Command* (1647), 11.

document declared it was the right of subjects to petition 'in a due manner' but attacked 'the tumultuous Assemblies' of petitioners and ordered that in future, petitions 'shall be brought up and presented only by a convenient number, not exceeding twenty persons' who were to remain orderly and peaceable.[12]

These restrictions on the right to petition were not forgotten and formed the basis of the 'Act against Tumultuous Disorders Upon Pretence of Preparing or Presenting Petitions or other Addresses to his Majesty or the Parliament', passed by the restored monarchy in 1661. Like its 1648 precedent, the 1661 act also associated petitioning with seditious assembly and limited the number of people who could present a petition (to ten rather than 20) and added a further restriction: no petition of more than 20 hands to any petition could be promoted unless its content had first been approved by three or more JPs or by 'the major part' of a grand jury. The act did not entirely eradicate the possibility that corporate bodies might press petitions on matters of national policy: indeed, the 1661 act specifically did 'not extend to debar any persons (not exceeding ten in number) to present any complaint to any member of parliament after his election, and during the continuance of parliament, or to the king, for any remedy to be thereupon had; nor to any address to the king by the parliament'. As such, the act was later claimed to have stated a right to petition, though that was clearly not the spirit of the law as it was passed in 1661 and (especially when combined with restrictions on the press) the new measure effectively suppressed mass petitioning until the succession crisis of 1679–81. The paradox of innovative petitioning was temporarily resolved by severely curtailing, even proscribing, a popular right to petition.

The right to petition parliament again became contested during the succession crisis of 1679–82. On 12 December 1679, during a mass petitioning campaign in favour of demanding parliament's sitting, a proclamation was issued against tumultuous petitions. But when parliament resumed sitting the following autumn, the Commons reasserted the subjects' right to petition. On 27 October 1680, the House voted first, that it was the 'undoubted right' of subjects to petition the king for the calling and sitting of parliaments, and second, that to represent petitioning as seditious was to betray the liberties of subjects, subvert the constitution and introduce arbitrary government. Impeachment proceedings were launched against Lord Chief Justice North for having prepared the 1679 proclamation, and against others for their opposition to petitioning. Yet this defiant stance was shortlived. A petition from the City of London in January 1681, again attacking the king's dismissal of parliament, provided one of the grounds on which successful legal proceedings were launched in 1682 against the London Charter. Indeed, the political tide had turned, and loyalist addresses flooding in to Whitehall during the so-called tory reaction in the early 1680s, were reminders that popular pressure was not always on the radical side.

It was left to the second revolution of the 17th century to establish a statutory right to petition; but clarity was only partial, since safeguards focused almost entirely on the right to petition the king rather than parliament. The Declaration (and subsequent Bill) of Rights did assert, in its fifth article, that 'it is the right of subjects to petition the King, and all commitments and prosecutions for such petitioning are illegal'.[13] But it said nothing about

---

[12] *LJ*, x, 273.

[13] Lois G. Schwoerer, *The Declaration of Rights* (Baltimore, MD, 1981), 283. The clause in part reflected the controversy generated by the seven bishops who had petitioned James II in 1688 and had been imprisoned. For

the right to petition parliament. Although the 17th century conflicts had explicitly raised the spectre of a tyrannous parliament as well as a tyrannous king, only one-half of this dual threat was tackled. This bequeathed a legacy of uncertainty and ambiguity about the relationship between people and parliament that was to plague future generations, especially as the power of parliament increased after 1688. Indeed, a history of key flashpoints in the 18th century could be told through a history of the right to petition parliament, a narrative that underlines that the legality and extent of popular pressure on the legislature remained contested.[14]

The right to petition parliament thus became controversial very soon after the revolution, when it took on partisan connotations. In 1701, a whiggish petition from Kent, urging MPs to engage in war against France, provoked a Commons' resolution that it was 'scandalous, insolent and seditious, tending to destroy the constitution of parliament, and to subvert the established government of this realm'.[15] The petitioners were ordered into custody by the tory majority.[16] This sparked a heated controversy over the right to petition parliament, a debate that rapidly evolved into an argument about popular sovereignty and the proper relationship between the people and their representatives. Tension was heightened by the 'Legion Memorial', written to support the Kentish petitioners, which purported to come to MPs 'from [their] masters (for such are the People who chose [them])' and asserted that:

it is the undoubted right of the people of England, in case their representatives in Parliament do not proceed according to their duty, and the people's interest, to inform them of their dislike, disown their actions and to direct them to such things as they think fit, either by petition, address, proposal, memorial or any other peaceable way.[17]

Moreover, if parliament did betray the trust imposed on them, it was claimed, it was 'the undoubted right of the people of England to call them to account for the same, and by convention, assembly or force may proceed against them as traitors and betrayers of the country'.[18] The dispute was never fully resolved and produced no clear statement of the right to petition.[19] Even so, the right to petition parliament remained relatively uncontested until 1721 (when Walpole was thought to threaten it) and again in 1733–4 during the excise

[13] (continued) the discussion during their trial of the right to petition the king, see The Stuart Constitution 1603–88, ed. John Kenyon (Cambridge, 1969), 442–6.

[14] For petitioning in the 18th century, see Eugene Black, The Association: British Extra-Parliamentary Political Organisation, 1769–1793 (Cambridge, MA, 1963); Seymour Drescher, Capitalism and Anti-Slavery: British Mobilization in Comparative Perspective (Oxford, 1986); John Phillips, 'Popular Politics in Unreformed England', Journal of Modern History, lii (1980), 599–625; Rosemary Sweet, 'Local Identities and a National Parliament, c. 1688–1835', in Parliaments, Nations and Identities in Britain and Ireland, 1660–1850, ed. Julian Hoppit (Manchester, 2003), 48–63; Harry Dickinson, The Politics of the People in Eighteenth-Century Britain (Basingstoke, 1994); Charles Tilly, Popular Contention in Great Britain 1758–1834 (Cambridge, MA, 1995).

[15] CJ, xiii, 518.

[16] The History of the Kentish Petition Answer'd (1701), 5; The Parliamentary Diary of Sir Richard Cocks, ed. David Hayton (Oxford, 1996), 114; CJ, xiii, 518; [J. Somers], Jura Populi Anglicani. Or the Subjects Right of Petitioning (1701).

[17] [?Daniel Defoe], 'Legion Memorial' (1701), 3.

[18] [?Defoe], 'Legion Memorial', 4.

[19] The issue became, again, one about addressing the crown as much as parliament: see Cocks Diary, ed. Hayton, 217–8.

crisis. Indeed, we could say that during the first half of the 18th century, the right became an assumed and implicit, even if not explicit, part of British liberties.

The revival of mass popular petitioning in the 1760s, nevertheless, reanimated controversy, though once again the right to petition the crown was as much at stake as a right to petition parliament. The right to petition became associated with Wilkite agitation, particularly in 1769–70 when it became the focus of attention because of both the parliamentary and the royal reaction to hostile petitions. Thus in March 1770, the lord mayor, aldermen, common council and common hall petitioned the king to say that parliament no longer represented the people and call for its dissolution. The king responded that the petition was 'disrespectful to me, injurious to my parliament and irreconcileable to the principles of the constitution'.[20] This provoked an outcry. 'Giving no answer to a petition but flinging it away as waste paper, seems to me a negative of the Right' to petition, wrote one observer.[21] Lord Chatham agreed, and on 4 May 1770 moved a resolution in the Lords against the contemptuous manner of the king's response which, he said, was of a dangerous tendency 'inasmuch as thereby the exercise of the clearest rights of the subject, namely to petition the King for Redress of Grievances' had been infringed. Indeed, Chatham asserted, 'the very essence of the Constitution, not only permits but requires petitioning the Throne and [was] what the Stuarts never dared to prevent in the zenith of their power'.[22] Petitioning the crown was thus, in his eyes at least, a duty as well as a right. Illustration 1 shows Lord Chief Justice Mansfield with a putative 'Law against Petitions' in his hand with Sir Fletcher Norton (top left), Speaker of the Commons, keen to prove the City of London petitioners traitors, and Lord Grafton (bottom left) wanting them 'whipt from Newgate to Tyburn'. The king tramples on a petition from Westminster.

Petitions from American colonies setting out the reasons for their defiance of the king again provoked debate about the right to petition the king.[23] But it was the petitions over reform in 1780 that highlighted the strained relationship between petitioners and parliament. The famous 'Dunning resolution' of 6 April 1780, that 'the influence of crown has increased, is increasing and ought to be diminished', sprung directly from the failure of petitions addressed to the Commons. Despite ministerial assurance that 'no man in his senses, who sat in that house, could be ignorant that the right of petitioning belonged to all British subjects', the petitions calling for reform had been criticized, slighted and ignored. Dunning, in order 'to bring both the points contested between the petitioners and ministers fairly to issue, [said] he should frame two propositions, abstracted from the petitions on the table'. The vote on the first of these, relating to the influence of the crown, was thus seen as one 'in behalf of the petitions'. The right to petition was also on the agenda that year when the mass petition to parliament promoted by Lord George's Protestant Association

---

[20] *The State of the Nation, as Represented to a Certain Great Personage, by Junius and the Freeholder: And the Petition of the Citizens of London* (1770), 33–4, 37–41.

[21] *Public Advertiser*, no. 11045, 20 Apr. 1770.

[22] *London Evening Post*, no. 6630, 3 May 1770; John Almon, *Anecdotes of the Life of the Right Hon. William Pitt, Earl of Chatham* (1792), 56–7.

[23] Colonists saw petitioning as their right as free-born Britons – see Richard Bailey, *Popular Influence upon Public Policy: Petitioning in Eighteenth-Century Virginia* (Westport, CT, 1979); Weldon Brown, *Empire or Independence; A Study in the Failure of Reconciliation, 1774–1783* (New York, 1966); and, for the wider petitioning movement, James Bradley, *Popular Politics and the American Revolution in England: Petitions, the Crown, and Public Opinion* (Macon, GA, 1986).

Illustration 1: *The Effects of Petitions and Remonstrances* (1770); BM Satires 4386. © Trustees
of the British Museum.

led to large-scale rioting, once again questioning how far popular pressure on parliament
could be sanctioned.[24]

The contest over the right to petition parliament intensified in the last years of the 18th
century, when mass petitioning was, arguably, the most important tool for the articulation
and animation of popular opinion on national affairs.[25] In 1795, the right to petition became
the centre of a political furore in the wake of the government's decision to introduce two

[24]See Mark Knights, 'The 1780 Protestant Petitions and the Culture of Petitioning', in *The Gordon Riots: Politics, Culture and Insurrection in late Eighteenth-Century Britain*, ed. Ian Haywood and John Rule (Cambridge, 2012).

[25]For the context, see *The French Revolution and British Popular Politics*, ed. Mark Philp (Cambridge, 1991); Clive Emsley, *Britain and the French Revolution* (2000); *Britain and the French Revolution 1789–1815*, ed. Harry Dickinson (Basingstoke, 1989); J.E. Cookson, *The Friends of Peace: Anti-War Liberalism in England 1793–1815* (Cambridge, 1982); John Oldfield, *Popular Politics and British Anti-Slavery: The Mobilisation of Public Opinion against the Slave Trade* (Manchester, 1995); Albert Goodwin, *The Friends of Liberty* (1979).

bills – the so-called 'gagging acts' – that included restrictions on the right to petition, assembly and free speech. The Seditious Meetings Act – all too clearly in the mould of 17th-century legislation – banned meetings of more than 50 people 'for the purpose or on the pretext of considering of or preparing any petition, complaint, remonstrance or declaration' unless notice of the meeting was given to local magistrates, who could attend; and if anyone proposed to alter anything in the constitution without parliament, the JPs were empowered to clear the meeting and make arrests.[26] The solicitor general, Sir John Mitford, claimed that the government's intention was not to deny a right to petition but 'to prevent the rights of petitioning from being abused and that it might lay other restrictions on those principles which were dangerous to civil liberty'.[27]

Yet the measure was immediately castigated in parliament as removing the right to petition. In attacking Pitt the Younger's measure, Charles James Fox argued that: 'whoever in future shall mention the right to petition will talk as absurdly as if he employed such language under the worst despotism'. Fox declared that the restrictions on meetings meant that it would be impossible to discuss grievances: 'if the people state their grievances or complain of their sufferings, they must call in a magistrate to listen to the language of their remonstrance and watch their proceedings with a jealous eye'.[28] Thomas Erskine, similarly, launched a formidable assault on the bill, arguing that it 'did absolutely destroy the right of the subject to petition'.[29] It was also noted that the bills were specifically aimed at popular urban radicalism – and that 'one of the most odious and obnoxious principles of the bill was the diabolical attempt to establish distinctions between different classes of subjects'.[30] Indeed, the attack on a *popular* right of petitioning introduced class overtones, since the bills specifically allowed meetings of the types of institutions of government likely to be dominated by the middling sort and gentry.

The measures temporarily reanimated the mass protests that the treason trials of the previous year had done much to quell and the focus of the agitation was the right to petition. On 12 November, the London Corresponding Society held a meeting attended by an alleged 300,000 to hear speeches defending the right to petition and to prepare to petition parliament against the bills.[31] Four days later, the inhabitants of Westminster met to discuss the bills which, it was said, raised the question 'whether all meetings to instruct our representatives or to petition the king or either House of Parliament are to be rendered ineffectual and contemptible, by submitting them to an officer of Government who is to be authorised to dissolve and disperse them at his pleasure?' They also asked 'whether we shall retain any right of petitioning for redress of grievances but the nugatory and ridiculous right of complaining precisely in such language as shall be agreeable to those against whom we complain?' Urged on by the parliamentary leaders of the opposition to the bills, several thousand of the 10,000–12,000 strong crowd signed a petition to uphold the right of

[26] 36 Geo. III, c. 8, reproduced in E.N. Williams, *Eighteenth Century Constitution 1688–1815* (Cambridge, 1960), 426–9.

[27] *London Paquet*, no. 4097, 16 Nov. 1795.

[28] *Star*, no. 2257, 11 Nov. 1795.

[29] *Courier*, no. 1034, 17 Nov. 1795.

[30] *An Impartial Report of the Debates that Occur [sic] in the two Houses of Parliament* (4 vols, 1796), i, 500.

[31] *Account of the Proceedings of a Meeting of the People, in a Field near Copenhagen-House, Thursday, Nov. 12* (1795), sig. A2.

petitioning: 'Your petitioners do in the language of their forefathers claim, demand and insist upon the free exercise of it, as their true, ancient and indubitable right' which they saw as the 'best security against the abuse of power'.[32] Many similar petitions followed and were collected into a *History of the Two Acts* that ran to over 800 pages. From this and other sources, it is evident that over 130,000 people signed the petitions, which were often promoted at large protest meetings. Bristol's had 4,000 signatures; Sheffield's 8,000; Newcastle's 3,000; Birmingham's 4,000; one from the London Corresponding Society an enormous 12,100 with a further 15,000 from London artisans. These easily outnumbered the total of 30,000 who signed petitions and addresses (including one promoted by Wilberforce) in favour of the bills.[33] The petitions poured into parliament, though they failed to stop the bill from becoming law.

Thus in 1800, as much as 150 years earlier, the right to petition parliament was contested. Indeed, the 18th- and 17th-century struggles were seen as linked. Any perceived denial of the right to petition was discussed in terms of Stuart tyranny and a breach of the rights allegedly codified in 1689. Thus in 1763 the *London Chronicle* quoted the Bill of Rights at the head of an editorial about the right to petition and in 1766, a pamphlet reprinted it together with the 1661 act – now ironically seen as proof of the right to petition.[34] In 1769, newspapers responded to the loyalist author known as 'Bull face', who had unflatteringly compared contemporary petitioners to 'their predecessors in the rebellion against Charles I',[35] by reminding readers of the Stuart experience.[36] Indeed, in 1769 there was a timely reprint of a 1721 tract about the right to petition, saturated in 17th-century precedent. The infringement of the Bill of Rights was repeatedly complained of in 1795 and that complaint was incorporated into petitions against the restrictive governmental bills.[37] Illustration 2 satirises Fox and Sheridan for trying to delay the passage of the bill restricting popular petitioning by deluging parliament with petitions, and on 23 November Fox moved for a delay on the grounds that the bill repealed part of the 1689 Bill of Rights. The historicised approach to the 1795 acts was highlighted by one MP, who observed that: 'All the stretches of the prerogative under Charles the First, who lost his head, and James the Second, who lost his crown, were but pigmy steps compared with the gigantic strides of modern despotism. Ship-money, arbitrary exactions, and even the infamous Court of Star Chamber were trivial to it.'[38] The 18th-century debate was, thus, often viewed through the lens of the 17th century.

---

[32] *Morning Chronicle*, no. 8135, 17 Nov. 1795; *Morning Post*, no. 7417, 16 Nov. 1795.

[33] *Star*, no. 2266, 21 Nov. 1795; *Oracle*, no. 19174, 26 Nov. 1795; *Courier*, no. 1048, 4 Dec. 95.

[34] *London Chronicle*, no. 987, 21 Apr. 1763, subsection called *The Monitor*, no. 403; *British Liberties, or the Free-born Subject's Inheritance* (1766). *London Evening Post*, no. 5536, 26 Apr. 1763, defended the right of the City to petition the king, with reference to the seven bishops' trial. *St James Chronicle*, no. 334, 26 Apr. 1763, and *Gazetteer and London Daily Advertiser*, no. 10650, 28 Apr. 1763, invoked the tyranny of Charles II.

[35] *A Reply to the Comments and Menaces of Bull Face Double Fee* (1769), 23–4.

[36] *St James's Chronicle*, no. 1314, 29 July 1769, reprinted the 1680 parliamentary resolutions. Cf. *Middlesex Journal or Chronicle of Liberty*, no. 61, 19 Aug. 1769 and *Gazetteer and New Daily Advertiser*, no. 12636, 31 Aug. 1769.

[37] *The Proceedings and Speeches, at the Meeting the Seventeenth November, 1795, at St. Andrew's Hall* (Norwich, [1795?]), 13, where Mark Wilks argued that the Bill of Rights' provision about petitioning was violated by the 1795 bills; a standpoint included in the resulting petition.

[38] *An Impartial Report of the Debates*, i, 516–7.

Illustration 2: *Petition Mongers in Full Cry* (1795); BM Satires 8697. © Trustees of the British Museum.

3

Having outlined some of the chronology and scale of the disputes, and having shown how the right to petition parliament was often entangled with a right to petition the crown and was still being debated in 1800, it is now possible to examine some of the arguments used to define, defend, or attack the right. The debate on the right to petition encompassed a variety of different questions about the relationship between people and parliament; about how far the right to petition implied a right to redress of grievance; about the nature and extent of the right to petition, including how far the right could be forfeited by the action or language of the petitioners; and about who enjoyed the right.

The assertion of an extensive right to petition implied, and sometimes explicitly stated, a claim to popular sovereignty and the supremacy of the people over their representatives. In 1648, 1701, 1769, during the American crisis, in 1780 and again in 1795, parliament asserted its sovereignty over petitioners; but petitioners frequently challenged this and sought to limit the right of MPs to speak for the people, in turn provoking parliament's anger. Thus in 1648, parliament criticized the Levellers, who used petitions to articulate grievances, for trying to 'give a rule to the Legislative power', as if they meant their petitions to be 'edicts' that 'the Parliament must verifie'.[39] In 1701, a similar conflict over sovereignty flared. The tories sought to uphold the supremacy of formal parliamentary representation over the informal representations of petitions. They suggested that the whig petitioners' claim to represent:

the Voice of the People is nonsense; for every little faction lays claim to that appellation and have wore it so thread-bare that tis scandalous to make use of it, as appropriating it to a party; for none can be truly called the people of England in a divided capacity; and they are only whole and entire in their representatives in Parliament.[40]

The people were not superior to their MPs, it was alleged, but 'by the choice of their representatives resign up all their authority to 'em'.[41] Indeed, on 26 February 1702, the Commons voted that anyone who asserted that the House was not the representative of the nation tended to subvert the rights and fundamentals of the constitution.

The clash between parliamentary and popular sovereignty, which the right to petition highlighted, continued to echo for the rest of the century. In 1780, Lord North agreed that the people had a right to petition and even to expect that attention would be paid to their views, but he protested that they could not compel his opinion and he would vote according to conscience 'whether his opinion coincided with the voice of the people or not'.[42] Thus, in response to Dunning's question whether 'the voice of petitions [could] reach the Royal ear without passing through the medium of that House?' North replied: 'the voice of the people of Great Britain could be heard only from that House where it was spoken by their Representatives'.[43] North's stance on domestic and colonial petitioning was thus of a piece: parliament was sovereign. Sir Peter Burrell agreed: the people had a right to petition but 'they had no right to dare to controul or direct the determination of that House, nor propose measures for their consideration', for this would be to usurp parliament; 'in this light he detested petitions and would set his face against them'. If petitioning was allowed to dictate to the House, he suggested, the liberty and constitution of parliament would 'be annihilated and gone for ever'.[44]

The right to petition candidates at election time through instructions – promoted in 1681, 1701, 1715, 1733, 1753, 1769, 1774, and 1783–4 – was also seen by critics as reducing representatives to mere delegates of the people.[45] This led to an attempt to distinguish 'instructions' from petitions. In 1733, when instructions on opposition to the excise were promoted, pro-government writers argued that the right to petition and the right to instruct

---

[39] *A Declaration of Some Proceedings of Lt. Col. Iohn Lilburn, and his Associates* (1648), [14 Feb 1647], 40.

[40] *History of the Kentish Petition*, 15; *Jura Populi Anglicani ... Answer'd, Paragraph by Paragraph* (1701), 79.

[41] *The Ballad or Some Scurrilous Reflections in Verse ... Answered* (1701), 27. Cf. *England's Enemies Expos'd* (1701), 31.

[42] *London Chronicle*, no. 3623, 22 Feb. 1780. In the version in the *General Evening Post*, no. 7172, 22 Feb. 1780, North added: 'Every subject had a right to petition, every subject had a right to give instructions to his representative; but no subject had a right to command his vote or control him in his judgement.' A third variant of the speech is given in the *Morning Chronicle*, no. 3360, 24 Feb. 1780.

[43] *London Chronicle*, no. 3651, 27 Apr. 1780.

[44] *Gazetteer and New Daily Advertiser*, no. 15936, 10 Mar. 1780.

[45] Paul Kelly, 'Constituents' Instructions to Members of Parliament in the C18th', in *Party and Management in Parliament 1660–1784*, ed. Clyve Jones (Leicester, 1984); Harry Dickinson, 'The Eighteenth Century Debate on the Sovereignty of Parliament', *Transactions of the Royal Historical Society*, 5th ser., xxvi (1976), 189–210.

MPs were very different – there was no right to the latter, which was said to be dangerous to the constitution.[46] Yet instructions were, nevertheless, seen by champions of the right to petition as important means to ensure that MPs did the bidding of their constituents, instead of pursuing their own, or the government's, interest. The right to petition MPs to mandate them to take a certain line was therefore a contested, but repeatedly invoked, one.

Yet such views were challenged. The Wilkites argued that whilst parliament conveyed to the king the 'presumed sense of the people' this had to be confirmed by petitioning.[47] Thus, whereas 'it has been alleged that the people have no right of judging public measures but by their representatives in Parliament … the contrary is manifest, from the right of the represented to instruct their representatives; and from their right to petition or address the throne'.[48] Indeed, claims to popular sovereignty, represented through a right to petition, could also lead in radical directions. A perception that petitioning, and hence the representative voice of the people, was deliberately ignored by parliament, led ineluctably to arguments that the voting system needed to be changed. This was the argument of *An Address to the Electors of Southwark* (1795), in which an 'elector' began by arguing that the people's petitions against the war had been treated with no more 'consideration than if you had no representatives in Parliament'. This led the author to the conclusion that 'all our national calamities originate in the present constitution of the House of Commons'. MP's, he claimed, were rightfully the servants, not the masters, of the people, and rotten boroughs and placemen should be swept aside. It was an 'evil' that there were so few electors; 'universal suffrage and annual parliaments' were the solutions.[49] Disdain of the right to petition parliament thus provoked demands for parliamentary reform and undermined parliamentary legitimacy. As a 1793 petition from Nottingham in favour of reform put it, the country was simply 'amused with the name of a representation of the people, when the reality was gone'.[50]

Closely tied to the debate about the supremacy of petitions as the voice of the people was one about what the correct response of those in authority (parliament or monarch) should be to them. During the 18th century, both parliament and the monarchy rejected petitions outright or gave them slighting replies and claimed that they thought they were justified in doing so. But for their critics, the right to petition conferred a right to redress of grievance, or else the right was an empty one. This conflict was clear in 1769–70 when the king cold-shouldered petitions and his supporters denied he had any duty to redress grievances raised by them.[51] One observer sympathetic to the Wilkites noted that: 'we have long been amusing ourselves with stating the subjects right to petition … Of what use is that right to us now?'[52] A conviction that a legal right to petition conferred a right

[46] *London Journal*, no. 755, 15 Dec. 1733.

[47] *A New and Impartial Collection of Interesting Letters, from the Public Papers; … Written by Persons of Eminence* (1767), 64.

[48] *London Chronicle*, no. 1184, 21 July 1764.

[49] *An Address to the Electors of Southwark* (1795), 4, 27–9.

[50] *Morning Chronicle*, no. 7401, 22 Feb. 1793.

[51] *A Petition of the Freeholders of the County of Middlesex, presented to his Majesty, the 24th of May, 1769, by Mr. Serjeant Glynn* [1769]; *Gazetteer and New Daily Advertiser*, no. 12,594, 13 July 1769: letter from Northants.

[52] *Middlesex Journal or Chronicle of Liberty*, no. 76, 23 Sept. 1769; cf. *Gazetteer and New Daily Advertiser*, no. 12830, 14 Apr. 1770; *General Evening Post*, no. 5685, 20 Mar. 1770: letter from Philolibertas invoking Magna Charta, also reprinted in *Gazetteer and New Daily Advertiser*, no. 12809, 21 Mar. 1770.

to redress could lead to suggestions that, if petitioning was denied, the use of force was justifiable. In 1680, Thomas Dare told Charles II that he could either petition or rebel. In 1721, an interesting tract linked the right of petitioning to the danger of ignoring the people. It argued that: 'the Right of Petitioning is a Privilege which mankind could never part with' and that 'when this has proved ineffectual' the people 'convinced their Sovereigns to their cost, how unreasonable a thing it is to be *Deaf to the Voice of the People*'.[53] Thus, the rejection of petitions was linked to threat of resistance. Similar arguments were heard in 1734 during the excise crisis. A tract called *The Right of British Subjects to Petition* (1733, reprinted 1734) ran to 121 pages rehearsing the 17th-century struggle to establish the right and emphasizing the need for MPs to listen to the people, and it included John Locke's dictum that where the right of appeal on earth was removed, the people had a liberty to appeal to heaven.[54] Indeed, the American crisis should be viewed in this context. The right to petition for redress of grievances was an essential part of the colonists' freedoms; denial of their petitions, slighting their right to submit them, justified a recourse to arms.[55] And in 1795, Charles James Fox warned that the consequence of the 1795 bill would, similarly, be to push the people into revolution: 'If you silence remonstrance and stifle complaint, you then leave no other alternative but force and violence.'[56]

Of course such statements tended to confirm the loyalist stance that there was an intrinsic link between petitioning and sedition. Loyalists thus argued that whilst a right to petition could be acknowledged, even embraced, a petition had to meet certain criteria for such a right to remain valid. First, it should be couched in moderate and humble language. ''Tis the right of the people to petition', acknowledged the author of *England's Enemies Expos'd*, 'provided always that it be done in decent words and submitting their opinions to the wisdom of the house'.[57] As another tract put it: 'not to distinguish between a modest petition and a scandalous, insolent and seditious one was to turn the world upside down'.[58] Second, the promotion of the petition and its presentation should be orderly, restrained and pursued through established institutions rather than riotous or seditious associations. After the riot that accompanied the presentation to parliament of the Protestant Association's petitions, the attorney general qualified the right to petition by saying that there had to be 'a decent and rational exercise of that right' and that it certainly did not confer 'a right to interrupt the deliberations of Parliament'.[59] Failure to meet the criteria of decorum and orderliness, loyalists argued, invalidated the right to petition, and special circumstances could force the government to curtail such a right for the greater good of peace and stability.[60]

For loyalists, the right to petition was thus contingent and even dispensable, subordinate to other considerations, rather than absolute and abstract. William Grant, urging a

[53] *A Letter to a Leading Great Man, concerning the Rights of the People to Petition* (1721).
[54] *The Right of British Subjects to Petition* (1733), xvi, appendix, 39.
[55] In Jan. 1775, the king referred a petition, from Benjamin Franklin and others on behalf of the Congress, to parliament which then voted, on 26 January, not to receive it (*American Archives*, Series 4, i, 1532; *CJ*, xxxv, 81). It had warned that rejecting petitions would 'end in universal rebellion'.
[56] *The Star*, no. 2257, 11 Nov. 1795. Cf. *An Impartial Report of the Debates*, i, 177; cf. i, 175: 'Mr Stanley said, if this bill passed into law we were upon the eve of a revolution'.
[57] *England's Enemies Expos'd*, 42.
[58] *History of the Kentish Petition*, 39. Cf. *The Old and Modern Whig* (1701), 46.
[59] *London Chronicle*, no. 3773, 3 Feb. 1781.
[60] *The Twelve Letters of Canana: On the Impropriety of Petitioning the King to Dissolve the Parliament* (1770), 4.

restriction on the right to petition in 1795, asked in parliament: 'Were all the benefits of the constitution lapped up in this one right? No! Estimate it as highly as gentlemen could, it was nothing when put in competition with liberty and constitutional happiness.'[61] To reformers, however, restrictions on petitioning destroyed the right itself. In 1793, Lord Grey warned that by applying such strict 'doctrines of decorum and respect to the House', the loyalists, 'while they admitted the right of petitioning [yet] they would deny the use of it'. Fox added that the House could reject a petition for disrespectful language but only if the language was not intrinsic to the plea, otherwise there could be no petitions for parliamentary reform at all and 'there was an end of the right of the subject to petition'.[62]

Another way of looking at the right to petition was not as a constitutional, so much as a natural, right. The Levellers had asserted it as a 'native right' of free-born Britons,[63] and in 1701, a Lockean tract, *Jura Populi*, talked about petitioning as the 'natural right of mankind'.[64] But it was in the later 18th century that this claim was most frequently made. In 1780, a meeting in Hertford heard a speech asserting petitioning to be 'an inherent right; it was before all statutes; it was an essential part of the constitution itself. The bill of rights at the revolution was only declaratory, not enacting'.[65] In 1791, it was said to be Britons' 'indefeasible right, as well as by the laws of nature, reason and common sense',[66] and in 1795, when defending petitioning, Fox defiantly stated that natural rights were the 'basis of a free government'.[67]

The shift towards a more insistent claim of petitioning as a natural right mirrored an increasing tendency to view the right to petition as part of a group of mutually-supporting rights, the most important of which were the right to assembly and the right to freedom of speech and print. Of course these had to some extent been associated together in the 17th century, as we have seen, and this continued to be the case in the early and mid 18th century.[68] But these rights became routinely grouped together in the later 18th century once mass petitioning campaigns were, again, underway. Thus in 1781, Wyvill argued in print that 'if the people have a right to petition parliament at all, they must have a right to meet and consult together, in order to exercise that right in a peaceable and orderly manner'.[69] It was, nevertheless, the 1795 bills that tied the rights together most explicitly, as

---

[61] *An Impartial Report of the Debates*, i, 524, 538. Wilberforce agreed, even though the anti-slavery petitions of 1792 had sought to mobilise mass pressure.

[62] *Evening Mail*, no. 654, 1 May 1793.

[63] *A Lash for a Lyar* (1648), 12–13, printed the petition 'to the Honourable the chosen and betrusted Knights, Citizens and Burgesses in Parliament Assembled', from East Smithfield and Wapping.

[64] [?Somers], *Jura Populi*, 33–4. This was part of a sophisticated discussion of a Lockean state of nature. A refutation of the tract argued that there was no state of extremis justifying an invocation of the 'great law of preservation': *Answer to Jura Populi*, 35.

[65] *London Courant*, 18 Apr. 1780. At the trial of Lord Gordon the attorney general admitted that: 'it is the inherent right of the subject to petition parliament' and that there was an 'innate right of the subject to petition': *Annual Register* (1781), 120.

[66] *St James's Chronicle or the British Evening Post*, no. 4777, 5 Nov. 1791: letter from 'a peaceable petitioner'.

[67] *An Impartial Report of the Debates*, i, 171–3.

[68] *The Right of British Subjects to Petition*, explicitly linked the right to petition with a free press. *The Public Ledger*, no. 1740, 2 Aug. 1765, said the right of free enquiry was 'evident from the indisputable right to petition against depending laws, to instruct their representatives' and to address the crown against existing laws.

[69] *London Courant*, 26 June 1781: letter from Wyvill, 14 May. This had already been stated in parliament by Fox who declared that 'the people had a right to associate, a right to delegate, and a right to petition the house

Illustration 3: *A Free Born Englishman* (1795); BM Satires 8711. © Trustees of the British Museum.

Illustration 3 shows.[70] The illustration suggests a 'Right of Petitioning reserved to Families only'; the Bill of Rights, enshrining the right to petition, lies trampled underfoot; and the right to petition is closely associated with the right to free speech. Yet one ultra-loyalist even thought the bills failed to go far enough because only the re-imposition of licensing on the press would remove the 'license of seditious remonstrance which they called a right to petition'.[71]

As the illustration of the gagged 'free born Englishman' suggests (see Illustration 3), there was a real fear that the government sought to erode or restrict the hard-fought right to petition and that 1795 marked a turning point in constitutional liberties. The passage of

69 *(continued)* by their delegates, and those rights were founded on the law and the constitution': *Morning Chronicle*, no. 3706, 3 Apr. 1781; *St James's Chronicle*, no. 3134, 31 Mar. 1781.

[70] See also John Baxter, *A New and Impartial History of England* [1796], x.

[71] *Morning Post*, no. 7417, 16 Nov. 1795: letter from a supporter of Reeves's Association.

the acts had, in the words of one critic, undone 1688 and led to the 'utter extinction of liberty'.[72] It is true that after 1688 it had become routine to petition parliament on a host of legislative proposals, that petitioning had grown in volume and that petitioning parliament had become an established part of the political culture. But at the end of the 18th century, the right to petition both parliament and (despite the Bill of Rights) the monarch, remained contested, particularly at moments of high political tension, and the nature and extent of any such right remained undefined and disputed. What is clear is that the right to petition in order to put pressure on parliament was seen in a historical way that linked the 18th and 17th centuries and that it raised fundamental questions about the location of sovereignty. The contest over the right to petition was so vigorous because petitioning was frequently resorted to as a means of articulating the voice of the people outside parliament. Parliament might claim a representative monopoly but this was hard to maintain against petitioners intent on claiming their own representative status. It was also clear that there was a set of controverted duties that the right to petition was said to generate – a duty to respond adequately on the part of the recipient, but also a duty to draft and present the petition in a humble and lawful manner. For some, that meant the right to petition was part of an associated bundle of rights, including free speech and freedom of assembly; but to others, the right to petition was a contingent right that could be curtailed, surrendered or invalidated, in order to preserve greater rights, such as those to security and the happiness of the whole. The former no doubt drew some consolation from the fact that the first amendment to the American constitution in 1789 included the very bundle of rights that were being contested in England.[73] Congress declared that it would 'make no law respecting an establishment of religion, or prohibiting the free exercise thereof; or abridging the freedom of speech, or of the press; or the right of the people peaceably to assemble, and to petition the Government for a redress of grievances'. But such a clear statement of the rights of Britons remained elusive. Petitioning was central to many of the early-19th-century reform movements, but it was still a contested right.

[72] *An Address to the English Nation; with … a Recommendation to Petition with Vigour* (1796), 5.

[73] The First Amendment prohibited laws against freedom of religion, of speech, of the press, of assembly and of petitioning. As early as 1641, The Massachusetts Body of Liberties had upheld a right to petition 'any publique Court, Councel or Towne meeting'. The right to petition the legislature was already acknowledged by constitutions in Maryland in 1765 and New Hampshire in 1783.

Conversations with Parliament: Women and the Politics of Pressure in 19th-Century England

SARAH RICHARDSON

In the long 19th century, women seized new opportunities offered by parliament and played a growing role in public politics long before well-known campaigns for the right to vote. As parliamentary politics grew more restrictive and formalised, women utilised older forms of interaction with the state and occupied spaces that were not explicitly barred to them. By looking at women's appearances before royal commissions and select committees, or women's participation in petitioning, this essay argues that women successfully pressured parliament and won their place in the blue books of government long before their names appeared on the electoral registers or in the columns of *Hansard*.

Keywords: parliament; petitions; pressure; royal commissions; select committee; women

Research has moved on since the 1970s and the groundbreaking analysis of 'pressure from without' published in a volume edited by Patricia Hollis with an array of leading 19th-century historians as contributors.[1] The index to that impressive collection contains only two entries on 'women's rights'; both are found in a chapter by Howard Temperley on 'Anti-Slavery', and both refer to the 'wrangle' at the World Anti-Slavery Convention which met in London in 1840 over the seating of female American delegates.[2] Hidden in the chapters on key associations, groups and people, there are references to influential women and female organisations such as the philosophical radicals, Harriet Grote and Sarah Austin, the sexual purity campaigner, Josephine Butler, and the British Women's Temperance Association. This is perhaps surprising given Hollis's later impressive contributions to the field of women and political history, but it reflected the prevailing orthodoxy of the time. This orthodoxy maintained that women were largely excluded, or at best played an auxiliary role in parliamentary and extra-parliamentary politics.[3] However, as *Pressure from Without* so clearly demonstrated, it is impossible to write a history of 19th-century pressure group politics without including women as key activists, policy shapers and organisers. Even if their contribution is not foregrounded, women are present on the pages of every historical record regarding public influence on parliament and on politics.

For women, the capacity to exercise influence on parliament to advance their favoured causes, virtually always came from 'without'. Although many could convince politicians

---

[1] *Pressure from Without in Early Victorian England*, ed. Patricia Hollis (1974).

[2] Howard Temperley, 'Anti-Slavery', in *Pressure from Without in Early Victoria England*, ed. Hollis, 46, 49.

[3] Patricia Hollis, *Women in Public, 1850–1900: Documents of the Victorian Women's Movement* (1979); Patricia Hollis, *Ladies Elect: Women in English Local Government, 1865–1914* (Oxford, 1987).

by using 'private' methods of patronage and informal lobbying, only the queen had ability to legislate, a power that was increasingly hypothetical as the century progressed. There were no female ministers, parliamentarians or civil servants, therefore women utilised other strategies. This essay focuses on women's increasing exploitation of parliamentary processes and procedures to get their voice heard. These were tactics that ran in parallel with the more familiar organised pressure groups and voluntary associations that proved successful in abolishing slavery and repealing the corn laws and centred on women's exploitation of the petitioning process and engagement with royal commissions and select committees of inquiry.

A major turning point in the historiography of women and the politics of pressure, came in 1980 with the publication of Alex Tyrell's influential article analysing the important rhetoric of 'woman's mission' which acted as a device to enable middle-class women to partake in pressure group politics by portraying their work as an extension of philanthropic and humanitarian activities.[4] Tyrell, like Temperley, focused on the prominent anti-slavery movement of the early 19th century. But rather than depicting female campaigners as troublesome, whose presence at the World Convention caused disputes between the American and British representatives, Tyrell demonstrated how they revitalised and transformed the movement, creating an environment where women could justifiably participate in crusades against 'moral, social and political unrighteousness'.[5] Clare Midgley furthered this argument, arguing that the women's anti-slavery movement allowed a distinctive political voice to emerge.[6] Women's groups changed both policy and practice. Their commitment to the immediate abolition of slavery contrasted with the views of the more cautious male leadership which favoured a gradualist approach. In May 1830, the pressure they applied succeeded in persuading the national Anti-Slavery Society to drop the term 'gradual abolition' from its mission statement.[7] At the practical level, women participated in a robust petitioning movement and led a campaign for morally informed consumption persuading neighbours and kin to boycott slave-grown cotton and sugar. They articulated their abhorrence of slavery through poetry, didactic novels and moral tales as well as more overtly political pamphlets.[8]

'Woman's mission' was a contested term in the early 19th century, with writers as diverse as Sarah Lewis, Marion Kirkland Reid, and Anna Jameson, debating the concept.[9] Whilst Lewis recognized women's capacity for social and moral regeneration, she considered that this influence should be exercised from a solely domestic and neighbourhood base. Jameson

[4] Alex Tyrell, ' "Woman's Mission" and Pressure Group Politics in Britain (1825–1860)', *Bulletin of the John Rylands University Library of Manchester*, lxiii (1980), 194–230.

[5] Tyrell, ' "Woman's Mission" ', 208.

[6] Clare Midgley, *Women against Slavery: The British Campaigns, 1780–1870* (1992).

[7] 'Proceedings of a General Meeting of the Anti-Slavery Society and its Friends Held at the Freemasons Hall on Saturday, the 15th of May', *Anti-Slavery Monthly Reporter*, iii (1830), 234–42. The motion was put by Thomas Fowell Buxton and seconded by Lord Milton.

[8] See Midgley, *Women against Slavery*, esp. ch. 3; Lynne Walker and Vron Ware, 'Political Pincushions: Decorating the Abolitionist Interior, 1878–1865', in *Domestic Space: Reading the Nineteenth-Century Interior*, ed. Inga Bryden and Janet Floyd (Manchester, 1999), 58–83.

[9] Sarah Lewis, *Woman's Mission* (1839); Marion Kirkland Reid, *A Plea for Woman: Being a Vindication of the Importance and Extent of her Natural Sphere of Action* (Edinburgh, 1843); Anna Jameson, 'Woman's Mission and Woman's Position', in Anna Jameson, *Memoirs and Essays Illustrative of Art, Literature and Social Morals* (1846).

observed tensions between woman's mission and woman's position, of which, she argued 'no one dares to think, much less to speak'.[10] She went on to note that:

Man's legislation for woman has hitherto been like English legislation for Ireland: it has been without sympathy; without the recognition of equality; without a comprehension of certain innate differences, physical and moral, and therefore inadequate, useless, often unjust and not seldom cruel.[11]

Reid offered a solution to the issue of men legislating on women's issues. She advocated the extension of the franchise to both men and women, arguing that this would allow female interests to be represented and inequalities to be redressed, in particular in the fields of marriage and education. The fact that 'woman's mission' spoke equally powerfully to conservative evangelicals and to radical proto-feminists, encouraged women of all political persuasions to embrace pressure group politics with enthusiasm and vigour during the mid 19th century. This rich seam of women's activism has now been carefully charted by historians.[12] For example, Simon Morgan, in his work on the women and the Anti-Corn Law League, noted that pressure group participation created a 'national community of women' working for a common cause. The League politicised women's role in the home, linking household economy directly to economic policy.[13] Kathryn Gleadle has charted how pressure groups for legal reform, sexual reform, and female education, were increasingly linked with calls for women's emancipation.[14]

The extent of the female contribution to extra-parliamentary lobbying was also recognized by contemporaries. In the 1840s, Henry Brewster Stanton, American journalist and politician (and husband of the women's rights campaigner, Elizabeth Cady Stanton) wrote an overview of progress of the British reform movement entitled *Sketches of Reforms and Reformers of Great Britain and Ireland*.[15] He devoted a chapter to significant women who were advocating change in a number of spheres. These included Lady Byron, Harriet Martineau, Amelia Opie, and Mary Howitt, but many more were cited in other chapters on particular pressure groups, including Maria Edgeworth, Elizabeth Heyrick, Elizabeth Fry, and Eliza Cook. And by the 1850s, Lord John Russell, speaking to the recently-established National Association for the Promotion of Social Science in Sheffield, could confidently assert:

Everyone must have observed the new influence which has not been asserted or sought, but is falling to the lot of women in swaying the destinies of the world. It is not a share

---

[10]Jameson, 'Woman's Mission', 134.

[11]Jameson, 'Woman's Mission', 132.

[12]To cite just a few indicative examples: Clare Midgley, 'From Supporting Missions to Petitioning Parliament: British Women and the Evangelical Campaign against *Sati* in India, 1813–1830', in *Women in British Politics, 1760–1860: The Power of the Petticoat*, ed. Kathryn Gleadle and Sarah Richardson (Basingstoke, 2000), 74–92; Lilian Lewis Shiman, *Crusade against Drink in Victorian England* (Basingstoke, 1988); Hilda Kean, *Animal Rights: Political and Social Change in Britain since 1800* (1998).

[13]Simon Morgan, 'Domestic Economy and Political Agitation: Women and the Anti-Corn Law League, 1839–1846', in *Women in British Politics, 1760–1860*, ed. Gleadle and Richardson, 115–33.

[14]Kathryn Gleadle, *The Early Feminists: Radical Unitarians and the Origins of the Women's Rights Movement, c. 1831–1851* (Basingstoke, 1995).

[15]Henry Brewster Stanton, *Sketches of Reforms and Reformers of Great Britain and Ireland* (New York, 1850).

in directing the patronage of ministers or guiding the councils of kings, as in former times, but a portion in the formation and moulding of public opinion.[16]

In fact, Russell underestimated the authority that women possessed. Pressure groups enabled them to influence policy and shape public opinion. However, women were also engaged in more direct dialogues with parliament and with politicians in the 19th century. Some of this took place out of public view. Thus the private correspondence of leading government ministers contained many letters from women claiming expertise in particular areas of policy. Sarah Austin, author and translator, was a fervent advocate for public education and undertook extensive research comparing educational provision throughout Europe which she published in an essay entitled *On National Education*.[17] Behind the scenes, she used her political connections centred on the powerful London group of Philosophical Radicals to promote her cause. Her correspondence networks included important politicians such as Strutt, Derby, Romilly, and Gladstone. She wrote frequently to Gladstone representing herself in conventional terms, as a middle-class woman unused to the rough and tumble of public debate. For example, on the issue of national education she wrote that:

seeing the violence and bitterness with which the subject is, I will not say discussed, but handled by the Press, I take fright. I have always shrunk from appearing before the public in my own person or behalf, as the author or champion of any opinions whatever … Will you read the few pages which I will ask Mr. Murray to send you? Will you tell me whether the party to which you in a wide sense belong are likely to attack me with the sort of rancour I see and hear now so much afloat on all sides. God forbid I should confound you with those who use such poisoned weapons. I judge you as I wish to be judged by you, and I look to you and the small knot of friends with whom you act with an anxious hope you can hardly imagine.[18]

Yet, as this and subsequent interactions demonstrated, she had a steely determination to further the cause of national public education, reminding Gladstone of his commitment to the cause just before he delivered his first budget speech as chancellor of the exchequer in 1853, 'Now is your time. The country is prosperous, the people in good spirits, and alive to all sorts of schemes of improvement.'[19] This 'private' method of campaigning was generally only available to political 'insiders', those with the necessary authority and personal connections to influence leading politicians. And women, as Sarah Austin noted, had to tread carefully so they were not seen to be transgressing gender boundaries. However, there were more public means for women, of all classes, to pursue 'conversations with parliament' to further their political and economic aims by utilising governmental processes and procedures to promote issues on which they had an interest.

The 19th century witnessed a spectacular increase in older forms of political engagement, and as access to these processes were open to all, the expansion enabled women's

[16] Lord John Russell, 'Presidential Address', in *Transactions of the National Society for the Promotion of Social Science, 1858*, ed. George Hastings (1859), 17.

[17] Sarah Austin, *On National Education* (1839).

[18] Janet Ross, *Three Generations of English Women: Memoirs and Correspondence of Susanna Taylor, Sarah Austin and Lady Duff Gordon* (1893), 150: Sarah Austin to William Ewart Gladstone, 27 May 1839.

[19] Ross, *Three Generations of English Women*, 285–7.

ability to pressure parliament to proliferate. They were able to draw on many historical precendents: petitioning parliament and the crown, and the use of commissions and committees to investigate key policy areas had been utilised as strategies by the ordinary public to engage in political affairs. Thomas Erskine May argued that entitlement to petition was a right that had been exercised successively since before the time of Edward the Confessor.[20] Numbers of petitions began to rise notably at the start of the 19th century from both men and women. However, the volume was considerably swelled when female anti-slavery activists adopted petitioning as a key campaigning strategy. By the middle of the century the numbers of petitions were reaching tens of thousands per year with hundreds of thousands of signatories.[21] As the formal arena of parliamentary politics grew more exclusive, many women looked to older forms of interaction with the state. They petitioned on key matters of political and economic policy including the franchise, repeal of the corn laws, the new poor law and protectionist legislation, but also on more minor issues such as copyright law or the state of public roads.[22] Signing petitions signalled that women (and others excluded from the formal political system) were able to perform a role as active citizens on a national stage notwithstanding their lack of a vote.

There was a corresponding increase in the production of parliamentary papers. Royal commissions were the most conspicuous of these, but select committees of both Houses also examined aspects of British society and issued blue books appended by long transcripts of hearings and additional documents.[23] Royal commissions may be traced back to the Domesday Book, but the 19th-century format of employing commissioners to gather expert witness advice dates from the Commission on Inclosures in 1517.[24] Select committees were sections or subdivisions of the house of commons and house of lords and reported to those institutions. From the 1790s, select committees were given their own index entries in the *Commons Journals* and from that date appear to have developed a clear role as investigating bodies on issues as diverse as copyright and the police.[25] Royal commissions possessed power via delegations by warrant from parliament and the crown which conferred authority on them. The evidence of the commissions, which often ran to over 1,000 pages, demonstrated a desire for official transparency. As was with the case with petitions, the sheer quantity of official publications emanating from these committees was breathtaking. From 1731 to 1800, there were only 110 volumes issued by parliament. Whereas from 1801 to 1851, there were 1,794 volumes. In 1800, the annual number of volumes printed was 20; by 1850 this had risen to 60.[26] Blue books were not destined to be consigned to libraries unread. They were enthusiastically read and consumed by an informed and engaged public seeking to understand the challenges of early industrial Britain. Women were often the disseminators of the vast quantities of knowledge contained in the pages of the reports.

[20]Thomas Erskine May, *A Treatise upon the Law, Privileges, Proceedings and Usage of Parliament* (1844), 300; see also Mark Knights's essay in this volume for 18th-century contests over 17th-century rights of petitioners.

[21]See also Colin Leys, 'Petitioning in the Nineteenth and Twentieth Centuries', *Political Studies*, iii (1955), 47.

[22]For a detailed analysis of women's petitioning in this period see Sarah Richardson, *The Political Worlds of Women: Gender and Political Culture in Nineteenth-Century Britain* (2013), ch. 5.

[23]Oz Frankel, *States of Inquiry: Social Investigations and Print Culture in Nineteenth-Century Britain and the United States* (Baltimore, MD, 2006), esp. 39–71.

[24]Thomas J. Lockwood, 'A History of Royal Commissions', *Osgoode Hall Law Journal*, v (1967), 172–209.

[25]Peter Jupp, *The Governing of Britain, 1688–1848: The Executive, Parliament and the People* (Abingdon, 2006).

[26]Hansard, Parl. Debs, 3rd ser., cxxiii, col. 1065: 7 Dec. 1852.

A notable example is Charlotte Elizabeth Tonna who published the best-selling, *The Perils of the Nation*, in 1843, summarizing evidence on the wealth and poverty of Britain.[27] The book contained a specific chapter on the role of female influence in improving living conditions. Tonna also used the evidence from the royal commissions on factories in her popular novel, *Helen Fleetwood*, published in 1841.[28]

At times, the publication of reports of both select committees and royal commissions turned into communal events, with the public eagerly awaiting the outcomes of particular inquiries. In 1852, there was without any sense of irony, a debate on whether a select committee should be established to consider whether parliamentary papers and reports should be freely distributed to the country's literary and scientific societies and mechanics institutes. In the debate, Disraeli celebrated the growth in the accessibility of this public official knowledge, maintaining it was a means to elevate the character of the people:

If we looked to manners, if we looked to the means of Government not only in this country but its dependencies, and indeed, to all those subjects which ought to afford the materials when the true history of a country was drawn, we should find that in Parliamentary literature, which had grown into importance in the last half-century resources were placed in the hands of public writers, such as never had been before possessed in any time or country.[29]

Many women activists accessed these key sources of knowledge to inform their interventions in debates on all aspects of public policy.

The upwards trend in the numbers of commissions and petitions was not without its critics. Following the establishment of the royal commission on the poor law, William Cobbett noted:

These *commissioners* sit in London, it seems, and send forth roving deputy-commissioners to collect information about the country. These rovers give in written accounts of the result of their inquiries. A parcel of *extracts* from these accounts have been collected together and printed in the form of an octavo book, and sold at *price* four shillings, 'PUBLISHED BY AUTHORITY', and the members of the House of Commons have each then been furnished with a copy of this book. This is a new way of doing the nation's business.[30]

Joseph Hume, the noted guardian of public expenditure, pointed out the irony of the millions of pages of paper that the Commons produced, which were read by very few, in contrast to the taxes on newspapers which were limiting the spread of knowledge to the working class.[31] Joshua Toulmin Smith also attacked the process of circumventing parliament and doing business by royal commission. He argued that commissions infringed on

[27] [Charlotte Elizabeth Tonna], *The Perils of the Nation: An Appeal to the Legislature, the Clergy and the Higher and Middle Classes* (1843).

[28] Barbara Kanner and Ivanka Kovacevic, 'Blue Book into Novel: The Forgotten Industrial Fiction of Charlotte Elizabeth Tonna', *Nineteenth Century Fiction*, xxv (1970), 152–73.

[29] Hansard, Parl. Debs, 3rd ser., cxxiii, cols 1069–70: 7 Dec. 1852.

[30] *Cobbett's Political Register*, 6 July 1833, p. 398.

[31] Hansard, Parl. Debs, 3rd ser., cxxiii, col. 1067: 7 Dec. 1852.

Table 1: *Royal Commissions of Inquiry*

Decade	Number of royal commissions
1830–9	48
1840–9	52
1850–9	85
1860–9	71
1870–9	50
1880–9	52
1890–9	39

Source: H.D. Clokie and J.W. Robinson, *Royal Commissions of Inquiry* (Stanford, CA, 1937).

old freedoms by assuming functions historically formed by local authorities. Commissioners were nominated by the crown with no opportunity to challenge appointments. They departed from accepted modes of inquiry by eradicating the adversarial dimension that was at the core of parliamentary hearings. He argued that:

> What evidence they please is taken and no more. All evidence is taken in secret; and so much published as, and when they like; and with such an accompanying gloss as they please to give it. No liberty of cross-examination, 'that is, of extracting dissimilitudes,' is admitted. Judgment is pronounced in the absence of every party affected, or whose property or interests are brought in question. An unlimited authority to squander money is assumed.[32]

Royal commissions were also criticized for the time they took to deliberate and the suspicion that they were merely there to prepare the way for predetermined government policies. *Punch* regularly satirised the establishment's propensity to turn to a royal commission to answer every burning question of the day. In 1888, following an enquiry into naval and military provision which urged retrenchment, they quipped that [John Bull] 'has neither Army nor Navy, but he has a Royal Commission and several voluminous Blue Books'.[33]

The number of royal commissions increased rapidly with the reforming whig ministries of the 1830s and quickly became an established mode of parliamentary life (see Table 1). The 1850s were the highpoint for the establishment of inquiries, with 18 inaugurated in 1853 alone. There was a similar increase in the number of select committees with numbers averaging between 30 and 40 each year by the middle of the century. The print culture of parliamentary knowledge became an industry in the early 19th century. In 1799, the expense of printing the journals, votes and all other papers was £8,000; in 1827, it rose to £46,000 and by the 1850s exceeded £100,000 a year. Parliament did make some cutbacks on the printing and publication of information by restricting the numbers of petitions that were printed. In 1829 (a high point), 84% of petitions presented were printed. In 1843, only

---

[32]Joshua Toulmin Smith, *Government by Commissions Illegal and Pernicious* (1859), 168–9.
[33]'The British Ollendorff', *Punch*, 9 June 1888, p. 268.

2.8% were published and the average for the period to 1858 was around 12%.[34] Disraeli gave an indication of the significance of commissions, committees and petitions in a report to the Commons in August 1848:

> there have been this year forty-five public Committees, some of more than usual impor-
> tance, with an average number of fifteen Members serving on each Committee. Then
> there have been twenty-eight Election Committees, with five Members serving on each
> Committee; fourteen groups on Railway Bills, with five Members on each group; seven-
> teen groups on private Bills, with five Members on each group; and there have been also
> one hundred and eleven other Committees on private business. Of the public Commit-
> tees, that on commercial distress sat thirty-nine days; that on sugar and coffee planting,
> thirty-nine days; that on the Navy, Army, and Ordnance expenditure, forty days; and that
> on the miscellaneous expenditure, thirty-seven days. There have, besides, been presented
> this year upwards of 18,500 petitions, showing an increase of 25 per cent above the
> greatest number presented in any former year, except 1843.[35]

Women were able to utilise these changing dynamics of parliamentary culture in order to gain a public voice. Petitions, requests for particular information and participation in select committees and royal commissions were all methods for promulgating views and promoting causes without the need for formal political representation. This contrasts with the views of some historians who have portrayed the period after the passage of the 1832 Reform Act as witnessing the growth of a masculine public sphere and the development of more formal, regulated political structures and institutions.[36] Obviously, the agendas of parliamentary commissions and committees were set centrally, by members of parliament (and increasingly by civil servants), but women, by dint of their experience, expertise, and authority, were able to play an important role once they had been established. In addition, petitions were generally initiated from the bottom up, allowing any citizen who had a grievance to make their point to parliament.[37] It was perhaps because of the closure of some avenues of informal political participation, that these older methods of interacting with parliament became so popular in the 19th century. Recent work on parliamentary space has revealed that women were always present, as spectators, participants and lobbyists.[38] Thus these modes of 'conversations with parliament' are an important source to gauge women's interaction with national politics and their ability to put pressure on the personnel and institution of parliament.

As royal commissions and select committees were established to explore in depth the key social, economic, cultural and political issues of the day, they needed expert witnesses in or-der to operate effectively; and women were often best placed to provide that service. Their contribution often went unrecorded. So, for example, the royal commission on fine arts,

---

[34] *Parliamentary Papers* (1854–5), liv: General Index to the Reports on Public Petitions, 1833–52.

[35] Hansard, Parl. Debs, 3rd ser., ci, col. 671: 30 Aug. 1848.

[36] The most articulate expression of the concept of 'closure of democratic political forms' in this period is James Vernon, *Politics and the People: A Study in English Political Culture, c. 1815–1867* (Cambridge, 1993).

[37] Richardson, *Political Worlds of Women*, ch. 5.

[38] See, e.g., Richardson, *Political Worlds of Women*; Kathryn Gleadle, *Borderline Citizens: Women, Gender, and Political Culture in Britain, 1815–1867* (Oxford, 2009).

which reported in 1842, relied heavily on the work of Mary Philadelphia Merrifield. Merrifield was an expert on Italian Renaissance art. In 1844 she translated Cennino Cennici's early-15th-century work, the *Treatise of Painting* (1844), which had been recently discovered and published in 1821 by the Italian antiquary, Giuseppe Tambroni. On the merits of this work, the royal commission employed her to investigate the history of painters' materials and techniques, which resulted in the publication of her book, *The Art of Fresco Painting*.[39] This reflected the commission's deep concern about the absence of a British school of history painting, and it was both a collection of historical texts on the techniques of 12th- to 18th-century fresco painters and a functional manual for the practising artist.[40] In 1857, Merrifield was granted a civil-list pension of £100 in recognition of her services to literature and art. Although she was a key researcher for the royal commission on fine arts, Merrifield's name appears nowhere in its published report. Her evidence was, instead, subsumed under the contribution of Sir Charles Eastlake.[41]

Five years after Merrifield's sterling work for the royal commission on fine arts, Caroline Chisholm gave evidence to two house of lords select committees examining aspects of Australian settlement. In contrast to Merrifield's experience, Chisholm was publicly listed as the only female witness to both committees and her immense specialist knowledge and expertise was readily acknowledged. At one point the peers asked if she was enabled to carry out her work by her 'own Influence and Authority, without any auxiliary Aid?' She replied: 'Entirely by my own Influence.'[42] Other witnesses to the committee heralded her skills and experience. Chisholm possessed formidable organisational skills but was also adept at promulgating her views. In Australia, she had tirelessly worked to provide services and employment for emigrants and convicts whose sentence was completed, taking on the colonial administration, magistrates, clergy and industrial vested interests. She collected evidence in the form of personal testimonies and economic statistics. In addition to her confrontations with the male establishment, she also challenged Australian middle-class women who employed female migrants as servants. She supported servants who had been penalised by having their wages docked for accidental damages (stating experience of 51 cases) and maintained that employers should use the magistrates to claim damages for breakages rather than take the law into their own hands.[43]

In April 1847, Chisholm, who had returned to England the year before, was summoned to the house of lords select committee on the criminal law. She was subject to rapid fire questioning but acquitted herself with aplomb. She gently steered the debate away from

---

[39] Mary Philadelphia Merrifield, *The Art of Fresco Painting, as Practised by the Old Italian and Spanish Masters, with a Preliminary Inquiry into the Nature of the Colours used in Fresco Painting, with Observation and Notes* (1846).

[40] Merrifield continued her major, if unsung, contribution to intellectual life. Her book, Mary Philadelphia Merrifield, *Original Treatises, Dating from the XIIth to the XVIIIth Centuries, on the Arts of Painting* (1849), was a collection of early technical information which was a standard reference book for artists well into the 20th century. Modern art historians consider her to be the pioneer in the field of art technological source research. In 1854, her book, Mary Philadelphia Merrifield, *Dress as a Fine Art* (1854), publicised the dress reforms of Amelia Bloomer and advocated practical, modest, and elegant fashions and displayed a considerable sympathy for the dress reforms of Amelia Bloomer.

[41] *Parliamentary Papers* (1842), xxv: 'Report of the Commissioners on the Fine Arts'.

[42] *Parliamentary Papers* (1847), vi: 'Report of the Select Committee of the House of Lords on Colonization from Ireland; Together with the Minutes of Evidence', 411.

[43] Caroline Chisholm, *Female Immigration Considered, in a Brief Account of the Sydney Immigrants' Home* (Sydney, Australia, 1842); see also Joanna Bogle, *Caroline Chisholm: The Emigrants' Friend* (Leominster, 1993).

conditions in Norfolk Island and Van Diemen's Land (where, she asserted she had no first-hand experience and thus was not prepared to comment on conditions or employment opportunities for convicts) to focus on Sydney and the interior. She provided factual and statistical information on employment opportunities both for ticket-of-leave men and for female emigrants, stating that she had aided around 14,000 people in the past seven years.[44] In July the same year she appeared before a select committee on colonization from Ireland where she set out a scheme to aid emigration by loaning potential emigrants a portion of their fare to Australia, which would be recouped once they obtained employment. Her testimony which ran to over 20 pages, is characterised by the substantial evidence-base she provided to support her statements on emigration and employment in Australia. This included statements from emigrants, reformed convicts, employers, and government officials; statistical information; and detailed business plans for emigration schemes. She was also judicious. Pressed on whether she favoured a particular class or ethnic origin of emigrant, she retorted:

> I made no Difference; the Good of the whole was my Object. I also included any Ticket-of-Leave Men, Emancipists, – any Persons that wanted Work that would go into the Country. My Object was to remove them into the Country to lessen the City Population. I had English, Irish, and Scotch, – Episcopalians, Presbyterians, Catholics, Orangemen, and Repealers, – and I never found any Difficulty beyond such Difficulties as must always be expected in a Work of the Kind.[45]

Caroline was the only woman to be heard directly by the committee, but she allowed the voices of many female emigrants to be heeded by reading out verbatim testimonies and by retelling their experiences.

The evidence she gave to the select committees was direct, straightforward and empowering. She set out her schemes to help those wishing to emigrate (and those already in Australia), in great detail, supported by comprehensive budgets and expected returns on investment. Little reference was made either by herself, or by the questioning peers, of her sex. Her authority was absolute and her experience transcended any barriers of gender. Chisholm's appearance before the committees received barely any attention from the press in England, although it was reported in detail by the *Sydney Morning Herald*.[46] By continual lobbying of the home office and ministers such as Earl Grey and Sir James Stephen, she achieved her immediate objective: that of obtaining free passage to Australia for wives and children of convicts now settled in the colony.[47] Her scheme to provide loans to those wishing to emigrate for employment or to join family members, received only lukewarm support, however. She kept up her propaganda offensive on the government, issuing a public letter to Earl Grey and by gathering a formidable array of influential supporters, including Charles Dickens and Angela Burdett-Coutts.[48] Eventually, in 1849, she established the

---

[44] *Parliamentary Papers* (1847), vii: 'Second Report from the Select Committee of the House of Lords appointed to Inquire into the Execution of the Criminal Law', 395–9.

[45] *Parliamentary Papers* (1847), vi: 'Report of the Select Committee of the House of Lords on Colonization from Ireland', 411.

[46] *Sydney Morning Herald*, 12 Feb. 1848.

[47] *Sydney Chronicle*, 11 Nov. 1847.

[48] Caroline Chisholm, *Emigration and Transportation Relatively Considered* (1847).

Family Colonisation Loan Society independent of the government, underwritten by Coutts Bank. Caroline Chisholm thus achieved mixed success from her appearances in front of the select committees but she had proven that women could wield influence and apply pressure to ministers if they possessed sufficient status and authority.

Chisholm's positive experiences of utilising the committees and commissions of parliament to pursue causes close to her heart were mirrored by those of Mary Carpenter a few years later. When Carpenter gave evidence to the select committee on criminal and destitute juveniles she spoke for over two days, and her evidence amounted to over 50 pages in the written report. Like Chisholm, she quickly set out the basis of her authority:

> the evidence which I now give particularly relates to Bristol as regards my personal experience; but I have besides, during the last two or three years, studied the reports of benevolent institutions connected with juvenile delinquents all over the kingdom and have corresponded with various individuals who have had opportunities of knowing their condition, particularly chaplains of gaols and others. Therefore the evidence which I give will be founded on the opinions which I have formed upon all these matters partly from my own experience and partly from other sources.[49]

She was grilled by the committee on aspects such as morality, religious instruction in reformed schools, the economic and financial aspects, and regulation. But her evidence demonstrates that she was well informed; knowledgeable; and robust in her responses. She was willing to contradict and challenge the commissioners on issues such as regulation and funding of reformatory schools. Her testimony did much to bring pressure to bear on parliament to recognize a need for reform. The Youthful Offenders Act of 1854, owed much to her influence authorising the establishment of reformatory schools by voluntary bodies, certified by the state and partly funded by the treasury. The act represented a major change in penal policy and established a pattern of relations between statutory and voluntary bodies that would serve as a model for the future. Her influence was also felt in the act of 1857, which applied similar procedures and support to industrial schools. Carpenter has often been categorised by historians as demonstrating the limits of women's influence in the public sphere. Her refusal to deliver her paper to the Social Science Association in 1851 for fear of 'unsexing herself' has been often cited to illustrate the dangers of women lobbying in public arenas.[50] She has been portrayed as the embodiment of maternalist policies which would be short-lived as the state gradually occupied spaces previously dominated by private philanthropists.[51] However, in spite of this shaky beginning to her career as a public lobbyist, Carpenter went on to deliver 36 papers to the Social Science Association, more than any other member, and gave evidence to the select committee on poor relief in 1861.[52]

---

[49] *Parliamentary Papers* (1852), vii: 'Report from the Select Committee on Criminal and Destitute Juveniles', 90.

[50] J.E. Carpenter, *The Life of Mary Carpenter* (1881), 126.

[51] Seth Koven, 'Borderlands: Women, Voluntary Action and Child Welfare in Great Britain 1840–1914', in *Mothers of a New World: Maternalist Politics and the Origins of Welfare States*, ed. Seth Koven and Sonya Michel (1993), 96–106.

[52] Lawrence Goldman, *Science, Reform, and Politics in Victorian Britain: The Social Science Association 1857–1886* (Cambridge, 2002), 144–5.

As their experience of engaging directly with parliament via royal commissions and select committees increased, many women linked their appearances more explicitly with feminist agendas. An article in the *English Woman's Journal* in the summer of 1861, celebrated the extensive evidence given by Louisa Twining, Mary Carpenter, and Ellen Woodlock, to a series of select committees appointed to consider and report on the subject of poor relief in England and Ireland.[53] With perhaps a hint of hyperbole, the article stated that the calling of these women 'to council' marked an 'epoch in social history'.[54] All three women argued forcefully against the institution of the workhouse, offering practical alternative solutions based on their own personal experiences.[55] They were subjected to vigorous interrogations. Ellen Woodlock, who had established an industrial school in Dublin to take poor and orphaned children away from workhouses, was asked repeatedly by the committee if the establishments could be reformed or modified to meet her concerns. Eventually she replied: 'I imagine the workhouse ought not to be made such an institution; it is only intended to relieve the destitute and poor, and I think orphan and deserted children should get such an education as would fit them to take their place in society like any others.'[56] All three women provided comprehensive evidence to the committees, giving practical examples underpinned by more theoretical and intellectual reflections from papers they had given to the Social Science Association. Twining brought formidable expertise from her role as president of the Workhouse Visiting Society; she was author of numerous pamphlets and periodical articles. Carpenter and Woodlock contrasted their positive experiences of youths educated in industrial (and in the case of Carpenter) reform schools with those who had been incarcerated in workhouses receiving limited education and training. Other (male) witnesses were also asked to testify to the women's reputation as reformers in the field, with all giving a favourable response. Thus the *English Woman's Journal* could fairly state that their, 'Intelligence, social position, wide experience, were superadded; so that nothing was wanting to impress upon their testimony the stamp of unquestionable authority.'[57]

The experience of testifying to the various committees was summarized evocatively by the *English Woman's Journal* which emphasized the women's proximity to the decision-making process:

> a summons which required the necessity of crossing the lobby of the House of Commons, confronting the chairman, answering methodically the interrogatories of the honourable gentleman who undertook to conduct the inquiry, and withstanding the shock of a cross-examination by members on the 'other side,' may have been received with a feeling more or less akin to a natural feminine shrinking from the obligation of occupying too conspicuous a position.[58]

[53] 'The Ladies' Evidence. Poor Relief', *English Woman's Journal*, vii (1861), 405–10.

[54] 'The Ladies' Evidence', 405.

[55] The evidence of Louisa Twining and Mary Carpenter is recorded in *Parliamentary Papers* (1861), ix: 'Fourth Report from the Select Committee on Poor Relief (England)', 1–31; and also in the indexes presented in *Parliamentary Papers* (1861), ix: 'Sixth Report from the Select Committee on Poor Relief (England)'. Ellen Woodlock's evidence was published in *Parliamentary Papers* (1861), x: 'Report from the Select Committee on Poor Relief (Ireland)', 216–27.

[56] *Parliamentary Papers* (1861), x: 'Report from the Select Committee on Poor Relief (Ireland)', 227.

[57] 'The Ladies' Evidence', 405–6.

[58] 'The Ladies' Evidence', 406.

All three women proved more than capable of the task, avoiding any 'feminine shrinking' which led the periodical to call for a wider scope for women to exercise public roles in their areas of expertise.

A similarly feminist agenda was pursued by women giving evidence to the royal commission on the consolidation of the factory and workshops act in 1875 which sought to impose maximum working hours for women and regulate their work.[59] There was an organised feminist opposition in the cities where the commissioners were to hold hearings and meetings of both middle- and working-class women to collect evidence to present to the commission and to drum up opposition to the acts among female workers. One striking example of how far women had progressed in their utilisation of parliamentary inquiries to advance their interests was in the large number of female witnesses who testified: over 60 women appeared before the commissioners, of whom over half were described as 'working women' as opposed to 'philanthropic ladies'. The report noted ruefully that save for a couple of nailmakers and bleachers who sought further protection, all the female contributors were opposed to the proposed legislation.[60]

The delegation from Leeds, for example, consisted of Lucy Wilson and Alice Scatcherd (both active in a number of women's causes), Miss Roberts (a saleswoman in a shop), Mrs Wood, Mrs Ellis, Miss Conron, and Mrs Marsden (all power loom weavers). The chief speaker was Lucy Wilson of Leeds, a member of the executive committee of the married women's property committee from 1876 to 1882, a leader of the Ladies National Association, a member of the executive committee of the Vigilance Association and founder of the National Union of Woman Workers.[61] Wilson accused the committee of seeking a ban for married women engaging in factory work as they 'ought to attend to their families'. She argued that such a ban would bring economic hardship to families and 'alter the conditions of marriage for women if you reduce them to an inability to maintain themselves'.[62] Dr Eliza Walker Dunbar, house surgeon of the Bristol Hospital for Sick Children, who was asked whether women who had been recently confined should be excluded from factory work for a period to recuperate, made the analogy with housework:

> I think that the demands of housework are just as great as any demands in factories, and it is very usual for working women to return to their house work, to scrub and wash, and do hard labour, within the eight days. I have allowed it myself, but they do it. You would not legislate for housework, and why, therefore should you legislate for factories work.[63]

[59] *Parliamentary Papers* (1876), xxix: 'Report of the Commissioners Appointed to Inquire into the Working of the Factory and Workshops Acts', i; see, e.g., the evidence from the Women's Provident and Protective League, 192–3.

[60] *Parliamentary Papers* (1876), xxix: 'Report of the Commissioners Appointed to Inquire into the Working of the Factory and Workshops Acts', i, p. cix.

[61] For more on the National Union of Woman Workers and links to the wider suffrage movement, see Sandra Stanley Holton, *Suffrage Days: Stories from the Women's Suffrage Movement* (2002), 35–6.

[62] *Parliamentary Papers* (1876), xxix: 'Report of the Commissioners Appointed to Inquire into the Working of the Factory and Workshops Acts', i, 321.

[63] *Parliamentary Papers* (1876), xxx: 'Report of the Commissioners Appointed to Inquire into the Working of the Factory and Workshops Acts', ii, 654.

Eliza Sturge who headed the Birmingham 'Deputation of Ladies' argued that men had given evidence on the subject of women's labour without taking the opinion of the women concerned. Sturge 'asserted the right of women to work, side by side with men, for the public good' and she was critical of the inability of politicians to suggest practical methods of making a living for women reduced to poverty, as well as the undervaluing of women's work and activities.[64] Sturge's evidence highlighted the fact that class, not gender, frequently dictated the treatment meted out to women, and that women were blamed for being the product of a social and educational system designed to restrict their intellectual and economic contributions.

Nearly 20 years later, the key contributions that women were able to make to royal commissions and select committees were finally recognized by the appointment of three female commissioners to the royal commission on secondary education in 1894.[65] Sophie Bryant, mathematician and headmistress of North London Collegiate School, Lucy Cavendish, a member of the Girls Public Day School Company and the Yorkshire Ladies Council of Education, and Eleanor Sidgwick, principal of Newnham College, Cambridge, were trailblazers yet their role was also limited. They were given a separate brief from the male commissioners: to consider whether girls required a different curriculum from boys, and how this might be delivered in a mixed-sex environment.[66] They were also described as either widows or, in the case of Sidgwick, as wife of Henry Sidgwick, Esquire, doctor in letters, professor of moral philosophy, University of Cambridge, though at least Sophie Bryant was accorded her status as a doctor of science. However, in spite of the restrictions, the last barrier had been breached and women were thenceforth able to play a full role in inquiries by the state giving full status credit to their extensive expertise, skills, knowledge and experience.

Alongside their work on royal commissions and select committees, women also took a full part in the revival of another form of parliamentary pressure: petitioning. The petitioning movement was revitalised in the 19th century, due in no small part to women's efforts particularly in raising the profile of the anti-slavery and anti-*sati* movements. The ability to make direct representations to parliament allowed women to articulate their concerns, and be heard by the foremost institution in the country. Further, it provided them with a political education, a chance to organise and mobilise public opinion, and ultimately to shape policy. Petitions were the consummate method of expressing 'pressure from without', and hundreds of thousands of men and women participated. The public appetite for petitioning may be summed up by this summary in a mid-century issue of the *Manchester Times*:

There are now 4,859 petitions against opening the Museum and galleries on the Lord's Day, signed by 599,870 persons, and 100 in favour of doing so, signed by 19,189 persons; 298 petitions against the abolition of church-rates without providing an equivalent, signed by 12,855 persons; 44 in favour of the Church rate Abolition Bill, signed by 3,559 persons; and 12 for the repeal of the Maynotth Act, signed by 2,083 persons. There are

[64] *Parliamentary Papers* (1876), xxx: 'Report of the Commissioners Appointed to Inquire into the Working of the Factory and Workshops Acts', ii, 337–41.

[65] *Parliamentary Papers* (1895), xliii: 'Royal Commission on Secondary Education: Report of the Commissioners', i, p. iv.

[66] Jane McDermid, *The Schooling of Girls in Britain and Ireland, 1800–1900* (2013), 87–97.

also 102 against the Police Bill, signed by 29,000 persons, and 13 for a repeal of the Scottish Public-houses Act signed by 6,117 persons. There is a long petition from 3,015 'women of Great Britain, married and single', for a law for the enforcement of the property rights of married women. The petition is headed by the signatures of Mary Howitt, Anna Jameson, and Jessie Meriton White.[67]

Women supported petitions for a wide range of public political and more private matters.[68] There were 'monster' petitions such as those against the institution of slavery, for the repeal of the corn laws, for universal suffrage, and for the reform of the contagious diseases acts. But there were also intensely personal appeals for redress, offering a glimpse of the strategies open to women under duress. Thus in 1849 Martha Wrede petitioned for relief, complaining that certain sums of money bequeathed to her by her husband had never been paid, in consequence of the neglect and mismanagement of the property by the executor.[69]

Appropriately, after having been so influential as a method for female political activism for most of the 19th century, petitioning played a pivotal role in the women's suffrage campaigns. The movement was inaugurated with a circular petition organised by the women's suffrage petition committee in 1865. A year later, 1,499 signatures were presented to parliament, marking the beginning of the continuous women's suffrage movement in Britain.[70] This was followed by further petitions culminating in the women's suffrage special appeal of the mid 1890s. More than 3,500 women worked to collect a total of nearly 250,000 signatures to the appeal, which was finally presented to parliament in 1896. Permission was granted by the Speaker to use the Westminster Hall to display the appeal, and the women maximised their opportunities to engage MPs directly:

Fifty feet of tables were arranged in a modest corner, and delegates from England, Ireland, and Scotland took charge of the precious volumes … By a coincidence the ladies found themselves at the feet of James the First, the monarch in whose reign their privileges were first whittled away. A little farther on Charles the First had his shoulder turned to them, ignoring the progress of thieving, and there the ladies passed the afternoon and evening. As the members began to arrive for the sitting of the House many visited the hall. Friends of the ladies brought down as many of the violent opponents as possible, and playfully introduced them to the lists of their own constituents, whose names were in evidence.[71]

There were further attempts to persuade parliament of the need for reform of the franchise (see Table 2). In 1902, Priscilla Bright McLaren wrote to her grandson: 'there is a very important Deputation of Women graduates going up to London to present a Petition today, in favour of Women's Suffrage – 1,800 names – there are about 2,000 graduates – but many of these are spread over the Globe, but have sent letters warmly approving it.

[67] *Manchester Times*, 5 Apr. 1856.

[68] For an in-depth analysis of women and petitioning, see Richardson, *Political Worlds of Women*, ch. 5.

[69] *Parliamentary Papers* (1854–5), liv, 983: General Index to the Reports on Public Petitions, 1833–52.

[70] Ann Dingsdale, ' "Generous and Lofty Sympathies": The Kensington Society, the 1866 Women's Suffrage Petition and the Development of Mid-Victorian Feminism', University of Greenwich PhD, 1995.

[71] *Englishwoman's Review*, 15 July 1896.

Table 2: *Support for Women's Suffrage, 1890–1906*

Session	Number of petitions in favour of women's suffrage	Number of signatures
1890	165	3,127
1890–1	147	3,277
1892 (session 1)	253	7,318
1893–4	344	19,765
1894	12	4,602
1895 (session 1)	16	312
1896	29	1,459
1897	1,289	43,399
1898	19	853
1899 (session 1)	192	6,127
1900 (session 1)	5	7
1901	21	30,178
1902	11	39,079
1903	10	13,990
1904	15	11,946
1905	55	8,153
1906	1	1

Source: *Return showing the Number of Petitions to the House of Commons in Favour of Women's Suffrage for each Session from 1890 to 1906, Inclusive; and the Number of Names Attached to Such Petitions* (1906). Note: the figures exclude the women's suffrage special appeal which was presented to parliament in 1896.

About 66,000 Textile weavers presented a like Petition last month. These Petitions are very educational – and the women will help to raise the men to see that justice ought to be extended to women and this would be well also for men.'[72] In 1903, Sarah Reddish was employed as a 'petition worker' for the north of England collecting signatories from Lancashire cotton mill factory women, Scottish textile workers, women trade unionists from the chain maker trades in Coventry and hosiers from Leicestershire.[73] However, it was the refusal of parliament to listen to the 'special appeal' which encouraged many women to turn to more militant tactics. The Pankhursts did not abandon the strategy entirely, and in 1914 Emmeline was arrested and imprisoned for attempting to present a petition to the king, after failing to engage his ministers.[74] The campaign for the extension of the female franchise exposed the limits of the petitioning system for women. Frustration with parliament's unwillingness to listen or engage in even moderate reforms of the electoral system encouraged many to pursue more confrontational and aggressive approaches. Women were no longer satisfied with raising their voices. They demanded to be heard and for action to be taken by parliament.

[72]Elizabeth Crawford, *Women's Suffrage: A Reference Guide, 1866–1928* (2003), 402–3.

[73]Crawford, *Women's Suffrage*, 593.

[74]June Purvis, *Emmeline Pankhurst: A Biography* (2002), 257.

Women thus seized the opportunities offered by parliament as a means of actively engaging in the public sphere. As parliamentary politics grew more restrictive and formalised, women were not excluded but utilised older forms of interaction with the state and occupied spaces that were not explicitly barred to them. Whether they were presenting petitions or attending commission and committee meetings, they demonstrated that parliament was not a closed institution to the women of England. Petitions enabled women of all social classes to express opinions and raise grievances. Women were able to utilise their authority as experts to contribute to committees and royal commissions. This signalled that they were performing a role as active citizens on a national stage that their voices should be heard and taken seriously and that the issues raised should be addressed. The function of these parliamentary procedures and processes as a device to mobilise and to politicise should not be underestimated. They demonstrated the blurred boundaries between the public and the private in the world of extraparliamentary pressure the wide space of debateable ground that needs to be explored to understand women's citizenship before the suffrage. The petitions, commissions and committees covered aspects as diverse as decimal currency, animal welfare, mercantile law, and bankruptcy, as well as key issues of concern such as health, education, and crime. They also provide an important source for understanding imperial and foreign affairs. Women's contributions are sometimes implicitly, but often explicitly, reflected in the burgeoning print culture of the blue books published by parliament, demonstrating their expertise in sometimes unusual areas. Women could, and did, make important interventions in matters of public policy in 19th-century England.

Petitions, Economic Legislation and Interest Groups in Britain, 1660–1800

JULIAN HOPPIT

Between 1660 and 1800, over 14,000 acts were passed at Westminster, with over a half of them directed at economic matters. Yet parliament was eager to ensure that proposed legislation had been duly considered. A key feature of this were the many thousands of petitions it received, mainly from interest groups, both for and against legislation, proposed and enacted. By systematically exploring the details of nine parliamentary sessions across the period, this essay considers the characteristics of petitions submitted to parliament regarding economic legislation. Controversies between petitioning groups overwhelmingly concerned economic matters, with many of the groups being constituted for the purpose. In this way, interest groups were usually much more important than parties in parliament. Two case studies show how such interests cohered and operated in practice.

Keywords: economic legislation; interest groups; petitions

1

nothing is more common than for traders to differ widely among themselves, in regard to measures proper to be taken by the legislature for the due encouragement or regulation of peculiar branches. Whence arise those opposite and contradictory petitions to parliament from traders, which often tend to mislead, and even confound the legislature itself. (Malachy Postlethwayt, *The Universal Dictionary of Trade and Commerce* (2 vols, 1751–5), i, p. vi)

Pursuing stability, order and prosperity, the Westminster parliament had always worried about economic life.[1] But in the 17th century such concerns intensified and evolved as economic matters rose to become a 'reason of state'. Four factors were especially important in this: the growing crisis of funding central government; the increasing importance to European interstate rivalry of economic power, especially imperial economic power; mounting worries about the scourge of poverty and social disorder; and a developing optimism in the prospects for improvement, not least that aided by political authority.

---

[1] I thank Richard Huzzey and Yale for the invitation to contribute to the conference behind this volume. This essay has been improved by discussions there, as well as at a UCL-Yale 'history and the social sciences' workshop in London. Joanna Innes and Mark Knights kindly commented on a draft. Some of the data used here were collected long ago in the project that led to a number of publications, including *Failed Legislation, 1660–1800: Extracted from the Commons and Lords Journals*, ed. Julian Hoppit (1997).

In that context, it was hardly surprising that from the middle of the 17th century, parliament increasingly sought to legislate on economic matters. Some of those efforts are well known, such as the Navigation Act of 1651 or the establishment of the Bank of England in 1694. But many are not, which is unsurprising given the numbers involved. Between 1660 and 1800, more than 7,000 acts were passed directly concerning economic life, while there were over 3,000 failed attempts to do so – together consuming at least a half of Westminster's legislative effort.[2] In contrast, the 'government', 'religion' and 'armed services' subject categories together accounted for only 11% of all acts passed, and 17% of failed attempts. It may be that spirited encounters over foreign policy, religion, and the constitution bulk large in the very incomplete records of debates available, but the bread and butter of parliament's work was legislating about the likes of infrastructure, property rights, market standards, trade, and debtor-creditor relations.[3] From such a perspective, of all the pressures put upon parliament in these years, those relating to economic legislation predominated.

General interpretive frameworks of pressure on parliament about economic matters in the period foreground the role of the central government and its alleged policies, with 'mercantilist' and 'fiscal-military' interpretations being especially important. In the first, protectionist and regulatory policies are argued to have been driven by the belief that bullion was wealth which could only be increased by ensuring a positive balance of trade. In the second, policies were mainly consequences of the need to raise revenue to wage war and patrol the oceans in an age of intense interstate rivalry, with measures primarily influenced by bureaucratic pragmatism, not abstract ideals. But stimulating though these general approaches have been, both depend on a partial view of the relationship between governance and the economy, particularly by failing to give due weight to the fact that in this period, 69% of economic legislation was sectional, local, or personal in scope and only 31% 'general'.[4] Most economic legislation emanated not from central government, but from scattered groups and individuals: it was overwhelmingly non-governmental, non-departmental, and non-partisan. One characterisation of this, consequently sees the central state as in significant measure 'reactive', as a resource exploited by propertied society.[5]

If mercantilist, fiscal-military, and reactive conceptions of economic legislation are clearly very different, all three give significant weight to interest groups affecting political processes of all three. From at least the 17th century, contemporaries often stressed that political actions were to be understood by the working out of selfish 'interests', an emphasis also

[2]Julian Hoppit, 'Patterns of Parliamentary Legislation, 1660–1800', *Historical Journal*, xxxix (1996), 109–31. 'Economic' is an anachronism for the period studied here and includes 'finance', 'economy', and 'communications', as set out in *Failed Legislation*, ed. Hoppit, 30–2. Any such categorisation is not cut and dried, and some economic legislation might have both economic and non-economic objectives in view (though the same is also true of non-economic legislation). There were also thousands of 'estate acts' that, in part, concerned landholding and so were also in a sense economic. Julian Hoppit, 'The Landed Interest and the National Interest, 1660–1800', in *Parliaments, Nations and Identities in Britain and Ireland, 1660–1850*, ed. Julian Hoppit (Manchester, 2003), 85, 87.

[3]Doohwan Ahn and Brendan Simms, 'European Great Power Politics in British Public Discourse, 1714–1763', in *The Primacy of Foreign Policy in British History, 1660–2000*, ed. William Mulligan and Brendan Simms (Houndmills, 2010), 84. This article is an interesting, but rather unpersuasive, attempt to gauge the importance of certain themes in public discourse.

[4]For discussion of the importance of this, see Stuart Handley, 'Local Legislative Initiatives for Economic and Social Development in Lancashire, 1689–1731', *Parliamentary History*, ix (1990), 14–37; Joanna Innes, *Inferior Politics: Social Problems and Social Policies in Eighteenth-Century Britain* (Oxford, 2009), ch. 3.

[5]An introduction to the existing literature is provided in J. Hoppit, 'Further Reading', in *Regulating the British Economy, 1660–1850*, ed. Perry Gauci (Farnham, 2011), 259–71.

made by 20th-century scholars of very different hues.[6] Indeed, there is now a rich and varied literature on local or sectional interest groups, such as studies of the West Indian or American colonial interests, or the history of particular pieces or categories of legislation where interest groups were especially important, such as the growth of turnpike roads.[7] Dietz and Gauci are unusual in providing important studies of sectoral interests, and Bennett has explored the chambers of commerce that began to appear in the late 18th century.[8] More general syntheses or interpretations are few, though Langford and Brewer have made especially important contributions.[9] However, no clear picture emerges from these studies of what types of groups were common, or of patterns of their activity. One survey noted that 'Economic interest groups were organized in many ways', but could only give a sense of the scale of those ways in terms of 'often', 'frequently', or 'usually'.[10]

This essay explores petitions to parliament systematically, to delineate rather more precisely the nature of economic interest groups in the period. As will become clear, petitions were just one weapon in the armoury of such groups, but their formality is particularly helpful in thinking about why some interests found it more or less easy than others to cohere and agitate. The approach focuses on identifying patterns in petitioning on economic issues by following Gauci's lead, while hopefully complementing several important studies of aspects of petitioning, especially by Brewer, Hayton, Knights, and Sweet.[11] It begins by

[6]J.A.W. Gunn, ' "Interest will not Lie": A Seventeenth-Century Political Maxim', *Journal of the History of Ideas*, xxix (1968), 551–64; J.A.W. Gunn, *Politics and the Public Interest in the Seventeenth Century* (1969).

[7]L.M. Penson, 'The London West India Interest in the Eighteenth Century', *English Historical Review*, xxxvi (1921), 373–92; A.J. O'Shaughnessy, 'The Formation of a Commercial Lobby: The West India Interest, British Colonial Policy and the American Revolution', *Historical Journal*, xl (1997), 71–95; Perry Gauci, 'Learning the Ropes of Sand: The West India Lobby, 1714–60', in *Regulating the British Economy*, ed. Gauci, 107–21; Michael Kammen, *A Rope of Sand: The Colonial Agents, British Politics and the American Revolution* (New York, 1968); Alison Gilbert Olson, *Making the Empire Work: London and American Interest Groups, 1690–1790* (Cambridge, MA, 1992); William Albert, *The Turnpike Road System in England, 1663–1840* (Cambridge, 1972).

[8]Vivien Dietz, 'Before the Age of Capital: Manufacturing Interests and the British State, 1780–1800', Princeton University PhD, 1991; Perry Gauci, *The Politics of Overseas Trade: The Overseas Merchant in State and Society, 1660–1720* (Oxford, 2001); Robert J. Bennett, *The Voice of Liverpool Business: The First Chamber of Commerce and the Atlantic Economy, 1774–c. 1796* (Liverpool, 2010); Robert J. Bennett, *Local Business Voice: The History of Chambers of Commerce in Britain, Ireland, and Revolutionary America, 1760–2011* (Oxford, 2011).

[9]Paul Langford, *Public Life and the Propertied Englishman, 1689–1798* (Oxford, 1990), 176–86; John Brewer, *The Sinews of Power: War, Money and the English State, 1688–1783* (1989), 231–49. Other general accounts include Samuel Beer, 'The Representation of Interests in British Government: Historical Background', *American Political Science Review*, li (1957), 613–50, which was an important general contribution in an older historiographical era; Peter Jupp, *The Governing of Britain, 1688–1848: The Executive, Parliament and the People* (Abingdon, 2006), 90–5, is a useful brief overview. There are two general surveys of economic interests that are relevant: Joel Mokyr and J.V.C. Nye, 'Distributional Coalitions, the Industrial Revolution, and the Origins of Economic Growth in Britain', *Southern Economic Journal*, lxxiv (2007), 50–70, provides a fairly broad-brush account from the perspective of new institutional economics; particularly penetrating points are made in Charles Wilson, *Economic History and the Historian: Collected Essays* (1969), ch. 9.

[10]Tim Keirn and Lee Davison, 'The Reactive State: English Governance and Society, 1690–1750', in *Stilling the Grumbling Hive: The Response to Social and Economic Problems in England, 1689–1750*, ed. Lee Davison, Tim Hitchcock, Tim Keirn and Robert B. Shoemaker (Stroud, 1992), xxxiv.

[11]Gauci, *Politics of Overseas Trade*, 210–20; Brewer, *Sinews of Power*, 233–6; *The History of Parliament: The House of Commons, 1690–1715*, ed. Eveline Cruickshanks, Stuart Handley and D.W. Hayton (5 vols, Cambridge, 2002) i, 390–8; Mark Knights, *Representation and Misrepresentation in Later Stuart Britain: Partisanship and Political Culture* (Oxford, 2005), ch. 3; Rosemary Sweet, 'Local Identities and a National Parliament, c. 1688–1835', in *Parliaments, Nations and Identities*, ed. Hoppit, 48–63. Somewhat separately, a good deal of work was done on political petitioning for the period from the 1760s, e.g., in relation to the Stamp Act crisis of 1765 and Wilkite radicalism of the 1760s and 1770s.

identifying from the *Journals* all petitions on economic matters presented to the Commons and Lords in nine of the 143 sessions from 1660 to 1800.[12] Some general patterns in those petitions will be considered, and then two case studies briefly outlined. The strengths and weaknesses of, and alternatives to, petitioning will then be considered to tease out some more general points about the nature of interests and interests groups. The final section considers some of the limits to interest group formation and how that then affects thinking about supposedly powerful interests. But before beginning it is important to clarify the meaning of 'interests' and 'interest groups'.

From Dr Johnson, an interest can be defined as a 'concern; advantage; good', associated with a 'Regard to private profit'.[13] They can involve needs, desires, concerns, and fears; people of course have many 'interests'.[14] When the interests of at least a few people cohere, historians and political scientists have resorted to a wide range of terms besides 'interest group', including lobbies, special or vested interests, pressure or sectional groups and, most recently, 'distributional coalitions'. For sake of simplicity, 'interest group' alone is used here. Alison Olson is unusual amongst historians in having carefully conceptualised the nature of interest groups in the period, identifying four sorts: ascriptive, based on kinship groups; institutional, such as guilds, town corporations, and trading companies; associational, based on voluntary membership, such as merchant groups; and the public opinion lobbies that emerged at the end of her period.[15]

Political scientists and economists have usefully explored the difficulties interests might have in acting as a group, and of the different motivations they might have. Particularly important here has been the work of Mancur Olson in showing that while everyone has interests, not all interests are politically influential.[16] In particular, he established logically how some interests, generally smaller ones, find it easier than others to act as groups seeking to influence central government. For example, consumers usually want better quality goods at lower prices, but they struggle to act as a group at a general level to seek to achieve this. Producers, however, more easily work together collectively to maximise their self interest. One key explanation for this is most easily thought of in terms of 'free riding', that people may not join a group if they think it will make little or no difference to the success of the group and/or their own ability to access the results of the efforts of the group. However, Olson also pointed out that groups well suited to collective action will exercise their power in relation

[12] Most petitions have not survived, though some are in archives, notably the records of the house of lords in the Parliamentary Archives. But the *Journals* do record all petitions presented by date, from whom, on what subject, usually summarizing their desire and, finally, what then happened to the petition – usually to 'lie on the table' to be perused, or referred to a committee, though sometimes they were quickly rejected, or even deemed frivolous. It is, therefore, impossible to explore systematically the number of signatories on petitions, or the social, economic, political or religious background of signatories. That can only be done unsystematically and occasionally, raising doubts about representativeness.

[13] Samuel Johnson, *A Dictionary of the English Language* (1755), see 'interest'. To him, a lobby was only an antechamber.

[14] L. Susskind, 'Arguing, Bargaining, and Getting Agreement', in *The Oxford Handbook of Public Policy*, ed. M. Moran, M. Rein and R.E. Goodin (Oxford, 2006), 272.

[15] Olson, *Making the Empire Work*, 2–4.

[16] M. Olson, *The Logic of Collective Action: Public Goods and the Theory of Groups* (Cambridge, MA, 1965). For a recent overview of the field, see W.A. Galston, 'Political Feasibility: Interests and Power', in *The Oxford Handbook of Public Policy*, ed. Moran, Rein and Goodin, 543–56. A good sympathetic summary of Olson's work is in A. Dixit, 'Mancur Olson – Social Scientist', *Economic Journal*, cix (1999), 443–52. R. Tuck, *Free Riding* (Cambridge, MA, 2008), is a recent challenge to aspects of Olson's work, relating it to certain intellectual traditions.

to the extent to which they have a medium- or long-term interest in the prosperity of society: 'it makes a huge difference whether individuals with coercive capacities have a miniscule or narrow stake in the society ... or an encompassing interest'.[17] Powerful groups may paradoxically, therefore, act with restraint. All told, it is not inevitable that large interests will become successful interest groups, or that powerful interest groups will act immoderately.

2

Petitions were submitted to parliament for various reasons, especially to seek legislation, to influence the passage of bills under consideration, to raise a more general matter for parliament to consider, to appeal a legal decision to the Lords and to contest an election return. Ignoring legal and election appeals, there were about 2,000 petitions for the nine sessions examined, even though legislation in 1661 had sought to prevent the submission of 'tumultuous' petitions, and petitions could not be submitted on money bills.[18] One way of making sense of some of this voluminous, yet varied, petitioning is to focus on issues (overwhelmingly bills) that attracted at least five petitions in a session – using this as a crude filter by which to focus upon issues involving interest groups.[19] (Obviously this has the negative effect of drawing attention away from certain types of issues that might have been very significant either in their own right or collectively.)

Some 48 issues elicited at least five petitions in the nine sessions, involving 759 petitions in all – 701 were presented to the Commons (92%), just 58 to the Lords. A little over a half of the issues related more or less to national concerns, and unsurprisingly, attracted more petitions on average than specific issues (19.8 as against 10.7). If a majority of legislation in the period concerned economic matters, this was even more true of issues attracting at least five petitions, accounting for 85% of the issues and 68% of the petitions (see Table 1).[20] The remaining discussion of petitions considers those relating to the 41 economic issues alone (hereafter 'the sample').

On average, issues in the sample attracted an average of 12.6 petitions each, with only seven attracting more than 20 petitions, with the case of the building of the London docks in 1795–6 attracting the most, 49.

The 41 economic issues in Table 1 related to 21 public acts, one private act, 15 failed attempts at legislation and four other matters. Of the 15 failed attempts, six were specific or local in their intended reach and nine were general. By subject matter, some 17 of the 41 economic issues (41%) dealt with infrastructural developments – turnpike roads, river navigations, canals and docks – and nine others (22%) dealt with matters of overseas trade, some of which related to exclusive rights, such as the Royal Africa (in both 1694–5 and 1708–9) and the Levant companies. There was a small amount of petitioning relating to

---

[17] M. Olson, *Power and Prosperity: Outgrowing Communist and Capitalist Dictatorships* (New York, 2000), 4.

[18] 13 Ch. II, c. 5. For an outline of the parliamentary procedures involved in petitioning, see P.D.G. Thomas, *The House of Commons in the Eighteenth Century* (Oxford, 1971), 17–19.

[19] These measures were also subject to a disproportionate number of divisions.

[20] Some economic issues were certainly not just that, such as those relating to overseas trade or the quartering of troops. The seven non-economic issues were: the general pardon, 1660; the building of London's 50 new churches and regulating the city's elections, 1724–5; the relief of protestant dissenters and a proposal to change charities, 1772–3; and the enormous reactions to the two acts on seditious meetings and treasonable practices, 1795–6.

Table 1: *Issues with at Least Five Petitions to Parliament in Selected Sessions, 1660–1800*

Session	Economic issues	Numbers of petitions on economic issues	Non-economic issues	Numbers of petitions on non-economic issues
1660	2	10	1	6
1674	0	0	0	0
1694–5	1	12	0	0
1708–9	7	126	0	0
1724–5	6	57	2	21
1740–1	7	100	0	0
1753	8	94	0	0
1772–3	6	46	2	17
1795–6	4	73	2	197
All	41	518	7	241

Source: *Journals of the House of Commons*; *Journals of the House of Lords*.
Note: 1674 was a short session, like many others in the Restoration era.

industry, such as regulating the West Riding cloth manufacture in 1724, and to the Framework Knitters Company in 1753, though other measures that mainly concerned overseas trade might have a marked industrial dimension: the 27 petitions about the failed bill regarding the clandestine export of wool in 1740–1 clearly needs, in part, to be considered in terms of an industrial raw material and a long history of attempts at its regulation. Notably, little petitioning on economic issues related to agriculture: there were just two such issues in the sample (5%), regarding corn exports in 1740–1, and enclosure in 1795–6.

Over 96% of petitions in the sample were submitted to the Commons; 94% came from groups rather than individuals and 87% were submitted from within England. Given that 7% of the sample cannot be placed geographically, obviously few petitions came from other parts of Britain and its empire – just 3% from Scotland, 1% from Wales, and 1% from the West Indies and North American colonies. These non-English shares were roughly in line with the patterns of specific legislation enacted, though, of course, somewhat less than the patterns of population distribution and economic activity.[21] Some explanations for that emerge by exploring more generally what types of groups generated petitions.

Because the *Commons Journals* routinely record who submitted petitions, it is possible to categorise the type of person or body from which they came, with a particular aim of distinguishing petitions sent by groups with established, and often formal, connections from those sent by groups appearing to have cohered specifically for the occasion (albeit probably usually based on previous informal connections of various sorts) – hereafter these are 'ad hoc' and 'established' groups.[22] As Table 2 shows, about 53% of the petitions came from ad hoc groups created for the purpose, about 42% from established groups.

[21]J. Hoppit, 'The Nation, the State and the First Industrial Revolution', *Journal of British Studies*, 1 (2011), 307–31. It is worth noting how, from this perspective, the secondary literature has given disproportionate attention to colonial lobbying.

[22]This categorisation rests on the summary details provided by the *Journals* and so may be wrong in a few cases.

Table 2: *Type of Petitioners in Sample*

Type	Number	Percentage
Ad hoc groups	276	53
Established groups:		
Local law, politics and administration	75	15
Central law, politics and administration	9	2
Companies, guilds, etc.	55	11
Imprisoned debtors	77	15
Others:		
Personal	25	5
Unknown	1	0
Grand total	518	101

Note: *local law, politics and administration* includes JPs, grand juries, civic corporations and agents for Caribbean and American colonies; *central law, politics and administration* are mainly those working at the central courts.

Clearly, it is important that so many petitions came from ad hoc groups. Established groups had many advantages in terms of preparing petitions, most obviously organisationally, but also in terms of drawing upon an existing, if not necessarily well worked out, interest and identity. Ad hoc groups lacked those advantages, depending on the energy of key individuals to mobilise opinion: common aims needed to be specified, possible adherents identified and pursued. Even so, certain issues were more likely to be the subject of petitioning from ad hoc, rather than established, groups. For example, ad hoc groups sent 86 of the 101 petitions in the sample on the subject of the monopolies or privileges of the Royal Africa, Levant, and Framework Knitters companies. With their exclusive rights targeted by those outside the companies, few other established groups than the companies themselves were likely to join the petitioning fray. Infrastructural developments, on the other hand, tended to engage both ad hoc and established groups, generally local. The nature of both established and ad hoc groups can be explored a little further.

Looking first at the types of established groups, debtors were highly distinctive and numerous. The contemporary law was such that debtors could find themselves imprisoned by their creditors, and if they lacked the means to pay their debts their release depended on either a parliamentary amnesty or creditors' goodwill. Parliament legislated for such amnesties about every other year, and debtors, accustomed to this pattern, played their part in reminding them of their need almost ritualistically. Their petitions bear witness to a structural limitation in credit-debt laws at the time, but one parliament failed fundamentally to reform, despite significant pressure, until the 19th century.[23]

Local government, law and administration provided the second highest number of petitions (75) from among established groups within the sample. A little over 80% of these

[23] P.H. Haagen, 'Eighteenth-Century English Society and the Debt Law', in *Social Control and the State*, ed. S Cohen and A. Scull (Oxford, 1983), 222–47.

came from urban corporations, just 12% from county administration (usually JPs and/or grand juries), with the rest, 7%, from colonial agents. The importance of urban centres to petitioning was more considerable still, as 55% of all petitions in the sample were submitted by groups within parliamentary boroughs (112 ad hoc, 54 established), and 19% of the sample came from London. It was, of course, easier for townspeople to organise petitions than for those in the counties and colonies. Civic officeholders of various sorts, such as mayors, aldermen, and burgesses, had a responsibility throughout their term to look after the interests of their jurisdiction – to be watchful of potential sources of damage and to aid the development of proposals to help their towns.[24] This was less true at the county level, where lord lieutenants, sheriffs and JPs often played more ceremonial, electoral and judicial roles. Arguably, political society generally was also more likely to be able to cohere and act at the specific urban level than at the wider county level. As locales with concentrated economic interests, legislative proposals were, similarly, more likely to emanate from the urban rather than the county level.

Three types of groups dominated petitions submitted by established companies, guilds, and the like: 19 of the 55 came from business companies; 16 from those directing infrastructure projects; and 14 from 'guilds'. The distinction between businesses and infrastructure is, arguably, insignificant, but even so, it is the small number of petitions from such groups which is striking. Plainly, they might easily petition, arguably more easily than town corporations, given that they were probably less likely to be politically or ideologically riven. Yet if corporate and collective enterprise and regulation caught the eye of both contemporaries and historians, they played only a small role in total economic activity in Britain and, consequently, were unlikely to figure much in terms of pressure on parliament as measured by simple counts of numbers of petitions submitted.

It is harder to categorise types of petitioners constituting ad hoc groups, not least because the summary in the *Journals* might give only a broad sense of who they were. Additionally, they were often composite groups, comprising a number of different elements, such as 'gentlemen, clergy, merchants, tradesmen and others'. However, by looking only at the first category of person mentioned in ad hoc petitions, on the grounds that they were likely judged by those managing the petition locally to be the most important, a very tentative summary can be provided. As Table 3 shows, using this method, five types of people were especially prominent, leading nearly three-quarters of ad hoc petitions.

Gentlemen and inhabitants, that is people essentially distinguished by status and locale, led nearly one-third of ad hoc groups petitioning. More widely, 29 petitions were sent by groups claiming to be the 'principal' members of their group, often of inhabitants, merchants or tradesmen. Such groups suggested their importance and authority less because of what they did than where, and who, they were. It is notable that nearly one-quarter of ad hoc groups were merchants. Some of these appear to have been inland merchants, or merchant manufacturers, but the majority were engaged in overseas trade, mainly petitioning about such matters. It was, of course, difficult for working people to involve themselves actively with parliament. But with sufficient encouragement and connections they might be able to do so. In 1755, poor weavers in the Gloucestershire woollen industry petitioned successfully

---

[24]An important overview of civic government in the period is provided in J. Innes and N. Rogers, 'Urban Government, 1700–1840', in *The Cambridge Urban History of Britain, 1550–1840*, ed. P. Clark (Cambridge, 2000), 529–74.

Table 3: *'Leading' ad hoc Petitioners in Sample*

	Number	Percentage
Clothiers	38	14
Gentlemen	49	18
Inhabitants	33	12
Innkeepers	13	5
Merchants	64	23
Subtotal	197	72
Total	276	

for an act confirming the principle of wage assessment by justices, catching the clothiers unawares.[25]

3

Petitioning parliament was well established before 1660. But the considerable unpredictability in the meetings of parliament in the Restoration period – in terms of when it met, for how long, and what business might be conducted – limited the opportunities for petitioning it. That changed quickly after the Glorious Revolution. The institutionalisation and regularisation of parliament within government revolutionised its legislative work, leading to more bills and acts and greater occasion for petitioning.[26] Interests immediately realized this, with significant petitioning activity becoming established in the 1690s.[27] This statistical overview has established a number of key features of that important change: that issues attracting five or more petitions were overwhelmingly about economic matters; that such petitions were very largely from interest groups rather than individuals; that such groups were ad hoc and established in roughly equal numbers; that very few were submitted from beyond England; and that a very high proportion were sent to the Commons. Some of the main types of ad hoc and established groups have also been established. While these statistics are drawn from the evidence of just nine sessions and, therefore, somewhat prey to the subjects which happened to crop up then, the broad patterns established are unlikely to change with a wider sample. As such, they pin down more securely than before some of the key features of interest groups in the period. However, such a picture is rather static, shedding relatively little light on how interests groups and petitioning worked in practice. To get some sense of this, two cases from roughly midpoint in the sample will be briefly considered, with attention directed mainly at the nature of the interests involved.

[25] W.E. Minchinton, 'The Petitions of Weavers and Clothiers of Gloucestershire in 1756', *Transactions of the Bristol and Gloucestershire Archaeological Society for 1954*, lxxiii (1955), 216–27. The act was 29 Geo. II, c. 33.

[26] Hoppit, 'Patterns of Parliamentary Legislation'; Julian Hoppit and Joanna Innes, 'Introduction', in *Failed Legislation*, ed. Hoppit, 1–24.

[27] Knights, *Representation and Misrepresentation*, ch. 3.

The first case study concerns the 35 petitions submitted in the 1708–9 session regarding the duty on imported Irish yarn. It built upon a substantial number of previous bills and acts. In the previous session, a bill on the matter had passed the Commons after two divisions, but was rejected in the Lords.[28] The point at issue was the growth of Irish yarn imports to circumvent an act passed at Westminster in 1699, which effectively prohibited the export of Irish cloth, to protect English woollen manufacturers.[29] In turn, this followed a ban on the export of Irish cattle in 1665 that had encouraged sheep grazing and, thereby, Irish woollen production. Many in England worried about the competitive threat posed by the low-wage Irish economy. Thus, England's fundamental interests – none was more fundamental than the woollen industries – had to be protected, while encouraging Ireland's economy to develop in complementary ways.[30]

The first of the petitions in 1708–9 was submitted on 27 January 1709, from the political and commercial elite in Exeter. It, like the subsequent 34 petitions submitted over the next two months, was presented to the Commons and referred to a select committee to consider. Seventeen of the 35 petitions came from town corporations, if often in association with other leading inhabitants and/or traders. A significant majority of these were against the increasing levels of imports of Irish yarn, claiming that it undercut local production – it was a commonplace in the 17th and 18th centuries that labour costs were lower in Ireland than in England. Generally these came from Cornwall and Devon, and the first 17 petitions submitted came from those counties alone and were almost certainly part of a concerted campaign. But there was some petitioning in favour of Irish yarn imports, with nine coming from weavers, especially in Gloucestershire, Somerset, and Wiltshire, eager to access cheaper materials. How many signed the petitions is unknown, but it was possibly considerable. A decade earlier, evidence survives of 22 petitions submitted to the Lords about the Woollen Manufactures Bill, which involved similar questions of the export of English wool and the import of Irish woollen goods. A total of 4,524 persons signed those petitions, an average of 206 each. The largest was from Exeter, signed by 1,365, and 13 petitions were signed by more than 100 persons.[31] However, rather more than a decade later, an average of just 64 signed eight petitions found relating to a bill to regulate the calico trade, ranging from 21 to 131.[32]

No bill appears to have been produced as a consequence of the 35 petitions in 1708–9: the woollen interests in Devon and Cornwall had failed to persuade the Commons to take the action they sought, despite having a disproportionate number of borough MPs to call upon. But it may be telling that no broadsheets or pamphlets appear to have been produced on this occasion, raising the possibility that the petitioners from Devon and Cornwall were further

---

[28] *Failed Legislation*, ed. Hoppit, 264–5, item 44.042.

[29] H. F. Kearney, 'The Political Background to English Mercantilism, 1695–1700', *Economic History Review*, xi (1959), 484–96; P. Kelly, 'The Irish Woollen Export Prohibition Act of 1699: Kearney Re-Visited', *Irish Economic and Social History*, vii (1980), 22–44.

[30] C.A. Edie, 'The Irish Cattle Bills: A Study in Restoration Politics', *Transactions of the American Philosophical Society*, lx (1970), 1–66; P.J. Bowden, *The Wool Trade of Tudor and Stuart England* (1962); E. Lipson, *A Short History of Wool and its Manufacture* (1953). A good discussion of textile legislation more generally in this period is in Tim Keirn, 'Parliament, Legislation and the Regulation of English Textile Industries, 1689–1714', in *Stilling the Grumbling Hive*, ed. Davison *et al.*, 1–24.

[31] HMC, Lords MSS, new ser., ii, 130–3.

[32] Parliamentary Archives [hereafter cited as PA], HL/PO/JO/10/3/213/30–5, 37–8.

testing the water of opinion in the Commons.[33] In fact, two years later there was a renewed petitioning effort by woollen interests in Devon and elsewhere to obtain regulation, which met much the same resistance as earlier. In this case, however, Irish interests, naturally against further restraints, petitioned and lobbied to defeat the proposed measure.[34]

Trade duties were always liable to throw up different points of views such as this. This was an issue that opened up divisions amongst English woollen interests, with a significant regional component, while developing common interests between some of those interests and Irish woollen interests.[35] It was also the case that while decisions on such questions were, in a sense, made in parliament, executive government (especially the treasury, the board of trade and the revenue services) were usually also actively, perhaps decisively, involved. As such, parliament weighed such petitions alongside other types of pressure, quite apart from the difficulties of deciding where, amongst these competing sectional or local interests, the national interest lay. The language of the petitions and the number of signatories was surely important in such cases, but could rarely be decisive where so much was at stake.

The second case study of petitioning is very different, concerning, as it does, a public act passed in 1725 to improve the navigation of the river Nene between Northampton and Peterborough.[36] As T.S. Willan showed long ago, such schemes became numerous in the second half of the 17th century, because of the obvious savings on transport costs, put at the time at nearly 90% compared with road.[37] If improving the infrastructure was widely seen as broadly beneficial to internal trade, river improvements, which usually required legislation, none the less frequently encountered opposition (as did canals later), especially from the owners of land, mills, weirs, and wharfs.[38] In the case of the Nene navigation in 1725, six petitions were submitted to the Commons and, unusually, seven to the Lords. This began with two petitions submitted together to the Commons in January, asking for a bill amending a sole earlier act to improve the river.[39] No more petitions were submitted until early March, between the first and second readings of the bill. One of these came from the corporation in Northampton, another from the 'gentlemen, tradesmen, freeholders and inhabitants' of the town, and two from notable local landowners. All of these related to mills on the river and the supply of water to the town, expressing concern that the

[33] When, in the 1790s, moves were underway to seek legislation to build new docks in London, a bill was introduced not to obtain an act, but to bring out into the open the different interests involved, 'in order to give a fair discussion to all parties and all interests' so that a better drafted bill could be submitted subsequently: W. Vaughan, *Reasons in favour of the London-docks* (1795), 3.

[34] Francis G. James, 'The Irish Lobby in the Early Eighteenth Century', *English Historical Review*, lxxxi (1966), 548–9. Because the proposal was considered as a clause within a bill that was enacted it does not register in *Failed Legislation*, ed. Hoppit.

[35] For a development of this last point, see T. Griffiths, P. Hunt and P. O'Brien, 'Scottish, Irish, and Imperial Connections: Parliament, the Three Kingdoms, and the Mechanization of Cotton Spinning in Eighteenth-Century Britain', *Economic History Review*, lxi (2008), 625–50.

[36] 11 Geo. I, c. 19.

[37] T.S. Willan, *River Navigation in England, 1600–1750* (Oxford, 1931). The calculation was by Sir Robert Southwell, Petty's friend, later printed in T. Birch, *The History of the Royal Society of London* (4 vols, 1757), iii, 208.

[38] Three excellent studies of such opposition are: T.S. Willan, *The Navigation of the River Weaver in the Eighteenth Century* (Manchester, 1951); T.S. Willan, *The Early History of the Don Navigation* (Manchester, 1965); Mark Knights, 'Regulation and Rival Interests in the 1690s', in *Regulating the British Economy*, ed. Gauci, 63–81 – which focuses on the river Tone in Somerset, but in the context of other schemes for river improvement.

[39] 12 Anne, stat. 2, c. 7.

proposed improvement might harm the town, as well as those of the businesses who had invested heavily in the mills and waterworks. They were clearly keeping a close eye on what parliament was doing, as after the bill passed to the Lords, these four petitions were re-sent there, along with two new ones.

As often with local legislation, it is possible in the instance of the Nene navigation to get behind the printed record in the *Commons Journals* a little. The trail begins in March 1723, when advice was sought from Paul Joddrell, clerk at the house of commons, about petitioning for a bill. It was claimed that large number of signatories could be obtained, because 'the people all here about seem very zealous for the navigation and wish very much for it', though, in fact, three days later the same correspondent acknowledged that there was opposition.[40] Indeed, in April, Northampton corporation decided unanimously against approving any change to the 1714 act, instructing the deputy recorder to write to the town's MPs 'to use their interest against & hinder as much as lyes in their power the said Bill … & that the Corporation Seal be affixed'.[41] Clearly, discussion had been taking place in and about Northampton well before parliament was petitioned for a bill, with opposing positions established. This perhaps explains the delay in formally initiating the legislation, with the proposers looking to marshal support. One pillar of that support was Sir Justinian Isham, a long-standing tory MP for Northamptonshire, who not only introduced the bill, but reported from the second reading select committee stage and carried the bill to the house of lords. Such weighty support was not enough in itself, not least because one of the petitioners against the bill, William Wykes, had been a tory MP for Northampton until defeated at the general election in 1722, and had invested heavily in the town's waterworks. Such was the strength of that opposition that two divisions were forced on the bill and printed cases prepared both for the original bill, and for an amended form of it, with a clause protecting Wykes's interests.[42]

In the Lords, the bill was, unusually for a local matter, considered in a committee of the whole House, with the proponents employing counsel to put their case. In his brief, it was optimistically hoped that the three petitions opposing the bill would be considered 'as only one petition – they being (as we apprehend) cast all in one mold and to one purpose'.[43] The proponents strongly believed that they had the support of the majority of both town and county, and that what they sought was truly in the public interest – Wykes was depicted as selfish and greedy. In fact, two of the petitions to the Lords have survived, one on each side. Some 113, headed by the mayor of Northampton, signed a petition from gentlemen, tradesmen, freeholders, and inhabitants of the town, calling for the bill to be amended to protect the interests and investments of Wykes and others. This was a notable number, but

[40]Northamptonshire RO [hereafter cited as NRO], W(A) box 4/parcel XIII/no. 9: Bramston to Joddrell correspondence, 27, 30 Mar. 1727.

[41]NRO, Northampton Borough Records, 3/2, assembly book, f. 437. No reasons for this opposition were given.

[42]For the original bill, *Reasons for passing the bill for making more effectual an act passed in the 12th year of the late queen Anne … as it now stands, without any alteration* (1725?); for an amendment, *The case in relation to a clause to be inserted in the bill for making more effectual an act passed in the parliament holden in the twelfth year of the reign of … queen Anne* (1725?). Probably these were available for the Commons' select committee, and/or at the divisions on the bill to engross it and pass it. The local paper, the *Northampton Mercury*, barely reported the measure, noting only its second reading in the Commons, and final passage: 1 Mar. 1725, p. 1146; 19 Apr. 1725, p. 1243. The paper generally reported very little local news at this time.

[43]NRO, W(A) box 4/parcel XIII/no. 9: 'A brief for the hearing before the committee of the house of Lords'.

it was dwarfed by the 736 who signed a petition from those landowners and inhabitants on, or near, the banks of the river for the bill to be passed unaltered.[44] This was an impressive mobilisation of opinion and support for a local measure.

Clearly, support for and against the Nene Navigation Bill involved constituting and representing interests groups: mainly between the corporation and Wykes on the one side, and between others from both town and county on the other. But the bill itself was the product of a somewhat different interest. Just who was behind the bill appears to be made clear by a document setting out contributions to the parliamentary costs involved. The earl of Westmorland contributed £90, with 10 guineas from the earl of Cardigan, the dukes of Montagu and Bedford, Lady Betty Germain, and James Joye, Esq. Finally, Charles and John Tryon, Esqs provided five and two guineas respectively.[45] Most, if not all of these, were substantial landowners close to the Nene – Westmorland at Apethorpe and Cardigan nearby at Deene Park – presumably activated by the hope that the improved river would help agricultural products from their estates obtain higher prices at more distant markets, thereby raising demand to rent their farms.

Obviously, proposals for change at a local level such as this were liable to prompt very different pressures upon parliament than considerations such as trade duties – though some local issues, such as the proposals in the 1790s to build London's docks, had national implications. If issues such as trade duties might make apparent different interests between, or within, particular sectors, or between particular regions or nations, measures such as roads or rivers might build upon, or open up, much more local divisions, involving both established and ad hoc groups. Those local divisions might be worked out in a number of venues, as well as in parliament, most obviously in local government, the press, by subscription, and in meetings. Nor was this restricted to the enfranchised, as work on opposition to enclosure legislation has shown.[46] Even so, for local or specific measures, the volume of petitioning was likely to be limited. Yet the executive was unlikely to take much interest in all of this, and, indeed, many parliamentarians away from the source of the conflict were probably similarly uninterested. (The Nene case was unusual in, so to speak, spilling beyond local confines in both houses of parliament.) MPs and peers from the relevant areas were the key figures, though sometimes, especially where legal niceties were involved, the lawyers were also liable to become heavily involved. In this case, external pressures could reasonably hope that their message would be listened to by the local MPs and peers, raising important questions about the nature of representation.[47] But for measures with a national scope, there must always have been some doubt by those exerting pressure upon parliament, whether their voice was heard across Westminster.

[44] PA, HL/PO/JO/10/3/218/7–8.

[45] NRO, W(A) box 4/parcel XIII/no. 9: 'A particular bill of charges relating to the act of parliament for making the river Nene navigable'.

[46] W.A. Tate, 'Parliamentary Counter-Petitions during Enclosures of the Eighteenth and Nineteenth Centuries', *English Historical Review*, lix (1944), 393–403; J.M. Neeson, *Commoners: Common Right, Enclosure and Social Change in England, 1700–1820* (Cambridge, 1993).

[47] Langford, *Public Life and the Propertied Englishman*, 186–96; Paul Langford, 'Property and "Virtual Representation" in Eighteenth-Century England', *Historical Journal*, xxxi (1988), 83–115; Paul Kelly, 'Constituents Instructions to Members of Parliament in the C18th', in *Party and Management in Parliament 1660–1784*, ed. Clyve Jones (Leicester, 1984), 169–89. Some MPs believed that they had to present petitions from their constituents, but others did not: Thomas, *House of Commons*, 18.

4

These two examples of petitioning have raised a number of the key general considerations. One has been to clarify how petitions built upon existing disputes. In the case of the petitions about Irish yarn in 1709, the issues at stake can be traced back over half a century. Even in the case of the Nene navigation, disagreements were clearly in evidence in 1723, two years before parliament was petitioned, and related to legislation from 1714 as well as prior decisions in Northampton corporation about the town's water supply. Petitions to parliament on legislative matters doubtless helped to cohere some interest groups for the first time. Even so, obviously this involved building upon existing similarities of circumstance, aspirations and beliefs. Three aspects were crucial. First, were regional or local identities and concerns. Place, locale and circumstance were especially important in petitioning, in part because of organisational considerations, but also mainly because of local or regional economic specialisation. Second, divisions expressed via petitions might also involve a sectoral or sectional element. In 1709, different types of manufacturers faced one another from their different regions. In Northamptonshire in 1725, a mainly urban manufacturing and service elite felt threatened by the efforts of large landowners. Here, third, is a hint of a wider phenomenon, the importance of social status in some petitions.

What the effect upon the parliamentary process of the petitions was in both cases is unclear. The impression is that the petitioners felt it important to express their views, that they thought they would be taken seriously, but that it was possible that their aim would not be met. Among the advantages of petitions was that it had a degree of formality about it. A case had to be prepared and agreed to, helping, thereby, to confirm or (re)constitute the interest involved and to clarify its arguments. Moreover, because petitions were public expressions, they perhaps reduced the extent to which the interests they expressed were viewed as narrow and particular. And because petitions were formally presented to parliament, they could not be ignored, and the claims were usually taken seriously and the information welcomed, even if ultimately parliament decided against them.[48] A range of factors affected that decision, but in terms of interest group formation, obtaining signatures was crucial.

Signatories gave the arguments of petitions an unambiguous weight; it is clear that both the number of petitions and the number of signatories was seen to matter. Indeed, it is striking that in the case of the Nene navigation, those peers and landowners pushing for the bill were supported by a petition signed by over 700 people. That said, an important feature of petitions is that they were very largely just lists of signatories (very few signed with a mark), overwhelmingly male, lacking addresses, occupations and titles.[49] Such details were, presumably, not thought to add weight to the petition, or might distract attention away from what was being sought. Yet if weight of numbers was obviously meaningful, that weight might look different when conceived of in terms of the numbers of possible

---

[48]'The stream of petitions from clothiers, merchants, poor weavers, guilds and companies and the like did not only represent an exercise of constitutional rights; they also represented the best, and often the only, source of information the government could obtain on complex economic problems.': Wilson, *Economic History and the Historian*, 143.

[49]Most petitions I have examined have no female signatories – both first and second names are usually signed, with marks very rare. An exception is that 17 women were among the 74 signatories (23%) to a petition from London calico retailers in Feb. 1721: PA, HL/PO/JO/10/3/213/37.

signatories. Local, yet extensive, interests such as that in the case of the Nene had, in fact, a fairly large pool of potential petitioners to draw upon – in this case along a 45-mile stretch of river.[50] Other groups did not. Gauci has found that for 50 petitions from West India interests between 1670 and 1720, the average number signing was only between 15 and 25.[51] Moreover, apparently smaller groups might be able to imply a higher concentration of expertise: that is, that their lack of numbers was significant. Kim has argued that some merchants may have sought to limit the number of petitioners to heighten 'the authenticity of their applications, at the same time avoiding the undesirable impression that they tried to exercise an unsolicited collective power to force their wills on decision-makers'.[52]

As is clear, petitions were important weapons to interest groups, not least because they could be used by such different types of groups. But they had clear limitations as a means of applying pressure upon parliament. They required, of course, a degree of organisation, literacy, funding, and connection that many lacked. An MP or peer had to be willing to present them; when presented they might be heard by very few in a thin House; even then they might quickly be forgotten, especially if they were ordered to lie on the table among many other petitions and papers; and it was difficult to make an elaborate argument, or present much factual detail, within the constraints of the genre – even the number of signatories was probably only glanced. As one guide put it: 'all Petitions ought to be drawn as short and in Terms as general as can possibly be conceived'.[53] But there was a further significant structural consideration, for if petitioners were notionally informed, they were certainly not disinterested. They sought a particular advantage, and their claims that such advantages would serve the wider good could not be taken on trust.[54] Ultimately, petitioners expressed private interests. Part of the job of parliamentarians was to be alert to that, to make judgments supposedly from a disinterested point of view, so that the public good would be maximised.

Weaknesses in petitioning obviously encouraged interests to present their cases by other means, though at the risk, of course, of further undermining the legitimacy of petitions. One way was to petition less publicly, in the hope of swaying important decision makers and, perhaps, reducing or eliminating the chances of counter-petitioning. Thus, for example, the Bristol Society of Merchant Venturers sent 100 petitions to parliament between 1698 and 1803, but additionally, 23 to the privy council, 13 to the treasury and six to the board of trade.[55] Other, related, modes of lobbying also existed. Much of that would have been unstructured and sometimes even opportunistic. Some bodies, however, gained considerable expertise in expressing themselves via a number of routes, such as Scotland's

---

[50] In the same session, a petition was submitted to the Commons on 13 Feb. 1725 from the coachmen, carriers, waggoners, salesmen, drovers, hagglers, and others of eastern England who used the main London to York road. How many signed is unknown, but it was potentially very many indeed.

[51] Gauci, 'Learning the Ropes of Sand', 110.

[52] D. Kim, 'Political Convention and the Merchant in the Later Eighteenth Century', in *Regulating the British Economy*, ed. Gauci, 131.

[53] *The Liverpool Tractate: An Eighteenth Century Manual on the Procedure of the House of Commons*, ed. C. Strateman (New York, 1937), 28.

[54] Sweet, 'Local Identities and a National Parliament', provides a telling discussion of the types of arguments employed to make compatible local and national advantage.

[55] *Politics and the Port of Bristol in the Eighteenth Century: The Petitions of the Society of Merchant Venturers, 1698–1803*, ed. W.E. Minchinton (Bristol Record Society, xxiii, 1963), p. xviii.

Convention of the Royal Burghs, which eventually had an agent in London to act for it, as did many of the West Indian and American colonies, helping to explain the rare occurrence of Scottish and colonial interests in the sample.[56] It is also significant that a number of bodies emerged in the 18th century, in part to represent the economic interests of their members politically, most commonly of societies of merchants or manufacturers, but also including some agricultural societies.[57] Most long-lived were the chambers of commerce, with the first being formally established in Jersey in 1767. Manchester had one, of sorts, in 1774, and those established at Glasgow, Dublin, Belfast, and Birmingham in 1783 still survive, if not always continuously since their foundation. Such organisations grew markedly in number after 1770, mainly because of economic growth in those places, and possible changes in Britain's commercial relations with France, Ireland, and the USA, as a consequence of American independence.[58] They might also adopt rather different tactics. Dietz has argued that by the end of the 18th century, manufacturers were more often submitting 'memorials' to departments of state, where the emphasis was upon an exclusive capacity to comment rather than upon numbers of signatories. As such, they may have been seeking to distinguish themselves from the growth of mass petitioning to parliament from the late 18th century.[59] Certainly, interest groups always have a nice decision to make as to whether they speak for a very wide body, in which case dangers of expressing the lowest common denominator come into play, or whether they were exclusive, with a high degree of specific expertise.

Another common way in which parliament was subjected to the expression of opinion about economic matters was via the press. The expansion of newspaper and periodical journalism was an element of that, but more important still was the growth of pamphleteering on particular legislative proposals. A good part of the great collections of the Goldsmiths' and Kress libraries have their origins in such purposes, and it appears, consequently, that economic literature was published in much greater numbers in Britain than in France in the 18th century, perhaps in a ratio of seven to one.[60] This crude quantitative imbalance, even more striking given the larger absolute size of France's population and economy, owed much to differences between political processes either side of the Channel. If British economic literature was often very short and momentary, it was certainly an essential part

---

[56]B. Harris, 'The Scots, the Westminster Parliament and the British State in the Eighteenth Century', in *Parliaments, Nations and Identities*, ed. Hoppit, 124–45; L.M. Penson, *The Colonial Agents of the British West Indies* (1924); Olson, *Making the Empire Work*.

[57]Three can be found once in the sample, petitioning for a general enclosure act in the 1795–6 session: the Bath and West of England Society, the Agricultural Society of Manchester, and the Berkshire Agricultural Society.

[58]Dietz, 'Before the Age of Capital', ch. 3; Bennett, *Local Business Voice*, 14–16, 121–7.

[59]Dietz, 'Before the Age of Capital', 292; Peter Fraser, 'Public Petitioning and Parliament before 1832', *History*, xlvi (1961), 195–211.

[60]C. Théré, 'Economic Publishing and Authors, 1566–1789', in *Studies in the History of French Political Economy: From Bodin to Walras*, ed. G. Faccarello (1998), 1–56; L.W. Hanson, *Contemporary Printed Sources for British and Irish Economic History, 1701–1750* (Cambridge, 1963); H. Higgs, *Bibliography of Economics, 1751–1775* (Cambridge, 1935). For the period 1705–74, Théré counts 1,487 works of economic literature published in France, while Hanson and Higgs list 10,008 works in English. The criteria for inclusion may differ somewhat between them (it is impossible to tell), but probably insufficiently to explain the huge difference. See also J. Hoppit, 'The Contexts and Contours of British Economic Literature, 1660–1760', *Historical Journal*, xlix (2006), 79–110. Britain also had greater newspaper circulation than France, perhaps by as much as fivefold: B. Harris, *Politics and the Rise of the Press: Britain and France, 1620–1800* (1996), 60.

of the environment within which parliament considered economic matters.[61] For example, when William Vaughan was helping to pave the way for legislation to authorise the building of London docks he adopted a common strategy and wrote a pamphlet entitled *Reasons in Favour of London Docks*, which he described as 'a little publication distributed in 1795, and reprinted in 1796 and 1797. About 3000 of these were printed off and given to friends and opponents, and contributed greatly to remove many objections to Docks, and to their proposed situations.'[62] Such 'reasons', 'remarks on', 'an answer to', and 'cases' were published in huge numbers in the period, frequently to be handed out freely to parliamentarians. Sometimes these might specifically seek to buttress petitions, as in 1781, when London sugar refiners petitioned parliament and printed off pro formas to remind MPs of the final meeting of the committee to consider it and to provide some key statistical data, an 'epitome of the sugar trade'.[63]

5

Interest groups expressed themselves in various ways, not simply via petitions. Some interests, however, tended not to petition, lobby, or publish, notably the landed interest. Superficially this is surprising, given how many historians have stressed political importance of landowners at the time.[64] Many have followed Beer's assertion that 'the landed interest was dominant and no one questioned its right to dominate'.[65] Here they have generally built upon what was said at the time. Many would have agreed with Arthur Young that 'the landed interest of this country, is of ten times the importance of all other interests … If interests are ever separately considered, it demands preheminence [*sic*], and it ought, and must have it.'[66] Yet Young implied that the landed interest did not then have that pre-eminence – and such a worry had been expressed earlier in the century when a new 'monied interest' was attacked as usurping its authority.[67] He was troubled that parliament paid insufficient regard to agriculture: that the corn laws were under attack; that obtaining statutory authority to enclose was fiddly, time consuming and expensive; and that exporting raw wool

[61] For two important examples: R. Wilson, 'Newspapers and Industry: The Export of Wool Controversy in the 1780s', in *The Press in English Society from the Seventeenth to the Nineteenth Centuries*, ed. M. Harris and A. Lee (Cranbury, NJ, 1986), 80–104; Bob Harris, 'Parliamentary Legislation, Lobbying and the Press in Eighteenth-Century Scotland', *Parliamentary History*, xxvi (2007), 76–95.

[62] W. Vaughan, *Tracts on Docks and Commerce, Printed between the Years 1793 and 1800* (1839), 30.

[63] *The sugar-refiners of London present their respectful compliments to* [blank] *and request the honor of his attention to the enclosed state of facts, and to inform him that the committee of the honble. the house of Commons sit on the business this day, when it is expected the Evidence in Support of the Petition will be closed* (1781?).

[64] E.g., J. Cannon, *Aristocratic Century: The Peerage in Eighteenth-Century England* (Cambridge, 1985); G.E. Mingay, *English Landed Society in the Eighteenth Century* (1963), ch. 11.

[65] Beer, 'The Representation of Interests', 623. Numerous more recent variants of this could be cited, e.g., J. Black, 'The Politics of Landed Power: England 1750–1800', *Revue Française de Civilisation Britannique*, viii (1995), 45.

[66] [A. Young], *The Expediency of a Free Exportation of Corn at this Time: With Some Observations on the Bounty* (1770), 41. On Young and the landed interest, see C. Veliz, 'Arthur Young and the English Landed Interest, 1784–1813', University of London PhD, 1959.

[67] On the 'clash on interests' under Queen Anne, see Geoffrey Holmes, *British Politics in the Age of Anne* (rev. edn, 1987), ch. 5.

was prohibited. He believed that the power of the landed interest was more apparent than real.[68]

Only one petition in the sample claimed to come from an element of the landed interest.[69] Most obviously, of course, this is to be explained by the landed being so numerous in central government that they had no need to act as a group. But it was, in fact, difficult for any interest to organise itself nationally as a group, even the landed, and only one petition in the sample came from a national body.[70] Thus, local agricultural societies generally proved more effective than the relatively short-lived national board of agriculture, whose purpose depended heavily on Young and Sinclair, founding secretary and president, respectively.[71] Similarly, the general chamber of manufactures died in infancy, 1785–7, despite being initially able to mobilise impressive volumes of support.[72] Broad interests were also liable to fracture over major political, religious and military questions, as well as those more particularly relevant to them – in the case of land issues such as tithes and corn bounties. The landed also struggled with two contradictions: in holding simultaneously to incompatible ideas of the supremacy of both parliament and property rights;[73] and by claiming that landowners were especially able to be disinterested, the room to articulate sectional views was thereby circumscribed. This relates to Olson's point about 'encompassing interests' having such an investment in their society that they are limited in what they can seek to extract from it – though an aspect of that is also about retaining legitimacy given the restraints consequent upon resistance to the growth of central, or police, powers. Finally, the landed might struggle to overcome the sense that their leisure made them unworldly and amateur. As Sir John Dalrymple put it in 1782: 'You must all ways [know] … that at General Meetings Merchants will beat country Gentlemen in Argument & plausibility, because men in the world must have great knowledge & of using it than men in Solitude.'[74]

6

By exploring patterns of petitions, this essay has established more clearly than before, some of the key characteristics of the pressures exerted on parliament by economic interests, in a period when the legislative work of parliament exploded. Certainly the ability to

---

[68] I provide a little more detail on this in Hoppit, 'The Landed Interest'. As ever, there is much of relevance in Langford, *Public Life and the Propertied Englishman*. An electronic search for 'landed interest' in the *Journals* of both Houses between 1660 and 1800 produces just 33 results (some of them duplicates), with one-half occurring in relation to the debate over Anglo-Irish trade in 1785.

[69] To the Commons on 11 Feb. 1741, against parts of the Calder Navigation Bill, from the 'gentlemen, freeholders, farmers and others concerned in the landed interest' in 21 villages and towns of Yorkshire.

[70] From papermakers in Apr. 1796: *CJ*, li, 585.

[71] R. Mitchison, 'The Old Board of Agriculture (1793–1822)', *English Historical Review*, lxxiv (1959), 41–69; K. Hudson, *Patriotism with Profit: British Agricultural Societies in the Eighteenth and Nineteenth Centuries* (New York, 1975).

[72] David R. Schweitzer, 'The Failure of William Pitt's Irish Trade Propositions 1785', *Parliamentary History*, iii (1984), 129–45, esp. 132; J.M. Norris, 'Samuel Garbett and the Early Development of Industrial Lobbying in Great Britain', *Economic History Review*, x (1958), 450–60.

[73] J. Hoppit, 'Compulsion, Compensation and Property Rights in Britain, 1688–1833', *Past & Present*, No. 110 (2011), 93–128.

[74] Quoted in H.B. Carter, *His Majesty's Spanish Flock: Sir Joseph Banks and the Merinos of George III of England* (Sydney, 1964), 36–7.

petition was very important, both to the interests and to parliament. But the weaknesses of petitioning and the absence of petitioning from supposedly powerful interests has thrown up important findings about the nature of interest groups. Two major points can be made by way of conclusion.

First, interest groups are a particular type of political organisation. Critically, they played a different role from political parties. If some economic questions, such as disputes over the old and new East India companies, had a party-political dimension to them, no such dimension is apparent in the two case studies considered earlier.[75] The different sides of the Irish yarn imports question argued in terms of their regional or local contribution to national advantage, not whether the question related to different ideas of economic prospects and policy. In the case of the Nene navigation, tories and whigs worked side-by-side for the navigation, and one strong tory was for it, but another against. This is hardly surprising. As has been seen, almost all of the expressions of group interest via petitions was local or regional. They did not claim to represent the nation, though, of course, they believed that their interest was more compatible with the national interest than that of their opponents. As Finer put it: 'It is the *métier* of interest groups … to put forward a sectional viewpoint.'[76] Parties, by contrast, articulated views about the nation, albeit by invoking what was happening, or might happen, in particular places – though, of course, they differed markedly from modern parties and were far from consistently significant during the period. That is, the ideological orbits of interest groups and parties generally differed, their paths crossing only occasionally. Moreover, interest groups had good reason to avoid expressing themselves in partisan terms for fear of immediately limiting potential support. Interest groups, then, are different from parties and, given the volume of local and specific legislation in the period, a critical means of understanding the history of that legislation: more important, indeed, than parties. Of course, interest groups at the local level might interact with party issues or in parliament their efforts might be considered within a party framework. But party considerations were rarely vital to the nature of the groups themselves.

The second important finding of this essay has been to raise the issue of the ease or difficulties with which interests might cohere to act as groups. If it might appear that 'from an economic viewpoint, parliament appears as the vortex of different pressure-groups', it must be recognized that some economic interests were better able to express themselves than were others.[77] Clearly, in a such a profoundly unequal society, many people lacked the money, time, literacy, or connections to act. Yet the difficulties the landed interest had in acting as a group also show that a range of other factors were also vital. Consequently, parliament did not simply act as an umpire, adjudicating between rival interest groups – though it certainly did do that – for if important interests were unable to express themselves coherently to parliament, they could simply be ignored. Parliament had to act in ways that did not damage the legitimacy of its authority – it had to appear to be fair to enough people and in some measure be so – while also being constrained by ideas of the national

---

[75] H. Horwitz, 'The East India Trade, the Politicians, and the Constitution: 1689–1702', *Journal of British Studies* xvii (1978), 1–18; C. Jones, ' "A Fresh Division Lately Grown Up Among Us": Party Strife, Aristocratic Investment in the Old and New East India Companies and the Division in the House of Lords of 23 February 1700', *Historical Research*, lxviii (1995), 302–17.

[76] S.E. Finer, *Anonymous Empire: A Study of the Lobby in Great Britain* (2nd edn, 1966), 114.

[77] James, 'The Irish Lobby', 543.

good that might sit awkwardly with the wishes of those groups who were able to pressure them. That is, parliament had to navigate between interest groups, between interests, and between groups and interests. To do so, which involved more than just umpiring, it necessarily stood somewhat apart from them. As Furner and Supple put it: 'the state's accumulation of information and application of models are related to the performance of functions that no private interest can adequately undertake, namely, adjusting to, or at least recognizing, different sectional interests, pursuing general objectives, and assessing particular policies in light of their consequences for society as a whole. The state, after all, is different.'[78]

Famously, Adam Smith had a low opinion of commercial and manufacturing interest groups, blaming them for the distorting effects of the mercantile system. He certainly exaggerated their influence to provide him with some intellectual leverage. More important for the purposes of this essay, he overlooked the vital role that interest groups could make to the working of parliament, providing it with information and opinions, refashioning connections between the centre and localities, identifying problems and suggesting solutions.[79] Within a political system that was formally rigid and exclusive, the creation and efforts of tens of thousands of interest groups provided a much-needed means of ensuring the system did not ossify. Across the period, such groups bear witness to the vitality of Britain's economy and an important openness in its polity. They were, indeed, a characteristic expression of several key features of 18th-century Britain: of the importance of the local and the specific; of lines of attachment via statutes from the present to the past; of the difficulties of collective action for many, and of relative ease for others; and of the importance of negotiation to authority. It was essential to Britain's economic performance that parliament could be pressured in such ways. Without it, the course of change would surely have been very different.

[78]M.O. Furner and B. Supple, 'Ideas, Institutions, and State in the United States and Britain: An Introduction', in *The State and Economic Knowledge*, ed. M.O. Furner and B. Supple (Cambridge, 1990), 11.

[79]Wilson, *Economic History and the Historian*, ch. 9.

Social Reform and the Pressure of 'Progress' on Parliament, 1660–1914

LAWRENCE GOLDMAN

In modern Britain, pressure on parliament for social reform has been transmitted not only by mass movements of the people, but by well-organised pressure groups and small coteries of experts. Driven by intellectual imperatives and by differing ideas of 'progress', these experts and activists have directed the impetus for measures to tackle poverty, working conditions, or inequality, mediating a broader sense of pressure from without. In contrast to political histories of social reform, this essay offers a history of ideas for social reform and the methods by which reformers shaped parliament's agenda.

Keywords: economics; parliament; poverty; pressure groups; progress; social reform; social science; statistics

1

The modern history of parliament and of extraparliamentary campaigns to introduce, amend, or repeal laws is intimately related to the history of social reform. Many of the most famous campaigns to change the law, from penal reform and anti-slavery in the 18th century, through suffrage extension and public health reform in the 19th century, to the welfare and educational reforms of the 20th century, have originated in pressure groups and mass action outside parliament. This essay will examine the relationship between extraparliamentary pressure and social reforms accepted by, legislated for, and administered from Westminster, but to discuss social reform in Britain across three centuries may require more than the usual techniques and approaches for this kind of history. In general, the history of social reform has been an account of discrete problems and interventions to solve them, often focused on a relatively few years, sometimes embracing a span of perhaps a generation. Treating the subject across most of modern British history is a challenge though one that offers opportunities to treat the history differently. In this case, thinking on a broad scale will reinforce an important recent trend in the historiography towards a focus on ideas as the most notable agents of social reform. As this essay will argue, in most existing accounts attention is focused on the individuals, campaigning groups and agencies which have discovered and investigated social abuses;[1] the bureaucracies, professional associations and political institutions which have designed solutions for them,[2] and the

---

[1] See, for a classic example, Royston Lambert, *Sir John Simon, 1816–1904, and English Social Administration* (1963).

[2] Lawrence Goldman, *Science, Reform, and Politics in Victorian Britain: The Social Science Association 1857–1886* (Cambridge, 2002).

parliamentarians – William Wilberforce, Michael Sadler, the 7th earl of Shaftesbury, Samuel Plimsoll, James Stansfeld, and their like – who have used their positions within the chamber to persuade fellow MPs to change their minds.[3]

In this essay, however, the argument will be advanced that social reform as an end of government and a social good in itself is best understood in relation to intellectual history. It is the outcome of changing conceptions, not only of the role of the state and its relationship with civil society – which is itself an old theme – but of the very nature of historical thinking. To understand the impulse to social reform is, in fact, to understand what might be termed the *telos* of modern history, something that includes, but which is, in truth, much larger than, the intellectual history of welfare reform. In many respects the modern history of Britain and of other developed western states is the history of the pursuit of, and the contestation over, social reform, however defined.

2. *Social Reform and the Idea of Social Progress*

Social reform can be conceptualised as a series of interventions, whether singly, simultaneously or in series, which are designed to deal with abuses, whether imagined or proven. Often in our period these interventions came from the central state; more frequently, at least earlier in this period, they emanated from local political authorities; and in many cases they were the initiatives of individuals, voluntary bodies, charities and so forth, which in due time were picked up by the expanding competence of public authorities. But social reform can also be understood more fundamentally as the product of a more basic aspiration to make society approximate to a desired model or ideal or outcome. In the mid 17th century it might have been a version of the puritan's godly commonwealth;[4] the mid 18th century aspired to a self-activating society of commerce and virtue;[5] in the mid 19th century reformers sought to build the infrastructure of a society characterised by economic and political individualism;[6] and by the mid 20th century the aim was a welfare state and society.[7] Today, for very many people active in British public life, and perhaps for all bar one of the main political parties, *the* purpose of the modern state in its present guise is to construct a more egalitarian society.

How has this come about? How is it that in modern Britain and modern western societies more generally, the essential task of government is now conceived as what we might term perpetual social reform, a never-ceasing effort to make social institutions, social behaviour, and social values, approximate to a desired model of the good society? This has usually been understood in terms of the development of the 18th-century military-fiscal state into a 20th-century welfare state.[8] It has been explained as the product of growing wealth, which

---

[3] *Pressure from Without in Early Victorian England*, ed. Patricia Hollis (1974).

[4] Christopher Hill, *God's Englishman: Oliver Cromwell and the English Revolution* (1970); Christopher Hill, *Milton and the English Revolution* (1977).

[5] *Wealth and Virtue: The Shaping of Political Economy in the Scottish Enlightenment*, ed. Istvan Hont and Michael Ignatieff (Cambridge, 1983).

[6] W.L. Burn, *The Age of Equipoise: A Study of the Mid-Victorian Generation* (1964); A.J. Taylor, *Laissez-Faire and State Intervention in Nineteenth-Century Britain* (1972).

[7] Pat Thane, *Foundations of the Welfare State* (2nd edn, 1996).

[8] John Brewer, *The Sinews of Power: War, Money and the English State, 1688–1783* (1989); T.O. Lloyd, *Empire to Welfare State: English History 1906–1976* (Oxford, 1979).

has invited social intervention and made it possible, and the growing demands of a larger, better educated, and more articulate population in a democratic political system where, to use the concept at the heart of this collection of essays, 'pressure from without' could be applied to achieve a wider and deeper distribution of social goods. But even this explanation fails to get to the root of the matter: it can explain why social reforms have taken specific forms and met certain social ends. It doesn't explain why, since the 17th century, it has been thought appropriate, or even possible, to pursue social reform in the second and wider sense of the term – as a constant process leading to the remaking of society according to a desired model.

When we speak and write about social reform we do so with an awareness that the term conveys social sanction and moral approbation. Social reform is always ethically endorsed, and it carries connotations of improvement, betterment, justice, above all, progress. It is understood to be a central aspect of those processes which have, for want of a better term, modernised society. But to those who lived before the late 17th century, progress was uncertain, the models to be emulated were more likely to be in the past than in an idealised future, and the word *reform* itself had quite other connotations.

Let us begin with '*reform*'. It denotes now, according to the *Oxford English Dictionary*, 'the action or process of making changes in an institution, organization, or aspect of social or political life, so as to remove errors, abuses, or other hindrances to proper performance'. These changes are socially approved; hence an ancillary meaning is 'the improvement or modernization of something no longer of sufficient accuracy or quality'. But an older meaning, caught in the very term 'Reformation' itself, denotes 'returning to an original rule or adopting stricter observances'. The early-16th-century protestant reformers sought to recover the innocence and virtue of a prelapserian past rather than develop the religion of the future. Indeed, the roots of the word *reform* are in Anglo-Norman of the 12th century when *réformer* meant 'to restore or change back (a person or thing) to an original form or state, or to a previous condition'. In the 15th and 16th centuries it carried connotations of redressing a wrong or grievance; making reparation for a loss or damage; of making good and making amends.[9]

More than linguistic chance may be involved here. Early-modern Englishmen took inspiration from the past and believed that they had lost contact with the wisdom and moral perfection of the ancients. The Tudor fascination with the Anglo-Saxons, which included the systematic collection of early documents for the first time, arose from the ideological impulse to prove that the English Reformation was returning to the spirit and principles of the earliest English churches before Roman corruption took hold. John Foxe, in his great *Acts and Monuments*, known as *The Book of Martyrs*, argued that the English Church was pure before its romanisation by Augustine at the end of the 6th century. The two great early-modern revolutions in the English world, in 1642 and 1776, arose in both cases from concerted opposition to the royal reforms of Charles I and George III. As J.G.A. Pocock, Bernard Bailyn, and others, have taught us since the 1960s, in both cases these were conserving revolutions led by men of property who were intrinsically hostile to innovation.[10] The hostility may have come from their desire to defend their privileges and purses from

[9] *Oxford English Dictionary* online.

[10] Bernard Bailyn, *The Ideological Origins of the American Revolution* (Cambridge, MA, 1967); J.G.A. Pocock, *The Machiavellian Moment: Florentine Political Thought and the Atlantic Republican Tradition* (Princeton, NJ, 1975).

ship money of 1634 in the one case and the Stamp Tax of 1765 in the other; yet they looked askance at reform as destabilising in itself and to be opposed in principle. The specifically English Civil War gave rise to its own brands of social radicalism in the shape of the Levellers and Diggers. But it had been made by men like Cromwell in defence of religious and personal liberties, who showed little tolerance in the 1650s for the proponents of levelling political reform and social radicalism.[11]

It follows from this that to get to the alternative, or what we might call the 'progressive' meaning of social reform, much wider intellectual changes were required, pre-eminently a belief in progress itself. British society, in this argument, could only embrace the concept of social reform if it had also embraced already the concept of social advancement, improvement, and progress, as among the very goals of social and political life. This identifies 'social reform' with what we call, for want of a better term, the enlightenment. In Renaissance historiography, history was circular, a cycle of examples to be imitated or avoided and without a *telos*, a direction, a purpose. But the *philosophes* broke with the past, which was barbaric, fanatical and warlike, and in its place they theorised history as linear, rational, and progressive – as a series of stages towards modernity. In Scotland, Robertson, Ferguson, Hume, and Smith plotted these stages and the development of human refinement and social sophistication. In England, Gibbon supplied 'a complete, secular account of human nature which was historically derived; an induction from 2000 years of historical record, which would as a result be different in kind from either philosophical or theological accounts'. Thus Gibbon contributed to 'the greatest of all Enlightenment "projects" – the construction of a secular science of man'.[12]

In the 19th century, this was brought to a culmination by the Liberal historicism which suffused all elements of British politics and culture – the so-called 'whig interpretation of history' – which conceived national history since the late 17th century as a story of advancement on a broad front, political, material, and also moral. The Victorians believed in progress because their history told them that it was real and immanent in Britain's recent past, and there was just about enough truth to this account to make it credible. In this version, judicious constitutional, religious, and political changes in 1688–9 had ushered in an age of stability and prosperity in which parliamentary institutions had flourished and the blessings of progress had been shared widely. It was not difficult to extend the argument in the late 19th century that similarly judicious social reforms would be the corollaries in a later age of these earlier, enabling political and constitutional changes.[13]

Yet the very complacency of whig historiography also encouraged the development of a more critical version of British history, albeit one still committed to progress and reform. Arnold Toynbee's *Lectures on the Industrial Revolution in England*, published in 1884, a year after his death, asked why the fruits of a century of industrialisation had been shared so unequally in British society, and influenced thereby a generation of progressive social and educational reformers.[14] R.H. Tawney's study of *The Agrarian Problem in the Sixteenth*

[11] Christopher Hill, *The World Turned Upside Down: Radical Ideas during the English Revolution* (1972).

[12] Peter Ghosh, 'Edmund Gibbon', in *Encylcopedia of Historians and Historical Writing*, ed. Kelly Boyd (2 vols, 1999), i, 462.

[13] J.W. Burrow, *A Liberal Descent: Victorian Historians and the English Past* (Cambridge, 1981).

[14] Arnold Toynbee, *Lectures on the Industrial Revolution in England* (1884); Lawrence Goldman, *Dons and Workers: Oxford and Adult Education Since 1850* (Oxford, 1995), 45–50.

Century, published in 1912 at the height of new liberalism, was the first of his works to establish a counter-whig narrative of the expropriation and exploitation of the common people, stretching from the Reformation to the industrial revolution, which informed all his subsequent research and publication in economic history and social ethics, including *The Acquisitive Society* (1921) and *Religion and the Rise of Capitalism* (1926).[15] In this perspective, the emergence of the disciplines of social and economic history in Britain in the late-Victorian and Edwardian periods as evidenced also in the work of J.L. and Barbara Hammond, and Sidney and Beatrice Webb, among others, can be understood as the response and answer to the whig historical tradition which underpinned 19th-century liberalism.[16] But in its influence over emerging British socialism, this critical account of British history was employed, as before, in the pursuit of progress, albeit in a new, more democratic guise.

What links together our period, therefore, and makes sense of social reform as an end to be achieved throughout its duration, is the idea of progress itself. Since at least the early 19th century, one sense of 'progress' has taken the form of a secular faith that modern societies have the capacity and technology to make social reforms work and endure. Indeed, to many over the past century, it has been the very badge and emblem of our success as a society that we have devoted resources on such a scale not only to existing social functions – education, health, welfare and so on – but to their further refinement and improvement.[17] When the first concerted reforms that began a welfare state were projected and introduced by the Edwardian Liberal administrations, the aim was to provide a minimum level of social support below which no one should sink. By the 1960s and 1970s, in Britain the aspiration was to provide optimum levels of support, as close as possible to those enjoyed by citizens who did not require the assistance of public authorities.

3. *Histories of Pressure and Social Reform*

It follows from this that our traditional ways of writing about social reform – and about extra-parliamentary 'pressure' which in older accounts has been taken as the primary driver of social reform – require development. If social reform is now conceptualised as an idea rather than a reactive process, and as a corollary to the historical imagination of the past 300 years, the traditional approaches begin to look a little threadbare. We could do worse as a point of departure than examine, again, the interpretation of A. V. Dicey in his *Lectures on the Relation Between Law and Public Opinion in England during the Nineteenth Century*, published in 1905, and the first attempt at a historical explanation of the growth of the Victorian state and its incursions into social policy. Dicey, at the outset, emphasized ideational factors in his interpretation. The effect of changing principles in public life, the development of a public opinion on these matters, the growth of ideological responses to the state and the impact of great minds, particularly Bentham's, were at the heart of his explanation of the growth of new social functions in public administration. The core ideas of 19th-century

[15] Lawrence Goldman, *The Life of R.H. Tawney: Socialism and History* (2013).

[16] Peter Clarke, *Liberals and Social Democrats* (Cambridge, 1978).

[17] Derek Fraser, *The Evolution of the British Welfare State: A History of Social Policy since the Industrial Revolution* (1973) (4th edn, Basingstoke, 2009). The 2015 British general election campaign saw the notable return into everyday political usage of the term 'progressive reform' by several of the parties, including the Scottish National and Labour Parties, as they vied for the votes of the Scottish electorate pre-eminently.

liberalism – reason, economy, efficiency, utility, responsibility – were used to explain how the Victorians came to view, and then accept, the need for state-sponsored social reforms. Yet Dicey's approach was largely overlooked when British historians returned to these questions more systematically in the 1950s and 1960s, impelled by the foundations of a welfare state in post-war Britain to uncover the roots of this development in earlier social interventions. This was at a time when, in the writing of political history, the dual themes of pragmatism and empiricism were especially notable. Under the influence of the 1930s and the Second World War, British historians were tempted to emphasize a cool and rational approach to social issues that differentiated their domestic history from other, and different, European narratives. To George Kitson Clark and his pupil, Oliver MacDonagh, the history of social policy was best approached through the essentially empirical responses of officials trying to devise workable solutions to problems as they arose, and then returning to those solutions and refining and improving them when it became clear that the original solutions were no longer adequate.[18] MacDonagh dubbed this 'the enforcement-inspection-amendment cycle'; it was the result of 'the most ordinary and everyday reactions' of well-meaning officials to the problems they faced. And this was dubbed, in turn, the 'Tory interpretation' of Victorian bureaucracy.[19] It was not only at odds with the many historians who wished to emphasize Bentham's impact on state and society, whether directly or through his many lieutenants and followers from the 1820s to the 1850s.[20] It was also an obstacle to any wider focus on the ideological and intellectual dynamics of social reform.

Whether the conventional literature on 'pressure from without' which was a feature of the 1970s took us much further is also open to question.[21] At a point in time when, in contemporary politics, the influence of pressure groups was a subject for debate, it was natural to want to show how social developments were the resultants of the collaboration (and sometimes conflict) of parliament and the executive with extraparliamentary agitation, be it for the abolition of slavery and the corn laws, the extension of the franchise, a free and unstamped press, or for the repeal of the Contagious Diseases Acts between the late 1860s and the mid 1880s. This was an advance on the internalist bureaucratic focus of the preceding literature, but the social model it endorsed with its clear separation between state and civil society, parliamentary politics and outside agitation, immovable Victorian object *versus* unstoppable popular force, was soon shown to simplify a more complex reality. The many intermediary institutions in these processes, from the Political Economy Club to the Fabian Society, were omitted. The existence of a genuine 'policy community' comprising parliamentarians, professionals, savants, journalists, and civil servants – the types who had founded the Statistical Society of London as early as 1834 – went unrecognized.[22]

---

[18] G. Kitson Clark, '"Statesmen in Disguise": Reflexions on the History of the Neutrality of the Civil Service', *Historical Journal*, ii, (1959), 19–39; Oliver MacDonagh, 'The Nineteenth-Century Revolution in Government: A Reappraisal', *Historical Journal*, i, (1958), 52–67; Oliver MacDonagh, *Early Victorian Government 1830–1870* (1977).

[19] Jenifer Hart, 'Nineteenth-Century Social Reform: A Tory Interpretation of History', *Past & Present*, No. 31 (1965), 39–61.

[20] S.E. Finer, 'The Transmission of Benthamite Ideas 1820–50', in *Studies in the Growth of Nineteenth-Century Government*, ed. Gillian Sutherland (1972), 11–32.

[21] *Pressure from Without in Early Victorian England*, ed. Hollis.

[22] Lawrence Goldman, 'The Origins of British "Social Science": Political Economy, Natural Science and Statistics, 1830–35', *Historical Journal*, xxvi (1983), 587–616.

The close contact of many parliamentarians with the reformers was overlooked. The model could not accommodate the many professional imperatives in the making of social policy and the advocacy of reform. Thus, in the 1980s the historiography began to explore such themes as the development of specialist knowledge and skills among Victorian public servants and members of new professional groups; the growth of expert opinion and 'expertise' as aspects of society in themselves; and, from the developing literature on professionalisation, a knowledge of how these experts sought to establish themselves in positions of high social status and authority.[23] The doctors who championed public health reform, the educationists who campaigned for decent systems of elementary and secondary education, and the penal reformers who campaigned for improvements in the prison regime, were often experienced, well qualified and well connected to parliamentarians. Indeed, in many cases they were from that elite themselves.[24]

The very concept of the 'statesman in disguise' to describe the powerful bureaucrats who, from the 1830s to the 1870s, tried to take control of social policy – men like Edwin Chadwick at the poor law board, John Simon at the privy council medical office and William Farr in the general register office – embodies a recognition that the bureaucrats were not unreflecting officials but men with schemes, blueprints for change, ideas for social improvement and professional advancement, and conduits between organisations like the Statistical Society of London and the Social Science Association (SSA) and government.[25] Yet the ideas which inspired them were not, in general, the broad ideologies that Dicey wrote about but grew from their professional training and experience in local social administration. As has been argued elsewhere, the SSA should not be conceived as just another Victorian pressure group because it cherished wider aims and broader influence as an aid and a shadow to government at a time when the official civil service was haphazard in organisation and when social questions were handled by the non-expert if handled at all. The SSA was never simply an extraparliamentary vehicle for one or more causes.[26]

If the historiography has moved on beyond this focus on professionalism and professionalisation, it has continued to probe the ideational, as opposed to the practical, roots of social reform. Jose Harris's study of the idealist ethics underpinning the origins of the welfare state in the period from the 1870s to the 1930s is an indication of what can be achieved and what remains to be done: the tying together of ethical and intellectual milieu with actual historical actors and situations.[27] In this way the focus is not on the proximate origins of any particular social reform – be it free schools meals for children, old age pensions, or national insurance in the early 20th century – but on the wider intellectual context which framed such developments and which set the parameters for social discussion and intervention. This approach works very effectively in the period Harris has investigated and knows best when late-Victorian philosophical idealism was inspiring the re-examination of the

[23] *Government and Expertise: Specialists, Administrators and Professionals, 1860–1919*, ed. Roy M. McLeod (Cambridge, 1988).

[24] Goldman, *Science, Reform, and Politics, passim.*

[25] Kitson Clark, '"Statesmen in Disguise"', *passim.*

[26] Goldman, *Science, Reform, and Politics*, 13–17.

[27] J.F. Harris, 'Political Thought and the Welfare State 1870–1940: An Intellectual Framework for British Social Policy', *Past & Present*, No. 135 (1992), 116–41.

relations between the individual, the community and the state, and helping to give rise to what was soon called collectivism. The argument advanced here is that to understand the ebbs and flows of parliament's attention to social reform in any period requires, pre-eminently, an intellectual history. It cannot account for all the details but it is much better at discerning the trends.

The intellectual history of welfare has its limits, nevertheless, at that point beyond which a history of ideas ceases to have explanatory force. The limits may have been exceeded by the pre-eminent intellectual historian of social reform in the modern era, Michel Foucault, whose brilliance invites correction even as it inspires respect and emulation. Foucault studied institutions – prisons, asylums, hospitals, reformatories – but always in the context of a structure of thought or a conceptual system, called by Foucault an 'episteme', which limits, directs, and controls, individual and societal outlooks and responses.[28] If not strictly innovatory – there have been many attempts to present the social and intellectual frameworks of the Victorian age, for example, in the work of historians like Halevy, Young and Burn – it has been both influential and revelatory.[29] But as a guide to social institutions as they functioned historically, Foucault has been found to be both empirically unreliable and also ideological in the present-minded antagonism he has shown to actors and social practices in the past, of which he evidently disapproved.[30] His explanation of these practices and assumptions in terms of power and authority – of the control that some groups, be they social classes, governing elites, doctors of the insane, penologists, or sanctioned experts of some other description, exercised over others – is both a truism and also a reduction. Power relations are ubiquitous, a feature of any social situation: they must be described and explained, but because of their universality are rarely sufficient explanations of any major innovation in social welfare.[31] And the implication that a single source of social power can be held responsible for all the 'reforms' ascribed to it by Foucault undervalues the significance of the decisions of myriad historical actors at local and institutional levels to conform to the dominant *episteme*, or indeed, to challenge it. History is made uniform and deterministic; the institutional and cultural complexity of social institutions is ironed out in ways that diminish the role of groups and individuals who may, or crucially may not, be servants of the dominant structures of thought. Foucault tended to generalize social history into a history of domination and subordination, arguing that the urge to control could be discerned in all human institutions; the scale became too broad and the argument too blunt.

Meanwhile, if an *episteme* can explain a structure of social thought synchronically, at a point in time, Foucault recognized the difficulty of explaining how societies move from one conceptual structure to the next, or diachronically, in his most original and brilliant work, *The Order of Things*. He expressed his doubts about the traditional drivers of policy change, be they technological, social or spiritual, but admitted that he had:

---

[28] Gary Gutting, *Foucault: A Very Short Introduction* (Oxford, 2005).

[29] Elie Halévy, *A History of the English People in 1815* (1924); G.M. Young, *Victorian England: Portrait of an Age* (Oxford, 1936); Burn, *The Age of Equipoise, passim*.

[30] Andrew Scull, 'Michel Foucault's History of Madness', *The History of the Human Sciences*, iii (1990), 57; see also Goldman, *Science, Reform, and Politics*, 41–2.

[31] G. Stedman Jones, 'Class Expression versus Social Control? A Critique of Recent Trends in the Social History of Leisure', *History Workshop Journal*, iv (1977), 163–70.

left the problem of causes to one side: I chose instead to confine myself to describing the transformations themselves, thinking that this would be an indispensable step if, one day, a theory of scientific change and epistemological causality was to be constructed.[32]

We have yet to develop that overarching theory of change in the history of social reform and it is doubtful if we ever will or can because the variables are many and their interactions complex. But what might be called 'middle order explanations' of the type offered by Harris for the period 1870–1950, which attempts to explain an intellectual structure within which many developments may be located and explained, offers a more plausible alternative. The scale is not so grand as to lose explanatory force; the detail can be marshalled so as to underpin the explanatory framework; the evidence and the theory cohere. The remainder of this essay will suggest how an explanatory framework might fit the broad sweep of parliamentary engagement with social reform across our period.

4. *Constant Causes and their Opposites: A Typology of Social Reforms*

Anyone examining the transitions in social reform will be aware of a set of social forces, for want of a better word, which in different combinations and at different times, have more and also less influence over the timing, nature and outcome of social welfare. These include the impact of science, humanitarianism, religion in its various forms, utilitarianism in *its* various forms, military and imperial preparedness and democratic pressure. There are more such categories, no doubt, but these will suffice to make the point that social reform across a period this long is best understood in terms of these constant causes, varying in intensity and primacy no doubt, but never without some discernible influence, though that influence is often more complex than might be imagined.[33] Often two or more of these categories combine in a single reform: the abolition of slavery owed much to both the wider growth of a humane spirit across the Atlantic world and the specific role of groups on both sides of the Atlantic who were moved by evangelical christianity.[34] In another case, social reforms inspired by military imperatives were the paradoxical outcome of quite different strategic situations. The mid-20th-century welfare state was the product and reward of military victory.[35] Conversely, the social self-scrutiny of the later 1850s and 1860s which provided the ideas and blueprints for the social reforms of the Gladstone and Disraeli administrations between 1868 and 1880, was the product of military defeat in the Crimea and the deficiencies of aristocratic government which were held to have contributed to it.[36] Meanwhile evidence of military weakness and unpreparedness as seen in the poor physical health and fitness of so many of the volunteers for the Boer War convinced a generation of 'social

[32] M. Foucault, *The Order of Things: An Archaeology of the Human Sciences* (1966), xiii.

[33] For a helpful typology of different 'perspectives' on welfare, see 'Introduction: Perspectives on the History of Welfare', in Fraser, *Evolution of the British Welfare State*, 1–15. Fraser identifies eight different perspectives: whig, pragmatic, bureaucratic, ideological, conspiratorial, capitalistic, democratic, and mixed

[34] Thomas L. Haskell, 'Capitalism and the Origins of the Humanitarian Sensibility', *American Historical Review*, xc (1985), 339–61, 547–66; Richard Carwardine, *Evangelicals and Politics in Antebellum America* (New Haven, CT, 1993); Christopher Leslie Brown, *Moral Capital: Foundations of British Abolitionism* (Chapel Hill, NC, 2006).

[35] Paul Addison, *The Road to 1945: British Politics and the Second World War* (1975).

[36] Goldman, *Science, Reform, and Politics*, 56–7; Olive Anderson, 'The Administrative Reform Association, 1855–57', in *Pressure from Without in Early Victorian England*, ed. Hollis, 262–85.

tories' that a national investment in health and welfare was required to sustain an imperial nation. In other contexts, movements seemingly unconnected, or even apparently opposed, share certain attributes. Benthamite utilitarians and Fabian collectivists, separated by almost a century, were united in the argument that social efficiency required social reform, and that the reform of social institutions – the old poor law for the Benthamites and the new poor law for the Fabians – was the key to social progress.[37] And they incited the same groups to hostility as well: christian tory paternalists like Oastler opposed utilitarian reforms in the 1830s, and christian socialists like R.H. Tawney steered well clear of the Fabians' fascination with mechanisms of social control and governmentalism in the 1900s.[38] In both cases their critics focused on the reform of individuals and not of society itself as the requirement for moral regeneration, arguing that only the alteration of individual behaviour and values could guarantee lasting social change.

Some of these constant causes set up their counter causes, therefore. Scientific and technological advances have been central to the initiation of social reforms and their implementation. But the anti-vaccination and anti-vivisection movements of the mid- and late-Victorian periods display different social values, respectively the hostility to social compulsion and moral opposition to the abuse of animals for human purposes.[39] There is a tendency, already noted, to write the history of social reform as an unalloyed blessing, ignoring, therefore, the very real tensions and struggles which reforms created or of which they were part. We sometimes refer to the 1830s and 1840s as 'the age of reform',[40] but it was also – and because of the nature of those reforms – an age of class conflict and social alienation caused in large part not only by what *was* done, such as the introduction of the New Poor Law of 1834 with its crucial criterion of 'less eligibility' but also by what was *not* done, notably the extension of the franchise. The first factory acts, the first grants of state funds for elementary education, the recognition of the rights of dissenters, the repeal of the corn laws and so on were the sites of intense dispute between different interests rather than the fruits of social consensus. In all these cases, extraparliamentary movements and agitations, in an age before mass representative politics, found their spokesmen inside parliament (and incited parliamentary opposition as well) so that 'pressure from without' had its undoubted effects on the legislative process and the history of social reform.

Models of consensus have dominated our thinking about social reforms; it would be more accurate to see them as products of conflict between different groups, often two or more extraparliamentary groups seeking to control the agenda of reform. The tripartite struggle between the Chartists, the Complete Suffrage Union and the Anti-Corn Law League in the early 1840s over the relative merits of suffrage extension and cheap food was won by the group – the League – with the most funds, the best organisation and the most support not only in the country but in parliament itself. Similarly, we recall with pride the struggles of Lloyd George and the new Liberals to pass the people's budget of 1909 and worst, the house of lords, forgetting that among those most suspicious of national insurance

[37] William Thomas, *The Philosophical Radicals: Nine Studies in Theory and Practice, 1817–1841* (Oxford, 1979); A.M. McBriar, *Fabian Socialism and English Politics, 1884–1918* (Cambridge, 1962).

[38] *R.H. Tawney's Commonplace Book*, ed. J.M. Winter and D.M. Joslin (Cambridge, 1972), 45–6; Goldman, *Life of R.H. Tawney*, 170–3.

[39] Nadja Durbach, *Bodily Matters: The Anti-Vaccination Movement in England 1853–1907* (Durham, NC, 2005).

[40] E.L. Woodward, *The Age of Reform 1815–1870* (Oxford, 1938).

were the trade unions themselves. Working people had internalised the Victorian gospel of self-help and constructed, in friendly societies and unions, their own collective response to personal adversity. They were not unnaturally suspicious of a new type of state support which threatened to marginalise their own hard-won institutions.[41]

But is evidence of conflict over social reform and suspicion of it enough to sustain the case that social reform has often been employed to buy off radicalism and genuine threats to social order from below? Has it been, for want of a better term, a method of social control?[42] The problem with this type of argument is its sheer profligacy: almost any concession from the state or ruling classes could be written off as a ploy to mislead the workers. Some reforms do look like concessions, though these are more evident and more famous in the realm of politics. But when we get close to these 'concessions' in the realm of social policy such simplistic analysis tends to dissolve. Take the Liberal welfare reforms before the First World War; it is commonly argued that these were concessions to the working classes to prevent them from drifting towards the new Labour Party and varieties of socialism. But there is little direct evidence that Liberal cabinet ministers said or thought in these terms, and much more evidence to suggest that the sequence of reforms was a largely unplanned response by particular individuals to long-standing social problems.[43] If anything, energetic Liberals were moved by progressive thinking and research into the causes of poverty and neglect, and they responded genuinely and sincerely to the evidence rather than with any thought for party advantage. If the latter really had been true then the new Liberals misunderstood the workers themselves, who, as the argument above makes clear, were certainly not expecting the state to come to their assistance; and they also miscalculated the electoral consequences of their actions. As is clear in the elections of 1910, in which the Liberal Party lost its majority of 1906, there were, as yet, few votes in the politics of welfare. The early Labour Party could not be tempted with social reform because, as Henry Pelling explained long ago, it had yet to define itself in terms of the extension of the competences of the state.[44]

This is not to deny that social reform has its political uses. It is a commonplace of sociological literature to recognize that modern business supports the welfare state and (sometimes) pays its taxes to sustain public services because a well-educated, well-fed, well-housed, and healthy, working population is evidently in its interests.[45] Social reform is not the privilege of workers only. In the mid 19th century there were many organisations, generally focused on the SSA, which sought to make the world safer and better for the Victorian middle classes. Nor can we overlook the fact that when the middle classes were most vocal in calling for reforms that would assist the working classes, they were also thinking of their

[41] H.M. Pelling, 'The Working Class and the Origins of the Welfare State', in Henry Pelling, *Popular Politics and Society in Late Victorian Britain* (1968), 1–18.

[42] For examples of this type of argument drawn from the history of workers' education, see Roger Fieldhouse, *The Workers' Educational Association: Aims and Achievements 1903–1977* (Syracuse, NY, 1977), 33–4; Roger Fieldhouse, 'Conformity and Contradiction in English Responsible Body Adult Education 1925–1950', *Studies in the Education of Adults*, xvii, 2 (1985), 123. For an answer to these arguments see Ross McKibbin, 'Why was there no Marxism in Great Britain?', in Ross McKibbin, *The Ideologies of Class: Social Relations in Britain 1880–1950* (Oxford, 1990), 1–41.

[43] Clarke, *Liberals and Social Democrats, passim*; Michael Freeden, *The New Liberalism: An Ideology of Social Reform* (Oxford, 1978); J.R. Hay, *The Origins of the Liberal Welfare Reforms 1906–1914* (1975).

[44] Pelling, *Popular Politics and Society, passim.*

[45] Fraser, *Evolution of the British Welfare State*, 9–10.

own needs. Cholera was no respecter of persons and cleaning up the streets, the drinking water and the drains in the poorest urban neighbourhoods was likely to also benefit those lucky enough to live in the outer reaches of the cities or high above the smog and miasma of urban river and canal basins.[46] But it is a large step to go from the acknowledgment of middle-class interests in reform to the belief in social reform as a weapon in the class struggle or a lever of group advancement. There were often class and group interests in play in the determination of social measures, but there is little convincing evidence that social reform was used as a means of control. Nor is there evidence that the working classes were seduced or duped by social reforms into political reformism (as opposed to political radicalism) and into paths they might not otherwise have followed. Trade unions, community organisations, and lobbyists for the poor and disadvantaged, have proved adept at extracting support from the state over the past century; in general, there has been a widespread acceptance that a welfare state in a mixed economy has been the best of all the realistic options for workers and dependent groups alike, in Britain as in most western societies.

5. Timing

Our generalizations about the development of social reform must inevitably minimise the degree of ebb and flow in the commitment of parliament and extraparliamentary opinion to reform at particular times. Why some generations were more engaged with social questions and their solution and some less so is an important, but sometimes neglected, element in the historiography. Our period, running up to 1914, ends at a time when enthusiasm for social reform in Britain was at some sort of historical high point. The Liberal welfare reforms after 1908 were themselves the outcome of intense social interest and reflection on urban squalor and inequality since the 1880s. The confluence from this time onwards of ambitious and widely-remarked social investigations by, among others, Charles Booth and Seebohm Rowntree; the writing of the first critical social histories of industrialisation in Britain such as Toynbee's *Lectures on the Industrial Revolution in England*; the urge among middle-class youth to work in social settlements such as the first, Toynbee Hall in Whitechapel, which was founded in 1884; and nothing short of a paradigm shift in the conceptualisation of both the reasons for poverty and the responsibility of the state towards the poor, ensured that for 30 years and more 'the social question' was examined, debated and addressed as never before in Britain.[47] Yet it followed a mid-Victorian equipoise so-called, when, according to the conventional narrative, social questions were largely ignored. And this generation, in turn, had followed a much more conflicted period of contested social initiatives in the 1830s and 1840s.

Part of the explanation for these changes in social consciousness may lie with the simple idea of the discrete historical generation which is defined by its commitment to certain issues and problems and not to others. As the context changes, as leading members of the

---

[46] A.S. Wohl, *Endangered Lives: Public Health in Victorian Britain* (1983); J.M. Eyler, 'William Farr on the Cholera: The Sanitarian's Disease Theory and the Statistician's Method', *Journal of the History of Medicine*, xxviii (1973), 79–100.

[47] Alon Kadish, *Apostle Arnold: The Life and Death of Arnold Toynbee 1852–1883* (Durham, NC, 1986); Werner Picht, *Toynbee Hall and the English Settlement Movement*, trans Lillian A. Cowell (1914); Asa Briggs and Anne Macartney, *Toynbee Hall: The First Hundred Years* (1984).

generation pass on, as some of the problems are resolved leaving behind only those which are intractable, so social focus alters in turn. One obvious contextual difference between the 'age of equipoise' in the 1850s and 1860s and the eras on either side, was the social and economic stability of the mid-Victorian period as opposed to the much more turbulent conditions of the early decades, and to the intimations and stresses of relative economic decline at the century's end. Social reform seems less compelling in periods of relative abundance and social calm. This is not to argue that social reforms were unnecessary between about 1850 and 1870; 'poverty is always with us' as Henry Mayhew's famous journalism for the *Morning Chronicle* at this time demonstrated.[48] What seems to have changed was sensitivity towards it and the compulsion to do something about it. But this argument has its paradoxes, none the less: why should social reforms have been background features in the 1850s and 1860s in a period of full employment and prosperity, and also in the 1920s and 1930s in a period of mass unemployment and slump? Hopes for social reconstruction were high and going higher in the last phases of the First World War and in its immediate aftermath. In the event, economic stagnation, high unemployment and industrial unrest, relegated creative acts of social reform to an inferior and subordinate position until the early 1940s.[49]

For want of a better term, the social mood is a crucial determinant of social reform. When the Reverend Andrew Mearns first heard the 'Bitter Cry of Outcast London' in 1882 and tried to alert others, his pamphlet seems to have coincided with a subterranean change in mood among the middle classes.[50] They were becoming unnerved by evidence all around them that for all the wealth of urban and industrial Britain, accumulated over more than a century, millions still lived in abject poverty. It is from this point that we may date the rising curve of social investigation and debate that formed the indispensable background to the reforms of the Edwardian period.

'Ripeness is all': Ken Loach's famous modern epic, *Cathy Come Home*, broadcast on BBC1 in 1965 and regularly voted the most significant British television programme ever made, also met a rising curve of social concern about homelessness, contributed mightily to the founding of charities and voluntary groups to address the issue, and formed a fixed point of reference in social debate for the next decade and more.[51] Yet Peter 'Poverty' Townshend at the University of Bristol spent the 1970s investigating social deprivation in Britain using the most sophisticated techniques, and published his results in 1979.[52] By then the mood had changed, with a newly-installed Conservative government ready to address a quite different set of issues, and Townshend's research never made its mark. Many of the social issues, and even some of the solutions debated and implemented after the 1880s in Britain, had been brought before the SSA a generation before. But public interest was limited at that stage and the state had not yet reached a size and a level of competence and expertise that might have allowed it to address such questions. Indeed, one of the most interesting aspects of the history of social reform between the 1880s and the First World War is the development of

---

[48] *The Unknown Mayhew: Selections from the Morning Chronicle 1849–1850*, ed. E.P. Thompson and Eileen Yeo (1971); Henry Mayhew, *London Labour and the London Poor*, ed. Robert Douglas-Fairhurst (Oxford, 2010).

[49] Philip Abrams, 'The Failure of Social Reform 1918–20', *Past & Present*, No. 24 (1963), 43–64.

[50] [Rev. Andrew Mearns], *The Bitter Cry of Outcast London: An Inquiry into the Condition of the Abject Poor* (1882)

[51] Stephen Lacey, *Cathy Come Home* (2011).

[52] Peter Townshend, *Poverty in the United Kingdom: A Survey of Household Resources and Standards of Living* (Harmondsworth, 1979).

bureaucratic expertise within government; figures of the calibre of Hubert Llewellyn Smith at the board of labour, and Michael Sadler and Robert Morant at the board of education, made possible all the stages of social reform from investigation and policy formation to legislation but then implementation.

The transition from mid- to late-Victorian social consciousness may merit special attention, not least because it laid down the parameters of political discussion over the role of the state in social reform which have structured British discourse ever since, and also because it demonstrates the place of intellectual history in the history of social reform. The transition of the 1880s may be understood in terms of a question once asked of the SSA: why, in the age of the Fabian Society, did the SSA cease to have a role? The question contains its own answer: because the Fabians approached social questions from a novel perspective which explicitly rejected the assumptions of the middle-class membership of the SSA. The SSA had been focused on the reform of social institutions by parliament to make them more efficient and to bend them to meet the needs of the hour. So a patchwork collection of existing initiatives in elementary and secondary education was, in the view of the SSA, to be patched further to fill in gaps in provision. Or, to take another example, the problem of how to deal with convicts hitherto shipped to the antipodes, could be solved by reforming the regime in British prisons to encourage right behaviour. Those who did not take this social medicine and reoffended might then be hounded as part of a new category of 'habitual criminal', as under the 1869 Habitual Criminals Act, which was passed by a parliament which followed the lead of speakers who had attended the SSA debates on this question.[53] Public health was a matter of better and more rational administration at central and county levels; science, if it had any part to play at all in matters of health, was left to others. Functioning within the individualist framework of Victorian liberalism, the association's conception of social reform was focused on the machinery of social administration. No one made the argument that the state should expend more on secondary education; rather, limited resources from historic and private sources might be better deployed by new bodies like the Endowed Schools' Commission.[54]

The very inadequacy of such methods was the reason for the intellectual shift of the 1880s. It was evident by then that Victorian liberalism, with or without more efficient forms of social administration, was failing the many millions who, by reason of defective education, poor health, inadequate support, and low incomes, were simply unable to take their place in a competitive society and economy as modelled by free traders in the 1840s, and were thus being excluded culturally as well as economically. This was the context in which T.H. Green in Oxford began to transmute the old into the *new* Liberalism, made aware by virtue of his own experiences in local government and in secondary and adult education, of the loss of human potential in a social system that failed to encourage and realize the talents of so many.[55] This was also the context in which the Fabians, meeting in London from 1884, began to theorise 'collectivism', the collective provision by the state and local government of the services which everyone required to achieve a decent standard of living and to a make a social contribution.[56] In Spencer's *Man Versus the State* on the one

[53] Goldman, *Science, Reform, and Politics*, 163–8.

[54] Goldman, *Science, Reform, and Politics*, 240–1, 267–8.

[55] Melvin Richter, *The Politics of Conscience: T.H. Green and his Age* (Cambridge, MA, 1964).

[56] McBriar, *Fabian Socialism and English Politics, passim.*

side (1884) and the *Fabian Essays in Socialism* (1889) on the other, the battle lines of the present and future were drawn up in the 1880s. In so far as they set out contrasting views of the size, competence and responsibility of the state we have not gone that far from these initial exchanges in more than a century. And these were intellectual conflicts between conflicting models of society, generated and sustained by writers and thinkers who, on the basis of their own social experience and the new research available – Charles Booth's first study of poverty in Tower Hamlets was published in 1886 – were engaged in a struggle of ideas. The prize was to change social consciousness and win access to the levers of the state, both of which the Fabians, for all their evident personal and class weaknesses in Eric Hobsbawm's jaundiced view, achieved between the 1890s and the First World War.[57]

6. Conclusion: 'Persons to Whom the Utmost Credit is Due'

The enthusiastic exploration by a new generation of historians of the 1960s and early 1970s of the role played by extraparliamentary campaigns, associations and pressure groups was encapsulated in the highly influential collection of essays, *Pressure from Without in Early Victorian England*, published in 1974. Yet it was not long before the assumptions of this group that the history of social reform – and the history of modern parliamentary politics more generally – could be written in terms of the impact of popular pressure in the era of emerging democracy, came under sustained scrutiny. The so-called 'Peterhouse School', taking their name from the Cambridge college to which many of them had been affiliated, whether as teachers or students, struck a self-consciously critical posture in response. In studies of 19th-century parliamentary and electoral reform focused on the Second and Third Reform Acts of 1867 and 1884, and of the home rule crisis of 1885–6, Maurice Cowling and his colleagues made a different argument emphasizing the closed nature of Victorian high politics in which key decisions were taken by a very small circle of leading figures at cabinet level, irrespective of public campaigns, press opinion and the extraparliamentary pressure in general. They emphasized the determination of leading statesmen in both parties to keep democracy at bay; they demonstrated that such men were often engaged in complex strategies to outmanoeuvre their rivals for power and far more alive to the needs of their careers than the needs of the people. In his study of the Second Reform Act, Cowling emphasized Disraeli's insecurity as a leader of Conservatism and his ambition to establish himself unrivalled rather than merely to 'dish the whigs'. In their analysis of the home rule crisis and bill of the mid 1880s, John Vincent and A.B. Cooke focused on Gladstone's use of the Irish question to undermine, and ultimately drive out of the party, his rivals for the leadership of Liberalism.[58]

Both interpretations of 1867 and 1886 have been questioned, but the renewed emphasis on high politics, careerism and personality in politics, and on the closed world that was mid- and late-Victorian Westminster, was salutary. A model of public pressure leading inexorably

---

[57] Eric Hobsbawm, 'The Fabians Reconsidered', in Eric Hobsbawm, *Labouring Men: Studies in the History of Labour* (1964), 250–71.

[58] Maurice Cowling, *1867: Disraeli, Gladstone and Revolution* (1967); Andrew Jones, *The Politics of Reform 1884* (Cambridge, 1972); A.B. Cooke and John Vincent, *The Governing Passion: Cabinet Government and Party Politics in Britain, 1885–86* (1974); Michael Bentley, *Politics Without Democracy 1815–1914: Perception and Preoccupation in British Government* (1984).

to parliamentary response was too easily employed and too often imprecise: close analysis showed many mediating and complicating factors, be they ideological, party-political or purely personal. The devil, moreover, was in the detail: the Reform League might demand the suffrage for respectable men at meetings and demonstrations, but who was enfranchised in the mid 1860s, on what basis, and where, were questions to be worked out in committee and cabinet by an elite making different calculations.[59]

Yet this was never a very well-focused debate because the two contending views had emerged from inquiries about different aspects of 19th-century reform. Those historians examining the effect of extraparliamentary pressure were largely interested in social and moral reform campaigns, from anti-slavery to religious equality, whereas the high-political Peterhouse school wrote about suffrage extension, parliamentary reform and national/constitutional issues such as Ireland. Though these latter questions engaged all levels of Victorian opinion and society, they directly affected the nature and composition of parliament and were of special interest to parliamentarians whose opinions and behaviour reflected intraparliamentary calculations and concerns far more than 'pressure from without'. Indeed, in their study of the home rule crisis, Vincent and Cooke were emphatic that Irish constitutional questions were of very limited interest to the English electorate at any stage and especially during the mid-1880s economic depression. The East End rioters who smashed the windows in clubland in London's West End in February 1886 were neither for nor against the Home Rule Bill that was then being debated in parliament, but were venting their frustration and class anger over unemployment and inequality.

Perhaps because of the difference between the political focus of one group and the social focus of the other, this debate petered out. In their respective spheres, both sides made persuasive arguments.[60] But these disagreements were also superseded in the 1980s by the new focus on 'intermediaries' – those professional organisations and associations which contributed their expertise, research and organisational skills to the solution of social ills and the making of social policies. The focus moved again from campaigning groups outside, and from parliamentarians inside parliament, to civil servants, social investigators, statisticians, journalists, economists, and savants who, from the 1830s, formed an emerging 'policy community' in Britain, however ill-defined and disorganised. Their emerging role was understood and explained by Lord John Russell when he addressed an audience of thousands at the SSA's second annual congress in St George's Hall, Liverpool, in 1858:

> I must say that the persons to whom the utmost credit is due are those men … who have not been able hitherto, to collect public opinion into a great force, who have not been able to direct it with great power, but who, in their several capacities of lawyers, political economists, and physicians, have patiently inquired into these subjects, have at great sacrifice of time (and in the case of the medical profession at a great risk to health and life also) devoted themselves to the improvement of their fellow-creatures.[61]

[59] For a more conventional account of events in 1866–7, see F.B. Smith, *The Making of the Second Reform Bill* (Cambridge, 1966).

[60] Goldman, *Science, Reform, and Politics*, 7–11.

[61] *The Times*, 13 Oct. 1858, p. 12.

Russell had been prime minister between 1846 and 1852; he would be again in 1865–6. His life was one of 'high politics' by definition, though he was a more public, accessible, and popular, figure than many statesmen of his generation, and in coming before the SSA he was signalling his respect for extraparliamentary politics and organised social reform. He could see, however, that between these two spheres was another on which both depended: an emerging group of professional men, who were soon to be joined at the SSA by professional *women*, whose 'patient enquiring' was required for social reform.[62] He was paying tribute to their skills, knowledge, expertise and idealism, and in so doing opening up an interpretation of social reform as an aspect of intellectual, as well as social, history.

In this sense, Russell had very early diagnosed the argument of this essay: that 'pressure on parliament' has been an ever-present aspect of social reform in modern Britain but is not the only, nor even the main, force for change, and has been transmitted not only by mass movements of the people, but by well-organised pressure groups and small coteries of experts driven by intellectual imperatives and by differing ideas of 'progress'.

---

[62] Goldman, *Science, Reform, and Politics*, 113–42.

From Estate under Pressure to Spiritual Pressure Group: The Bishops and Parliament

STEPHEN TAYLOR and RICHARD HUZZEY

This essay traces the mutating place of the anglican bishops within the house of lords to explore revolutionary changes in the relationship between religion, parliament and political pressure from the late 17th to the 20th centuries. After the Restoration, the lords spiritual reoccupied a contested position in the upper chamber as representatives of the clerical estate of the realm. During the 18th century, they began to act as representatives of the church's lay and clerical members. In the 19th century, they made a strong target for thwarted reformers and nonconformist pressure groups which resented the privileged place of these appointed legislators. However, by the 20th century we can detect an inclusive role for the bishops as conduits of spiritual pressure and ecumenical concerns in a legislature which might otherwise neglect those anxieties. These contortions, then, exemplify changing patterns of parliamentary pressure and the place of religion in politics. The essay concludes that the bishops' evolving role demonstrates the permeability of legislative deliberations, where clerical legislators might claim a role as channels for extraparliamentary pressure and under-represented interests rather than the continuing supremacy of the state church.

Keywords: anglican; bishops; catholicism; Church of England; disestablishment; judaism; lords spiritual; nonconformity; parliament; pressure; religion; representation

1

The position and role of the lords spiritual offers a unique opportunity to explore pressure both within and without the chambers of parliament. In keeping with many other essays in this volume, which go beyond pressure as a purely external force on legislators, it is helpful to explore the channels between parliamentarians and those who sought to pressure them. The bishops, of course, not only had seats in the house of lords, but they were also widely regarded as the leaders of the Church and clergy. It would be easy to exaggerate the extent to which even figures like the archbishop of Canterbury were believed to speak and act on behalf of the Church as an institution in any part of this period; informed observers were all too aware that individual bishops had little authority to speak on behalf of anyone other than themselves, but there was no one with a stronger claim to articulate anglican opinion. Precisely because of the ambiguities and contradictions of their position, a study of anglican pressure on parliament may use the role of the lords spiritual as a window into the politics of religion throughout our period.

The bishops had been deprived of their seats in the Long Parliament, even before the abolition of the order in 1646, and their position came under ferocious attack again in

1679.[1] On the latter occasion the debate ostensibly focused on the right of the bishops to vote in capital cases, though in fact it ranged much more widely. In the ensuing pamphlet controversy one tract was produced on the bishops' side which was regarded as particularly effective and which was quoted as a statement of the bishops' rights for many years afterwards. Edward Stillingfleet's *The Grand Question concerning the Bishops Right* (1680) argued that the bishops sat in parliament in two different capacities: as barons, summoned by the king's writ in the same manner as any of the temporal lords; and as representing the estate of the clergy, one of the three estates of the realm, alongside the lords temporal and the Commons.[2] This essay will explore the bishops' strange journey, in subsequent centuries, from the third estate; to the target of pressure from those outside the anglican establishment; to a conduit for religious pressure from the state Church – and even from other churches and faiths.

Of course, religious groups have long occupied a significant place in the literature on parliamentary pressure, with a tradition of dissenters exerting pressure against the privileges of the anglican establishment, of which the bishops constituted just one. In the increasingly pluralist society which emerged in England after the passage of the Toleration Act in 1689, the position of the Church of England was a focus for 'pressure from without' organised by groups excluded from a full role in public life or persecuted in their exercise of religious liberty.[3] Norman Crowther-Hunt persuasively argued that, in the early 18th century, protestant dissenters created two of the earliest extraparliamentary political associations, developing techniques and patterns of organisation which were imitated and adopted by most later pressure groups.[4] In the 19th century, the Liberation Society – with a full title of 'the Society for the Liberation of Religion from State Patronage and Control Society' – was founded in 1844 especially to marshal popular pressure against discriminatory measures such as church rates and the provisions for denominational education in the Factories Bill of the previous year.[5] Scholars have also noted that organisations such as the National Free Church Council (later the Federal Free Church Council), founded in 1896 to co-ordinate many local interdenominational committees, included lobbying amongst the collaborations they pursued into the 20th century.[6]

However, despite this long genealogy of religious pressure against the establishment, the role of pressure from the Church of England itself has been largely neglected by

---

[1] By the Bishops' Exclusion Act, passed in February 1642. Peter King, 'The Episcopate during the Civil Wars, 1642–9', *English Historical Review*, lxxxiii (1968), 523–37; John Morrill, 'The Attack on the Church of England in the Long Parliament, 1640–2', in *History, Society and the Churches: Essays in Honour of Owen Chadwick*, ed. Derek Beales and Geoffrey Best (Cambridge, 1985), 105–24; Mark Goldie, 'Danby, the Bishops and the Whigs', in *The Politics of Religion in Restoration England*, ed. Tim Harris, Paul Seaward and Mark Goldie (Oxford, 1990), 75–105.

[2] Edward Stillingfleet, *The Grand Question concerning the Bishops Right to vote in parliament in cases capital, stated and argued* (1680), esp. 151, 162.

[3] Andrew C. Thompson, 'Early Eighteenth-Century Britain as a Confessional State', in *Cultures of Power in Europe during the Long Eighteenth Century*, ed. Hannah Scott and Brendan Simms (Cambridge, 2007), 95; James Bradley, *Religion, Revolution, and English Radicalism: Nonconformity in Eighteenth-Century Politics and Society* (Cambridge, 1990).

[4] Norman Crowther-Hunt, *Two Early Political Associations: The Quakers and the Dissenting Deputies in the Age of Sir Robert Walpole* (Oxford, 1961).

[5] D.M. Thompson, 'The Liberation Society, 1844–1868', in *Pressure from Without in Early Victorian England*, ed. Patricia Hollis (1974), 210–38.

[6] David Bebbington, *The Nonconformist Conscience: Chapel and Politics, 1870–1914* (1982), esp. ch. 4.

historians. There are a number of reasons why the Church has not figured more prominently in accounts of pressure on parliament. In part, it is because, in Convocation and, later, the National Assembly and then the general synod, the Church possessed its own representative assembly, and debates in those bodies have tended to dominate the attention of both churchmen and later historians. In part, it is because, until the late 20th century, the Church lacked any central organisation, and thus the structures required either to articulate or to mobilise pressure. In part, it is because the Church, unlike any other institution or corporation in British society (apart from the universities), possesses its own formal representation inside parliament in the person of 26 bishops. It is also, paradoxically, because parliament was an anglican institution. This is not simply to say that parliament was, at least until the mid 20th century, composed overwhelmingly of baptised members of the Church of England, though that certainly has something to do with it. Rather, the Church was established – or so most parliamentarians believed – by parliamentary statute, and members of parliament took very seriously their responsibility to legislate for the Church, as the Prayer Book controversy of 1927–8 demonstrated.[7] The legislative supremacy of parliament in ecclesiastical affairs was, of course, part and parcel of establishment, but it was not a necessary condition of that establishment. In Scotland, an established Church existed with much greater autonomy, bolstered by the constitutional guarantees of the Act of Union of 1707 and by a firm opposition to Erastianism.[8]

An episode from the early 18th century reveals quite a lot about the bishops' understanding of their role at the start of our period. The Quaker Tithe Bill appears to have had its origins in some effective lobbying of both ministerial and opposition whig MPs by the quakers, the most impressive element of which was their ability to persuade the ministry to offer cautious, but definite, support. Walpole 'unwarily espous'd' the measure, failing to appreciate the implications of what appeared to be a minor measure of relief for the quakers. There is no doubt that the clergy quickly took fright at a piece of legislation which they saw as a direct attack on the rights and privileges of the Church; one which would certainly make much more difficult the collection of tithes, to which they had an undoubted legal right, and which also implicitly threatened the tithe system and the jurisdiction of the ecclesiastical courts.[9]

The Quaker Tithe Bill was not the only piece of anticlerical legislation to be introduced into parliament in 1736. An attempt by the dissenters to secure the repeal of the Test and Corporation Acts met with opposition from the Walpole administration and the motion to bring in a bill was defeated in the Commons. The Mortmain Bill reached the statute book, but it attracted a lot of support from moderate whigs, including some of the bishops. The Tithe Bill, however, was a different matter. In the political climate of the mid 1730s it appeared all the more threatening. In the eyes of some of the bishops, particularly Edmund Gibson, bishop of London and the ministry's ecclesiastical adviser, Walpole was failing to keep to the terms of the Church-whig alliance, agreed in the 1720s, by which the ministry's guarantee of the revolution settlement in the church was to be used to help win over the

[7]John Maiden, *National Religion and the Prayer Book Controversy 1927–8* (Woodbridge, 2009).

[8]C.R. Munro, 'Does Scotland have an Established Church?', *Ecclesiastical Law Journal*, iv (1997), 639–45; *The Constitution and Laws of the Church of Scotland*, ed. James L. Weatherhead (Edinburgh, 1997).

[9]Stephen Taylor, 'Sir Robert Walpole, the Church of England, and the Quakers Tithe Bill of 1736', *Historical Journal*, xxviii (1985), 51–77 (quotation at p. 71).

clergy. By 1736, Gibson and some of his allies had become so disillusioned that they had come to believe that it was essential, if they were to retain any credit with the clergy, that they demonstrate their commitment to the Church. It was hardly surprising, therefore, that the bishops decided to make a stand over the Tithe Bill. Even so, the unanimity shown by the bench was striking – 15 bishops were present in person to vote against the second reading in the house of lords, and a further six had made their proxies available. This vote was the culmination of a carefully organised campaign – a series of meetings had been held through the session, and a key moment had been the concerted refusal of the bench to consider any compromise while the bill was passing through the Commons.[10]

It would, however, be a mistake to focus narrowly on the high political arena and on what pressure the bishops could bring to bear *inside* parliament. One of the most striking and novel features of the controversy over the Tithe Bill was the extraparliamentary campaign. In a two-week period in late March and early April, 40 petitions were presented to the Commons from clergy in different parts of the country petitioning to be heard by counsel against the bill – this compares with the 'extraordinary' scale of the popular response to the excise proposals of 1733, which generated 'instructions' from 54 constituencies.[11] None of these petitions has survived, so it is impossible to determine the extent to which this was a spontaneous grass-roots campaign. But contemporaries had little doubt that it was co-ordinated by the bishops and, in particular, by Gibson. Nor did the campaign stop with the defeat of the bill. Over the next two years the bishops organised the production of printed pamphlets, diocese by diocese, considering the cases of 'persecution' adduced by the quakers in support of the bill, controverting them one by one.[12] Given concerns about the legitimacy of this sort of politics, it is hardly surprising that Gibson was denounced by Walpole as the 'Ringleader of Sedition'.[13] What is interesting, in the context of the present discussion, is the way in which the bishops recognized that the interests of the Church could be defended not only by them as members of the house of lords but also through a popular campaign designed to bring pressure to bear on parliament from without. It is hard to find a similar petitioning campaign organised by the bishops before 1736, and there is little doubt that it helped to change perceptions of the legislation.[14]

This marshalling of extraparliamentary pressure in support of the bishops' campaign during the 1736 controversy over the Tithe Bill suggests a metamorphosis in progress. While Stillingfleet's constitutional analysis of the bishops as representatives of a clerical estate may have been convincing during the Restoration, by the mid 18th century their role was

---

[10] Taylor, 'Sir Robert Walpole', 51–77; Stephen Taylor, ' "Dr Codex" and the Whig "Pope": Edmund Gibson, Bishop of London, 1716–48', in *Lords of Parliament: Studies 1714–1914*, ed. R.W. Davis (Stanford, CA, 1995), 9–28, 183–91. On anticlericalism in the mid 1730s more generally, see also Stephen Taylor, 'Whigs, Tories and Anticlericalism: Ecclesiastical Courts Legislation in 1733', *Parliamentary History*, xix (2000), 329–56; T.F.J. Kendrick, 'Sir Robert Walpole, the Old Whigs and the Bishops, 1733–6: A Study in Eighteenth-Century Parliamentary Politics', *Historical Journal*, xi (1968), 421–45.

[11] Paul Langford, *The Excise Crisis: Society and Politics in the Age of Walpole* (Oxford, 1975), 47.

[12] The first to appear, unsurprisingly, was for Gibson's own diocese: *An Examination of a Book ... intituled, A Brief Account of the many Prosecutions of the People called Quakers ... So far as the Clergy of the Diocese of London are concerned in it* (1737).

[13] St Andrews University Library, Gibson Papers, MS 5303: 'The Case of the Bishop of London's retiring from publick Business'.

[14] See the remarks of Queen Caroline: HMC, *Egmont Diary*, ii, 254.

crystallising into denominational and theological spokesmen more generally. How and why had Stillingfleet's 1680 analysis become anachronistic? The fundamental problem lies in the language of estates, which was used less frequently in 18th-century political discourse and, in as far as it was used, increasingly referred to king, Lords and Commons, rather than clergy, Lords and Commons.[15] As parliament developed into an institution, rather than an occasional event, the notion that it was summoned by the king, as Stillingfleet put it, 'to advise and debate about the great and difficult Affairs of the Kingdom', was articulated less frequently.[16] Moreover, with the passage of the Toleration Act and the establishment of *de facto* religious pluralism, the idea of the confessional state, in which Church and nation were coterminous, was dealt a severe blow. Even so, it remained possible for some anglicans to claim throughout the long 18th century, until the repeal of the Test and Corporation Acts in 1828 and the completion of catholic emancipation in 1829, that the established Church and the *political* nation were identical.[17] That, for example, was the implication of Blackstone's remarks on the Toleration Act, and was one reason why the *Commentaries* were so fiercely attacked by the dissenter Philip Furneaux.[18]

However, the idea that the bishops in parliament represented the clergy as an estate of the realm had died during the 18th century. Already, their church was in competition with other religious groups for the allegiance of the English people and, when parliament was prepared to grant some privileges, however half-hearted and limited, to some of the Church's rivals, religious pluralism was enshrined in law as much as establishment. Recognition of these changes can be seen in the ways in which the bishops described their actions in 1736. There was no ringing defence of the clerical estate; rather, they claimed that they were defending the 'rights' of the Church and clergy against its enemies. Their arguments were essentially sectional; they claimed that the Test Act and the toleration, as established in 1689, had to be maintained because they were the bulwarks of the establishment, protecting it against the demands of other subjects of the crown who did not share its benefits.[19] In this sense, the role, as opposed to the survival, of the lords spiritual suggests a greater and more subtle evolution of the Church's place in England's 'ancient regime' than J.C.D. Clark has credited.[20] Establishment itself had to be defended, and the bishops were thus transformed

[15]On changes in the language of estates, see J.G.A. Pocock, *Virtue, Commerce, and History: Essays on Political Thought and History, Chiefly in the Eighteenth Century* (Cambridge, 1985), 268; J.A.W. Gunn, *Beyond Liberty and Property: The Process of Self-Recognition in Eighteenth-Century Political Thought* (Kingston, ON, 1983), 43–57.

[16]Stillingfleet, *Grand Question*, 3.

[17]Thompson, 'Early Eighteenth-Century Britain', 86–107. For the survival of the confessional state until 1832, see J.C.D. Clark, *English Society, 1660–1832: Religion, Ideology and Politics during the Ancient Regime* (2nd edn, Cambridge, 2000), 24–36. For a summary of reservations with the argument of his book's 1985 first edition, which has significantly different emphases, see Richard W. Davis, 'The Politics of the Confessional State, 1760–1832', *Parliamentary History*, ix (1990), 38–49.

[18]William Blackstone, *Commentaries on the Laws of England* (4 vols, Oxford, 1765–9), iv, 51–3; Philip Furneaux, *Letters to the Honourable Mr Justice Blackstone, concerning his Exposition of the Act of Toleration, and some Positions relative to Religious Liberty* (1770).

[19]See, e.g., the views of Archbishop Wake and Bishop Gibson: Christ Church, Wake MSS, Arch.W.Epist. 8, no. 87: 'The Heads of my Speech in the H. of Lords agt Repealing the Occasional Conformity Bill'; [Edmund Gibson], *The Dispute Adjusted, about the Proper Time of Applying for a Repeal of the Corporation and Test Acts: By Shewing, That No Time is Proper* (1732), 6; Huntington Library, San Marino, CA, Gibson Papers, bound volume, no. 14: 'A Letter to Sr Robert Walpole, prepar'd during Archbp Wake's indisposition, in case ye Archbishopric should be offer'd to me.'

[20]Clark, *English Society, 1660–1832*, 12–34.

from the representatives of the clerical estate into the spokesmen of an established Church in an increasingly pluralist nation.

2. *The Unreformed Bishops*

The bishops thus formed a very distinctive group in the Lords – they sat apart on their own benches, they dressed differently, and they were there for life as crown appointees. This left them very vulnerable to criticism – as has been seen, both in the early 1640s and in the late 1670s the tendency of the bishops to support royal policy provoked attacks on their rights and privileges by the opponents of those policies. This pattern continued after the 1688 revolution. In 1733, for example, the Walpole ministry was saved from defeat on a key vote in the Lords during the excise crisis by the support of 25 of the 26 bishops, provoking denunciations of their political subservience in the opposition press.[21] Throughout the 18th century there was a succession of opposition proposals to limit the influence of the bishops as a way of limiting the influence of the crown. A favourite proposal was to prevent the translation of bishops, thereby, it was claimed, making them more independent once they had been appointed. Bills were introduced into the Commons for this purpose in 1701 and 1731, the first by a tory and the second by a whig – anticlericalism was never the exclusive preserve of whigs and liberals. Later in the century, Richard Watson, who had just been promoted to the bishopric of Llandaff by the earl of Shelburne and supported his programme of economical reform, advocated the introduction of a bill 'to render the Bishopricks more equal to each other, both with respect to income and patronage'. The aim was the same – removing the attraction of translations to wealthier sees would secure 'a greater independence of the Bishops in the House of Lords'.[22]

The problem for the bishops was that the perception of them as ministerial lackeys was not wholly without foundation. Following the development of long, annual parliamentary sessions in the 1690s, the bishops took seriously their duties to attend in parliament. Indeed, analysis of their attendance in the House, from the 1730s to the 1750s, as recorded in the *Lords Journals*, suggests that, while there may not have been a formal rota, a degree of co-ordination occurred to ensure that a group was always present, with the burden tending to fall on the more junior.[23] Most of them saw their role there as the care of the Church and religion, and on these issues both individually and collectively they acted with a considerable degree of independence. On other issues, as M.W. McCahill's study of the Lords in the later 18th century suggests, the bishops' intellectual engagement with the business of the House was greater than popular judgment gave credit.[24] Even so, it was rare for them to intervene in debates on non-religious issues; on broader questions most were content much of the time to give their support to the king's government. It is always possible to find dissidents, but much of the time, most bishops gave their votes to the administration. This behaviour inevitably provoked attacks from opponents of the ministry, as during the American war,

[21]E.g., 'The Knight and the Prelate', in *Political Ballads Illustrating the Administration of Sir Robert Walpole*, ed. Milton Percival (Oxford, 1916), 92.

[22]Richard Watson, *A Letter to His Grace the Archbishop of Canterbury* (1783), 7–11.

[23]Stephen Taylor, 'The Bishops at Westminster in the Mid-Eighteenth Century', in *A Pillar of the Constitution the House of Lords and British Politics, 1640–1784*, ed. Clyve Jones (1989), 137–63.

[24]M.W. McCahill, *The House of Lords in the Age of George III, 1760–1811* (Oxford, 2009), 89–92.

when whigs and Chathamites excoriated the bench for its readiness to support the sending of armies to make war on fellow Englishmen. But the bishops' willingness to rally pressure from without in support of the Church could also attract criticism, Earl Fitzwilliam, in 1813, wishing that they would 'get a little scratched' in the debates initiated by petitions at their behest.[25]

By the beginning of the 19th century the bishops had been transformed from the representatives of one of the three estates of the realm into a group which represented the interests of the established Church and whose reputation for political subservience meant that they were not widely regarded as having much to contribute to debates which did not touch on religion. But if there was scepticism about the value of the bishops' contribution to the proceedings of the House, their right to be there went unchallenged. When the Act of Union of 1800 merged the British and Irish legislatures, the Irish bishops were allocated four seats, with membership rotating between them at the end of each session. This provision has received little attention from historians, perhaps because it was not inconsistent with the wider treatment of the Irish peers, who were allowed to elect 28 of their number, each of whom then sat in the Westminster parliament for life. But the provision also suggests that concerns about the size of the episcopal bloc in the Lords pre-dated the creation of new bishoprics in England.[26] In the following year, when the election of the radical clergyman, Horne Tooke, provoked debate on the eligibility of a priest to sit in the house of commons, Charles James Fox asked what difference between the two houses of parliament made the clergy's place 'in the one not only harmless but useful, and in the other dangerous and destructive'. Tooke was definitively excluded by the 1801 Clerical Disqualification Act, but it is striking that his supporters, not his opponents, highlighted the role of the bishops; those in favour of clerical disqualification tended to emphasize the pastoral impact of electing clergymen, rather than the adequacy of the bishops in representing them as an estate.[27] By this point, then, the bishops tended to be seen as representing the established Church as an entity rather than just its ordained members.

For growing numbers of nonconformist critics, the bishops were vestiges of a historical accident which had accorded to a particular pressure group the privilege of representation in parliament. However, the bishops' apparent conservatism in temporal affairs riled anglican reformers as well as dissenters. The struggle for electoral reform and the expansion of the franchise, peaking with popular protest and parliamentary intrigue in 1831–2, crystallised 18th-century criticism of the bishops' role in the Lords. When an episcopal bench appointed by a succession of tory governments provided 21 of the 41 votes against the whigs' Reform Bill in autumn 1831, it provoked an outburst of virulent anticlericalism in the press. At a Hyde Park meeting of reformers, protesters believed 'it was the bishops and the bishops only, whose vote decided the fate of the Reform Bill'.[28]

In fact, as Michael Brock long ago noted, many of the bishops had feared just such a reaction and hoped, with moderate opponents of reform such as Lord Harrowby, to see

[25]McCahill, *The House of Lords in the Age of George III*, 87–8.

[26]K. Theodore Hoppen, *Ireland since 1800: Conflict and Conformity* (1989), 16.

[27]*The Parliamentary History of England from the Earliest Period to the Year 1803* (36 vols, 1803–20), xxxv, 1390–1401 (quotation at p. 1394).

[28]Eric J. Evans, 'Some Reasons for the Growth of English Rural Anti-Clericalism c. 1750 – c. 1830', *Past & Present*, No. 66 (1975), 84–109; quotation from William Gibson, *Church, State and Society, 1760–1850* (Basingstoke, 1994), 106–7.

compromise emerge from this rejection.[29] Work by Robert Saunders suggests that, in fact, parochial clergymen tended to be far more invested in opposing reform than their bishops, who were 'a body of political appointees operating in a political arena'.[30] Yet, effigies of the anglican prelates replaced Roman catholic villains on the nation's bonfires of 5 November 1831.[31] In Manchester, some residents refused to pay the church rate as a way of protesting against the perfidy of the lords spiritual.[32] The mood of reformers was epitomised when a pro-Reform mob burned the bishop's palace in Bristol and tried to do the same in Exeter.[33]

After the Great Reform Act had passed, it is hardly surprising that a radical MP, Gateshead's Cuthbert Rippon, moved the first bill since the 1640s to 'relieve the Arch-bishops and Bishops of the Established Church from their legislative and judicial duties in the House of Peers'.[34] The government refused to engage in the debate that he initiated in March 1834, but Rippon's arguments are instructive: he mocked the traditional claim that the bishops 'represent the Clergy' by querying whether 'a Bishop can be called the representative of his Clergy, when they have no voice in his election – when he is, in fact, a mere State-made Father in God'. He suggested that the role of the prelates as legislators undermined parliament's duty to reform the Church, especially where that might concern bishops' livings. His seconder, Lanark's William Gillon, added that for those who worried about how to 'represent the Church', the prelates could still be 'received with respect, and treated with favour, by that Parliament, upon a formal representation from the Bishops', but without risking the partisan discord involved in acting as legislators themselves.[35]

The whigs sought to appease nonconformist grievances while re-strengthening an es-tablished church 'as the most efficient means of guaranteeing social and political stability and promoting a moral society'.[36] In 1836, Lord John Russell's 'liberal anglican' ministry made permanent the Ecclesiastical Commission created to pursue reform of church finances and government, following a series of temporary commissions under both tory and whig premiers. As Richard Brent notes, opposition to this move crossed party boundaries and reflected differences between anglican groupings.[37] Crucially, Russell expressed his contin-uing support for the bishops remaining in the Lords and 'was not prepared to make that invidious distinction between the spiritual and temporal Lords of Parliament', which was involved in the attempts of the lower chamber to revise membership of the upper. At the same time, when creating new bishoprics to serve the growing towns of the north and midlands, he sought to maintain the parliamentary status quo by merging other bishoprics, limiting the number of English and Welsh lords spiritual to 26.[38]

[29]Michael Brock, *The Great Reform Act* (1973), 237–47.

[30]Robert Saunders, 'God and the Great Reform Act: Preaching against Reform, 1831–2', *Journal of British Studies*, liii (2014), 380.

[31]Angus Hawkins, *Victorian Political Culture: 'Habits of Heart and Mind'* (Oxford, 2015), 9, 12–13, 67.

[32]J.P. Ellens, *Religious Routes to Gladstonian Liberalism: The Church Rate Conflict in England and Wales, 1832–1868* (State College, PA, 1994), 21–4.

[33]Gibson, *Church, State and Society*, 107.

[34]Richard Masheder, *Dissent and Democracy: Their Mutual Relations and Common Object: An Historical Review* (1864), 41–2; *Spectator*, 15 Mar. 1834, p. 3.

[35]Hansard, *Parl. Debs*, 3rd ser., xxii, cols 133–4, 140–1: 13 Mar. 1834.

[36]Ellens, *Religious Routes to Gladstonian Liberalism*, 6–7.

[37]Richard Brent, *Liberal Anglican Politics: Whiggery, Religion, and Reform, 1830–1841* (Oxford, 1987), 3–4, 6–7.

[38]Hansard, *Parl. Debs*, 3rd ser., xxxiii, cols 1154–5: 30 May 1836.

Russell claimed that the general support of the bishops for the commission demonstrated that they would 'yield to the general opinion of the country' in 'the correction of defects' in management of the Church, largely relating to inequalities in the income of livings. Yet, in conceding to his more radical back benchers that the presence of the bishops in the house of lords made it politic to avoid too steep a curb in episcopal incomes, Russell reduced the prelates to the role of stakeholders with a personal interest in Church governance, rather than an estate of the realm.[39] In rejecting measures to prevent the translation of bishops between sees, which would have been a restriction of crown prerogative in appointments, he insisted that the commission's equalisation of livings would ensure that 'those filling the inferior bishoprics would be more likely to act independently of political parties, by whom they might otherwise be influenced, for the sake of preferment'.[40] Hence, adaptations in the episcopate, like the Reform Bill which the bishops had fruitlessly opposed a few years earlier, were designed to reform in order to preserve.

As a critic of the Established Church Act of 1836, the bishop of Hereford did dispute the archbishop of Canterbury's claim of unanimous support from the clergy of the Church, referring to 'distrust and dismay' among those with whom he had corresponded or met. However, in challenging the primate's accuracy in representing clerical opinion on financial reform of the Church, Hereford introduced internecine conflict rather than reasserting any traditional doctrine of estates.[41] It was left to the eccentric MP, Sir Robert Inglis, not the bishops as representatives of the clerical estate, to criticize the commission as 'an inquisitional proceeding into the property of one class of the King's subjects' whose recommendations would be passed 'by an Act of the Legislature, unsanctioned by the Church itself' and would assert that 'Church property was public property'.[42] Indeed, the creation of the permanent Ecclesiastical Commission offered an alternative forum to parliament for overseeing government of the Church, even if the archbishops and some of the bishops also had seats in this new body.

Indeed, when parliament debated the creation of another new bishopric, for Manchester, in 1847, the old language of the clerical estate had disappeared altogether. Lord John Russell, bowing to a campaign by churchmen in Wales such as the earl of Powis, reversed earlier plans to maintain the number of diocesan bishops (by joining the sees of St Asaph and Bangor). By increasing the overall size of the episcopate for the first time since the Reformation, his ministry introduced a table of seniority which would determine which of the bishops took up the existing 26 seats in the Lords. There was, it is true, some fierce criticism of the provision in the 1847 bill limiting the number of bishops in the house of lords to 26, but it came from a small group of Conservative peers and bishops who denounced it as an infringement of the privileges of the crown and of the peerage. They were concerned not with the role of the bishops as *spirituali*, but in their capacity as barons, and the exclusion of a bishop from the Lords was seen as a limitation on the royal prerogative and, perhaps threateningly, as 'a dangerous precedent, at variance with the precedent of an hereditary Peerage'.[43] With similarly constitutional, not clerical, concerns, the reactionary

---

[39]Hansard, *Parl. Debs*, 3rd ser., xxxv, cols 354–6, 523–4: 19, 25 July 1836.

[40]Hansard, *Parl. Debs*, 3rd ser., xxxv, col. 17: 8 July 1836.

[41]Hansard, *Parl. Debs*, 3rd ser., xxxv, cols 921–2: 5 Aug. 1836.

[42]Hansard, *Parl. Debs*, 3rd ser., xxxv, cols 344–9: 19 July 1836.

[43]Hansard, *Parl. Debs*, 3rd ser., xciii, col. 797: 22 June 1847.

bishop of Exeter, Henry Philpotts, opposed the innovation as inconsistent 'with the law, and the privileges of the House'.[44] Indeed, almost all of the bishops who spoke treated the question as one of expediency. Bishop Blomfield of London alone referred to the issue of 'representation', but he was concerned with the representation of 'the Church' as a whole rather than the clerical estate and, while he felt that it could not be accomplished effectively with fewer than 26 bishops, he did not see the need for any increase.[45] The bishops' re-formation as representatives of the Church and symbols of establishment was complete.

3. *The Bishops as Spiritual Pressure*

While the bishops had occasionally rallied public support from outside parliament in support of their concerns, stretching back to the 18th century and earlier, they started to play this role more in the second half of the 19th century. That fact, in large part, reflects the growing sense of siege among anglicans, who became 'sufficiently resentful and insecure to adopt methods of organisation first developed by their religious and political rivals', as M.J.D. Roberts astutely judges. The 1859 foundation of the Church Institution, to repel those pushing for disestablishment, won the support of bishops from the high, low, and broad parties in the Church. Though numbers of subscribers never matched the success of the rival Liberation Society, the initiative marked a growing desire to organise support for the Church rather than rely on the representation of the lords spiritual and other anglican parliamentarians. The group's reorganisation as the Church Defence Institution in 1871 remained controversial, but it always enjoyed the active participation of at least some of the bishops.[46] In the 1885 election, the Institution played an active role in opposing the election of those who seemed to threaten disestablishment, such as the Liberal liberationist, Joseph Chamberlain. The bishops, variously, encouraged anglicans to seek pledges against disestablishment and decried 'an infidel, democratic and socialist upheaval against religion and against our Lord Jesus Christ'.[47]

However, the Irish home rule controversy in the final decades of the 19th century may have marked a peak of the bishops' role as parliamentary tribunes for pressure for the established Church's supremacy.[48] While seeking new avenues to support their defence of the Church in parliament, the bishops continued to act as champions of causes adopted by particular groups of churchmen or involving clear questions of christian morality. Samuel Wilberforce, as bishop of Oxford, opposed equalisation of the sugar duties in the 1840s on the grounds of fidelity to his father's principles and the claims of 'morality and duty'.[49]

[44] Hansard, *Parl. Debs*, 3rd ser., xciii, cols 788–90: 22 June 1847.

[45] Hansard, *Parl. Debs*, 3rd ser., xciii, cols 794–5: 22 June 1847.

[46] M.J.D. Roberts, 'Pressure-Group Politics and the Church of England: The Church Defence Institution 1859–1896', *Historical Journal*, xxxv (1984), 560–82 (quotation at p. 561).

[47] Alan Simon, 'Church Disestablishment as a Factor in the General Election of 1885', *Historical Journal*, xviii (1975), 791–820 (quotation at p. 804).

[48] Alan Megahey, '"God will Defend the Right": The Protestant Churches and Opposition to Home Rule', in *Defenders of the Union: A Survey of British and Irish Unionism since 1801*, ed. D. George Boyce and Alan O'Day (2001) 160–1; S.J.D. Green, *The Passing of Protestant England: Secularisation and Social Change, c.1920–1960* (Cambridge 2011), 35.

[49] Richard Huzzey, *Freedom Burning: Anti-Slavery and Empire in Victorian Britain* (Ithaca, NY, 2012), 107.

Support for nonconformist causes, such as temperance, from some bishops, offered a platform in the house of lords and a model of interdenominational co-operation on matters of spiritual unity against secular mores.[50] But before the First World War, the episcopate, with inevitable exceptions, were reluctant to take a prominent role in debates which did not impinge directly on questions relating to the Church and religion. Thus, in the controversy about the 1909 budget and then the Parliament Act of 1910, the bishops, led by Randall Davidson, adopted a policy of studied neutrality, desperately trying to avoid aligning themselves with the Conservative opponents of reform.[51] At the same time, when they did speak out, it was often still as members of the Church of England, defending the Church's privileged status, as over the disestablishment of the Church in Wales. The latter measure, indeed, deprived the Welsh bishops of their seats in the house of lords.[52]

By the end of the First World War, the bishops were more ready to speak on matters beyond the limited concerns of anglicanism, and the leaders of the other christian churches also demonstrated a willingness, in certain circumstances, to accept the leadership of the bishops and perhaps even to look to them as spokesmen on some issues.[53] In the 1920s and 1930s, the English bishops appear to have acquired a new confidence to speak out on a range of issues. Through the 1920s and 1930s the bishops, led by the archbishop of Canterbury, were intervening regularly in debates on foreign policy – on Russia, Abyssinia, Spain, Italy, Germany – on unemployment, on housing, on education, as well as on rather more predictable subjects like divorce.[54] But it was not simply that they were speaking more often and on a wider range of subjects, the tone of their speeches was also changing. Thus, when Archbishop Lang intervened in the debate on war aims on 5 December 1939, it was to remind the House that the nation's war aims needed to be an expression of 'Christian principles', founded on faith, without which there would be little hope of building 'anything that we can call a Christian civilization'.[55] These words were not chosen accidentally, nor were they a response to the outbreak of war. Repeatedly through the 1930s, Lang and his colleagues claimed to be speaking on behalf of the 'Christian people'[56] and appealed to the principles of 'Christianity', sometimes linking the latter with the principles of humanity. Moreover, the claim to be speaking on behalf of other christian churches was not simply rhetorical – Lang incorporated within his speeches material which he received from other religious leaders, including the secretary of the Baptist World Alliance, and even, on one occasion, from the chief rabbi.[57]

---

[50]Lillian Lewis Shiman, *Crusade against Drink in Victorian England* (New York, 1988), 12–13, 89, 107, 236; John R. Greenway, 'Bishops, Brewers and the Liquor Question in England, 1890–1914', *Historical Magazine of the Protestant Episcopal Church*, liii (1984), 61–75.

[51]Derek W. Blakeley, 'The Archbishop of Canterbury, the Episcopal Bench, and the Passage of the 1911 Parliament Act', *Parliamentary History*, xxvii (2008), 141–54.

[52]P.M.H. Bell, *Disestablishment in Ireland and Wales* (1969); Roger L. Brown, 'The Disestablishment of the Church in Wales', *Ecclesiastical Law Review*, v (1999), 252–64.

[53]Philip Williamson, 'National Days of Prayer: The Churches, the State and Public Worship in Britain, 1899–1957', *English Historical Review*, cxxviii (2013), 323–66.

[54]E.g., Hansard, *Lords Debates*, 5th ser., lxxvi, cols 1131–48: 2 Apr. 1930; xci, cols 300–10: 21 Mar. 1934; xcii, cols 830–6: 5 June 1934; xcix, cols 290–6: 19 Dec. 1935; cx, cols 1318–24: 3 Oct. 1938.

[55]Hansard, *Lords Debates*, 5th ser., cxv, col. 97: 5 Dec. 1939.

[56]Hansard, *Lords Debates*, 5th ser., lxxxv, col. 519: 4 July 1932.

[57]Hansard, *Lords Debates*, 5th ser., lxxvi, cols 1143–4: 2 Apr. 1930.

How do we account for this change in the role and behaviour of the bishops in parliament?[58] It seems clear that the experience of the First World War provides part of the
explanation; all the churches shared a challenge to respond to the spiritual crises posed
by the horrors of war.[59] It is notable, for example, that there was far more co-operation
between chaplains of different denominations on the western front, while, at home, both
the free churches and the Roman catholics were content to follow the lead of the archbishop of Canterbury in organising national days of prayer in a way which simply had not
been true before 1914.[60] But the experience of war was not the only factor. Apart from
anything else, there were clear signs that denominational conflict was easing before 1914:
Welsh church disestablishment, for example, signally failed to ignite a campaign for the disestablishment of the Church of England – it may be going too far to suggest that it ceased
to be a nonconformist grievance after the First World War, but it certainly ceased to be
an issue for agitation. Other factors can also be adduced. Theological changes were taking place not only within anglicanism, but also, to some extent, within the other christian
churches, which emphasized the duty of christians to take a more active role in improving
social conditions. As a result it became possible for bishops to denounce the 'evils' (the
language itself is significant coming from christian leaders) of slums and overcrowding in a
manner which had a clear moral meaning and which, at the same time, provided points of
shared concern with the leaders of other churches. And, then, there was the direct threat
to christianity and christian civilization posed by the emergence in Russia of a godless and
anti-christian regime expounding 'an unflinching materialism'.[61] Thus, in the years around
and following the First World War, there crystallised a series of social, political and intellectual debates, which overshadowed earlier denominational differences and contributed to
the emergence of the archbishop of Canterbury in particular as a spokesman for christian
principles and christianity, both of which appeared to be under attack from godless forces
in modern society.

4. Conclusions

Given what we know about the demographics of religion since the mid 19th century
and the 20th-century secularisation of British society, we might expect bishops to have
disappeared from the house of lords by the 21st century.[62] Yet they are still there. Indeed,
the 1999 royal commission on the reform of the house of lords recommended not only that
there should be 'formal religious representation' in a reformed second chamber, but also that
the Church of England should 'continue to be explicitly represented'.[63] In its submission

---

[58] The changing role of the bishops in the house of lords is the subject of a Durham PhD dissertation, to be
submitted in 2017, by Tom Rodger: 'Bishops as Legislators: The Lords Spiritual, *c*.1904–74'.

[59] Alan Wilkinson, *The Church of England and the First World War* (1978); Alan Wilkinson, *Dissent or Conform
War, Peace and the English Churches* (1986), ch. 2.

[60] Michael Snape, *The Royal Army Chaplains' Department, 1796–1953: Clergy Under Fire* (Woodbridge, 2007)
231–5; Williamson, 'National Days of Prayer', 328–32.

[61] Hansard, *Lords Debates*, 5th ser., lxxvi, col. 1135: 2 Apr. 1930.

[62] On contested chronologies of secularisation, see, e.g., Callum Brown, *The Death of Christian Britain: Understanding Secularisation, 1800–2000* (2001); Green, *Passing of Protestant England*, 15–32.

[63] *A House for the Future: Royal Commission on the Reform of the House of Lords*, Cm. 4534 (2000), 152.

to the commission the Church put forward a justification for episcopal membership of the Lords which confirms the evolution of the bishops' role traced in this essay. The submission specifically rejected the idea that the bishops represented 'the Church as an organization', claiming instead that their position flowed from 'a function lying at the core of the spiritual, ethical and social dimensions of the nation's life'. Thus, the bishops in the house of lords spoke 'not just for the Church of England, but for its partners in other christian churches, and for people of other faiths and of none'.[64] The commission received this claim with some scepticism, but it acknowledged not only that the Church's representation in the Lords during the 20th century had 'served to acknowledge the importance of philosophical, moral and spiritual considerations ... in the conduct of public affairs', but also that 'other Christian denominations and faith communities' had acknowledged that the bishops had provided 'a voice in Parliament for religion in general, not simply for the Church of England'.[65]

The judgment of the 1999 royal commission only confirms those dramatic changes we have found in the bishops' own conception of their role as members of the house of lords and the way in which they were regarded by others. Over the course of the period from the Restoration to the mid 20th century, the bishops transformed from representatives of the clerical estate, to guardians of the Church of England and its clergy, to spokesmen for christian values and civilization. This story reveals much about the changing ways in which pressure was brought to bear on parliament in relation to religious issues, not only by the established Church, but also by dissenters. But the story is not a simple one. If, in some ways, we can trace the increasing marginalisation of the Church in parliamentary affairs, the 20th century has also seen a growing confidence on the part of the bishops, for long a largely silent presence, to intervene on a range of non-religious issues and to do so as the representatives of the christian churches in general. This underlines the ways in which it is the dynamics of representative pressures on parliament, rather than the force of the one upon the other, which are fruitful in uncovering the politics of religion in modern Britain.

[64] *The Role of Bishops in the Second Chamber: A Submission by the Church of England* (May 1999), 3, 4; a copy may be consulted at Lambeth Palace Library, H5157.C4.

[65] *A House for the Future*, 152, 153.

Reforming Expectations: Parliamentary Pressure and Moral Reform

AMANDA B. MONIZ

'Reforming Expectations' argues that English and British moral reformers' agendas, including their relation to, and expectations of, parliament, were shaped, and increasingly so, by the world beyond England and Britain from the 17th to the early 20th century. Reformers' efforts have fallen into three distinct eras of reform activity – the European phase, the Atlantic phase, and the global phase – which each had a distinct emphasis. In the European, early-modern phase, activists participated in European conversations about the moral regulation and care of the poor, but they worked locally. In the Atlantic phase, from the Glorious Revolution to the American revolution, transatlantic ties supplanted European connections and activists aimed to reform morals both locally and at a distance. With the American revolution and the sustained attention it gave to parliament's role in governing the nation, reformers' expectations about parliament's role in governing moral life expanded. In the global phase, from the end of the French revolutionary wars to the early 20th century, activists sought to have a worldwide impact. British reformers undertook moral improvement projects aimed at peoples throughout Britain's now more heterogeneous empire. Building on the new expectations of the previous era, they looked to parliament and foreign legislatures to achieve those aims. For over three centuries, English and British moral reformers' approach to parliament was influenced by interactions with foreign colleagues.

Keywords: Anglo-American networks; Atlantic world; British empire; European networks; globalisation; lobbying; moral reform; parliament; philanthropy; protestant reformers; public opinion; voluntary associations

1

This essay argues that English and British moral reformers' agendas, including their relation to, and expectations of, parliament, were increasingly shaped by the world beyond England and Britain from the 17th to the early 20th century. Reformers' efforts have fallen into three distinct eras of reform activity – the European phase, the Atlantic phase, and the global phase. Reflecting larger political developments, each phase had a distinct emphasis, although older practices continued. In the European, early-modern phase, activists participated in European conversations about moral reform, but worked locally. In the Atlantic phase, from the Glorious Revolution to the American revolution, transatlantic ties supplanted European connections and reformers' expectations about parliament's role in governing moral life blossomed with the American revolution and the sustained attention it gave to parliament's role in governing the nation. In the global phase, from the end of the French revolutionary wars to the early 20th century, activists sought to have a worldwide impact and, building on the new expectations of the previous era, looked to parliament and foreign legislatures to achieve that aim.

2. *The European Phase: Long-Distance Networks, Local Efforts*

English and British efforts to improve society morally through parliamentary action date back hundreds of years. Over the centuries, they encompassed an amazing array of undertakings, from regulating the poor to evangelising American Indians, East Indians, slaves, and the lower sorts, to fighting vice, slave-trading, and juvenile delinquency, to promoting Sunday schools, poor law reform, prison reform, resuscitation, and vaccination, to building parks, libraries, and social housing, and more.[1] Reformers and philanthropists in all those movements cited the moral dangers of leaving their pet causes unaddressed and the moral benefits of pursuing their proposed programmes: Their many and varied initiatives, which activists would, from the mid 1700s, have explained as growing out of their broad moral concern for others, would both improve the moral condition of individuals and improve the functioning of society as a whole.[2] Hence, in the early 17th century, Dorchester's new hospital promised to improve morality by 'the training up and instructing the children of the poor in honest labour'.[3] A century-and-a-half later, the Philanthropic Society, founded in 1788, saved children who would have been 'the pests and annoyers of society' from 'ruin, temporal, and perhaps eternal', to the benefit of the nation's virtue, and also its wealth.[4] A succeeding generation's reformers looked to the kind treatment of animals to elevate morals.[5] Often, reformers grew interested in new causes as they learned from their experiences, both successful and frustrating, in earlier undertakings.

The types of projects have changed and expanded, but a constant has been that English and British moral reformers have been involved in long-distance religious and intellectual networks that influenced their efforts. In the early modern period, these networks were European. The 16th and 17th centuries saw a Europe-wide effort of new or renewed ordinances, policies, and institutions for the regulation and care of the poor, with moral aims at least as important as social aims. Spurred first by civic humanist thinking and gathering force with the reforming energies of protestant leaders, cities around Europe, but especially in protestant areas, revamped welfare infrastructures to centralise charitable institutions and assert secular control over them. Reformers also worked to curb

---

[1] Joanna Innes refers to some (and by implication many) of these initiatives as 'social policy'. That term, as she notes, was not commonly used in the period under consideration and nor was there a clear line between what we might call social and moral policy. See Joanna Innes, *Inferior Politics: Social Problems and Social Policies in Eighteenth-Century Britain* (Oxford, 2009), 1, 21–47.

[2] Many scholars have explored the expansion of understandings of moral responsibility on both sides of the Atlantic in the 18th and 19th centuries. A good starting point into this literature is *The Antislavery Debate: Capitalism and Abolitionism as a Problem in Historical Interpretation*, ed. Thomas Bender (Berkeley, CA, 1992); see also Michael Barnett, *Empire of Humanity: A History of Humanitarianism* (Ithaca, NY, 2011), 57–65.

[3] David Underdown, *Fire from Heaven: Life in an English Town in the Seventeenth Century* (New Haven, CT, 1992), 110.

[4] *The Philanthropic Society, Instituted 1788, for the Prevention of Crime, and for a Reform among the Poor* ([1789?]), 4.

[5] Keith Thomas, *Man and the Natural World: A History of the Modern Sensibility* (New York, 1983), 149–50.

begging.[6] These trends spread across Europe through travel and emigration, especially by reforming protestants, and by the later 17th century through printed works, including charitable manuals.[7]

Reformers pursued societal regeneration through various, complementary means. Philanthropy was one method. Acting individually, early-modern Englishmen and women bequeathed great sums to local ventures to house the poor and set them to work, educate the young, relieve prisoners, and much more designed to right souls and communities.[8] Reformers also sought to promote the commonweal through central government direction with crown orders touching on everything from vagrancy and begging to street-cleaning.[9] In addition, moralists worked through local government. Between 1570 and the interregnum, many town councils, especially in the robustly puritan area of East Anglia, pursued godly reformation with a host of ordinances to prevent or punish immoral behaviour and encourage right living.[10]

Finally, they worked through parliament. In the late 16th and early 17th centuries, parliamentary power ebbed as crown power grew. Parliament, none the less, passed many laws to regulate manners – morals – with the signal achievement of the poor law first and foremost a moral measure.[11] In the mid 17th century, parliament, now sitting annually, was a 'focus for reforming aspirations'.[12] Puritan activists' key welfare innovation, with familiar concomitant moral goals, was corporations of the poor.[13] Proponents and opponents of the corporations in some towns, notably Bristol and King's Lynn, lobbied MPs, providing them with printed broadsheets advocating their views.[14] These reform endeavours, however, did not involve mobilising public opinion, as they would in later eras. Moreover, parliamentary efforts reflected MPs' local orientations, with legislation, such as the acts to establish corporations of the poor, pertaining to specific localities, not to the kingdom as a whole.[15] Participation in European trends but a focus on local communities defined the early-modern phase of moral reform activity.

[6]John Bossy, *Christianity in the West 1400–1700* (Oxford, 1985), 143–59; Paul Slack, *Poverty and Policy in Tudor & Stuart England* (1998), 8–10.

[7]Ole Peter Grell and Andrew Cunningham, 'The Reformation and Changes in Welfare Provision in Early Modern Northern Europe', in *Health Care and Poor Relief in Protestant Europe*, ed. Ole Peter Grell and Andrew Cunningham (1997), 4, 13, 15, 26–8; *Pietas Hallensis: Or a Publick Demonstration of the Foot-steps of a Divine Being Yet in the World: In a Historical Narration of the Orphan-House, and Other Charitable Institutions, at Glaucha near Hall in Saxony*, trans. Josiah Woodward (1705), i, xii. On Woodward and the SPCK's role in the publication of *Pietas Hallensis*, see W.R. Ward, *The Protestant Evangelical Awakening* (Cambridge, 1992), and Paul Slack, 'Hospitals, Workhouses, and the Relief of the Poor in Early Modern England', in *Health Care and Poor Relief*, ed. Grell and Cunningham, 244.

[8]W.K. Jordan, *Philanthropy in England, 1480–1660* (New York, 1959); Underdown, *Fire from Heaven*, 109–10.

[9]Paul Slack, *From Reformation to Improvement: Public Welfare in Early Modern England* (Oxford, 1999), 14–15.

[10]Slack, *From Reformation to Improvement*, 30–1.

[11]Slack, *Poverty and Policy*, 130; see also Paul A. Fideler, *Social Welfare in Pre-Industrial England: The Old Poor Law Tradition* (Basingstoke, 2006).

[12]Slack, *Poverty and Policy*, 103; Slack, *From Reformation to Improvement*, 102.

[13]Slack, *Poverty and Policy*, 154–5.

[14]Slack, *From Reformation to Improvement*, 109.

[15]Slack, *From Reformation to Improvement*, 103. On the ongoing importance of policy making for municipalities or counties and the relationship to national governance, see Innes, *Inferior Politics*, esp. 21–47, 78–105. On the late-18th-century terms, 'inferior officers' and 'officers of the crown' or 'officers of the state', that Innes uses to distinguish the two arenas of policy making and political activity, see pp. 2, 5–6.

3. The Atlantic Phase: Legislative Approaches in a Revolutionary Era

The Glorious Revolution began a new phase in moral reform activism. In the long 18th century, reformers stayed connected to their European counterparts, but over time transatlantic ties became primary. In addition, Britons and their fellow subjects in America favoured collectivist means for charity and moral reform and they increasingly aimed to reach far beyond their local communities. Historians have considered moral reform efforts in the last few decades of the long 18th century to be the province of the many voluntary associations founded in the era.[16] A closer look at the Atlantic phase of activism, however, shows that reformers' vision of parliament's role in national moral supervision intensified over the 18th century as the legislature's reach expanded after the Glorious Revolution and with repeated wars and a growing empire. They also now considered it acceptable to call publicly for such a role. Pressuring parliament was just one of reformers' strategies for bringing about the changes they sought and not the most successful one. Nevertheless, they left later generations not only a robust voluntary associational infrastructure but also a new set of expectations about parliament's role in the moral life of the nation.

The Atlantic phase in moral reform began, ironically, with an event shaped deeply by European affairs. With both sides inspired by European examples and considerations, William of Orange overthrew James II in a revolution that would lead to parliamentary supremacy.[17] William, none the less, continued policies that the absolutist James had pursued to exert greater control over the American colonies. As a result, the North American colonies, which had been largely autonomous in the 17th century, became more closely integrated with metropolitan Britain.[18] The growing transatlantic reach of moral reform projects reflected Britons' growing interest in the American colonies.

Activists began a new wave of moral activism in response to the Glorious Revolution. Believing that political regeneration required moral regeneration, a number of anglican men in Tower Hamlets, London, founded a society for the reformation of manners in 1690. Their model spread, with support from the new monarchs seeking legitimacy, and within a few years, societies for the reformation of manners were a national phenomenon. These groups fought vice by prosecuting people who broke laws prohibiting immoral behaviours, such as swearing, blaspheming, and breaking the Sabbath.[19] Later, middle-class reformers might

---

[16] On the rise of associated philanthropy and activism broadly construed, see Donna T. Andrew, *Philanthropy and Police: London Charity in the Eighteenth Century* (Princeton, NJ, 1989), and Peter Clark, *British Clubs and Societies 1580–1800* (Oxford, 2000). On the voluntary nature of 18th-century moral reform in contrast to later eras, see M.J.D. Roberts, *Making English Morals: Voluntary Association and Moral Reform in England, 1787–1886* (Cambridge, 2004), 15, and Patricia Hollis, Preface, in *Pressure from Without in Early Victorian England*, ed. Patricia Hollis (1974), vii.

[17] Steve Pincus, *1688: The First Modern Revolution* (New Haven, CT, 2009).

[18] Alan Taylor, *American Colonies* (New York, 2001), 276–88.

[19] Dudley W.R. Bahlman, *The Moral Revolution of 1688* (Hamden, CT, 1968), esp. 31, 33, 34, 37–40; Robert Shoemaker, 'Reforming the City: The Reformation of Manners Campaign in London, 1690–1738', in *Stilling the Grumbling Hive: The Response to Social and Economic Problems in England, 1689–1750*, ed. Lee Davison, Tim Hitchcock, Tim Keim and Robert B. Shoemaker (New York, 1992), 99–120. For anglican ideas of voluntarism in the late 17th century, see John Spurr, 'The Church, the Societies, and the Moral Revolution of 1688', in *The Church of England c. 1689–c. 1833: From Toleration to Tractarianism*, ed. John Walsh, Colin Haydon and Stephen Taylor (Cambridge, 1993), 127–47; see also Tony Claydon, *William III and the Godly Revolution* (Cambridge, 1996); Faramerz Dabhoiwala, 'Sex and Societies for Moral Reform, 1688–1800', *Journal of British Studies*, xlvi (2007), 290–319.

consider these behaviours as typical of the unruly lower classes. To earlier generations, they constituted public vice that demanded attention.

Activists did not necessarily have transatlantic perspectives. Transatlantic ties or components, however, were common in the era's moral reform endeavours, starting with the Reformation of Manners Movement: British North Americans founded societies in Boston and Delaware.[20] The groups that built on the Societies for the Reformation of Manners foundation of voluntary associational action had stronger American ties or components. Indeed, the premier moral reform pressure group of the early 18th century owed its start to colonial concerns. Unhappy with the strength of dissenters, especially quakers, in British North America, the Reverend Thomas Bray and colleagues founded the Society for Promoting Christian Knowledge (SPCK) in 1699. Initially, the SPCK aimed to strengthen the Church of England in the colonies. Within a few years, the SPCK changed course and instead focused its mission domestically, with its foremost undertaking encouraging the founding of charity schools to provide religious education among the poor in communities throughout the country. Meanwhile, its colonial work had been spun off to the Society for the Propagation of the Gospel in Foreign Parts (SPG).[21] A transatlantic vision was also central to the Society in Scotland for Propagating Christian Knowledge (SSPCK). Set up in 1701 by a number of gentlemen with experience in a Reformation of Manners Society, the group was chartered to spread christian knowledge at home and in 'Popish and Infidel Parts of the World' – in practice, North America.[22] Similarly, the associates of Dr Bray, established in 1723, evangelised in North America, in its case to people of African descent.[23] Two final endeavours that were transatlantic in scope were the Georgia colony and Bethesda, George Whitefield's orphanage in Georgia. Formed in 1731–2, the Georgia Trust, an offshoot of the Associates of Dr Bray, worked to found a new colony in North America where the dregs of English society could be rehabilitated. Whitefield's Bethesda would help draw poor people to the new colony by assuring potential migrants that if they died in a strange land, their children would be cared for.[24]

Many of these moral reform groups were truly Atlantic in inspiration and organisation. First, they drew on both European and American models. In setting up his missionary groups, Dr Bray looked to both the Roman catholic congregation for the propagation of the faith and to American quaker activity. As time passed, ideas and institutions from continental Europe – especially from Halle, Saxony, a university city that had an outsized influence on international protestantism and on charitable agendas in the 18th

[20] Christine Leigh Heyrman, 'A Model of Christian Charity: The Rich and the Poor in New England 1630–1730', Yale University PhD, 1977, pp. 159, 163, 166; Jon Butler, *Power, Authority, and the Origins of American Denominational Order: The English Churches in the Delaware Valley 1680–1730* (Philadelphia, PA, 1978), 72.

[21] H.L. Thompson, *Thomas Bray* (1954), 36; Craig Rose, 'The Origins and Ideals of the SPCK 1699–1716', in *The Church of England c. 1689–c. 1833*, ed. Walsh, Haydon and Taylor, 180; Tim Hitchcock, 'Paupers and Preachers: The SPCK and the Parochial Workhouse Movement', in *Stilling the Grumbling Hive*, ed. Davison, Hitchcock, Keirn and Shoemaker.

[22] Margaret Connell Szasz, *Scottish Highlanders and Native Americans* (Norman, OK, 2007).

[23] *Religious Philanthropy and Colonial Slavery: The American Correspondence of the Associates of Dr. Bray*, ed. John C. Van Horne (Urbana, IL, 1985).

[24] *London Magazine*, July 1732, p. 198; Gillian Wagner, *Thomas Coram, Gent: 1688–1751* (Woodbridge, 2004) 46–52; Frank Lambert, *'Pedlar in Divinity': George Whitefield and the Transatlantic Revivals, 1737–1770* (Princeton NJ, 1994), esp. 139; 'Continuation of the Account and Progress &c. of the Orphan House' (1746), in *The Works of the Reverend George Whitefield* (6 vols, 1771), iii, 463.

century – shaped SPCK programmes. Thanks to ongoing exchanges, activists in Scandinavia, Holland, Switzerland, and elsewhere, in turn borrowed from England. Similarly, Halle's orphanage inspired Whitefield, while America offered a place to experiment.[25] Second, the groups had people from Europe to America in their networks. From the outset, the SPCK had corresponding members in Europe. A leading member in London was German while the long-time secretary was Boston-born and Harvard-bred.[26] And it was a Huguenot in the Hague who left the bequest that funded the associates of Dr Bray.[27] For his part, Whitefield not only corresponded with leading American reformers such as Benjamin Colman of Boston, but also raised funds from thousands of Britons and Americans alike.[28]

These groups were also Atlantic in objectives. Unlike their early-modern forebears, who had drawn on European trends but aimed locally, the 18th-century reformers aimed to reform morals both locally and at a distance. Most notably, they included people in America in their moral reform agendas. The missionary groups sought to tame unchurched Euro-Americans, fanatical dissenters, and uncivilized Indians and Africans. Doing so would benefit the converts' souls and it would also benefit Britain by binding diverse peoples in the colonies to the British interest. Although the SPG, the SSPCK, the Bray Associates, the Georgia Trust, and Whitfield's Bethesda all promised rewards to Britain, some – not least the *Gentleman's Magazine* – carped that charitable and reform endeavours in America meant the neglect of problems at home.[29] For those Britons, a transatlantic approach to reform was too expansive. For leading early-18th-century activists like Dr Bray, however, moral reform abroad and at home were integrally intertwined.

Also integral to the 'general "moralist" lobby', as one historian has termed it, was working through parliament.[30] Direct action to save the souls and change the behaviour of the immoral and unregenerate was most common. But the men in the moralist lobby had establishment ties and included members of parliament in their number, and they looked to parliament for support for their endeavours. Both the Societies for the Reformation of Manners and the SPCK pursued reform through legislation, not necessarily successfully. The Reformation of Manners Movement's only legislative victory was an act against profane swearing and cursing and blasphemy.[31] The SPCK, the leading moral pressure group of the early 18th century, had more clout. It 'acted as a sophisticated parliamentary pressure group, and continually advised the dozen or so MPs among its members on legislation', lobbying for changes, for instance, to the corporations of the poor and for the establishment of

[25] Thompson, *Thomas Bray*, 36; Butler, *Power, Authority, and the Origins of the American Denominational Order*, 25, 65; Eamon Duffy, '*Correspondence Fraternelle*: The SPCK, the SPG, and the Churches of Switzerland in the War of the Spanish Succession', in *Reform and the Reformation: England and the Continent c1500–c1750*, ed. Derek Baker (Oxford, 1979).

[26] On the SPCK's international links, see Duffy, '*Correspondence Fraternelle*'.

[27] Van Horne, Introduction to *Religious Philanthropy and Colonial Slavery*, ed. Van Horne, 4–12.

[28] Ebenezer Turell, *The Life and Character of the Reverend Benjamin Colman, D.D. late Pastor of a Church in Boston New-England: Who Deceased August 29th 1747* (Boston, MA, 1749); Lambert, '*Pedlar in Divinity*', 58, 62, 176.

[29] *Gentleman's Magazine*, xxxvi (1766), 197.

[30] Lee Davison, 'Experiments in the Social Regulation of Industry: Gin Legislation, 1729–1751', in *Stilling the Grumbling Hive*, ed. Davison, Hitchcock, Keim and Shoemaker, 29. On the reach and limits of parliament in shaping social policy, see Innes, *Inferior Politics*.

[31] Shoemaker, 'Reforming the City', 102.

workhouses for the reform of the poor.[32] Pressuring parliament was not at the forefront of early-18th-century reformers' activism, but it was a familiar tactic. Public pressure, however, was not.[33]

As the press grew over the next decades, so, too, did the role of publicity in moral reformers' campaigns for parliamentary action. A case in point is the effort to restrict gin consumption in response to the 'gin craze'. Anxious about moral breakdown of society due to poor people's easy access to gin, reformers, including men associated with the SPCK, the SPG, and the Georgia Society, sought to raise the cost and restrict the sale of gin with a series of laws passed between 1729 and 1751. Until 1751, these laws were more cosmetic than meaningful. The advocacy was important, however, because reformers increasingly appealed to public opinion. Unlike the campaign for the 1729 Gin Act, the debate over the 1736 act received 'near constant' coverage in the London newspapers, while the problem garnered less, yet still 'significant', attention in the early 1750s.[34]

Over the next decades, more and more men, and eventually women, embraced voluntary associations to organise all manner of activity from sociability to intellectual endeavour to charity and reform.[35] In the familiar story, activists turned to parliament to reform morality only after 1815 and especially 1832.[36] And indeed, although activists had long expected more parliamentary intervention in moral life more than historians have previously appreciated, reformers in the late 18th century and beginning of the 19th century, did place great faith in voluntary approaches to moral betterment.

These committed men and women sought to change moral behaviour with three distinct, though not mutually exclusive, strategies. The first was to *foster* moral behaviour, as the Humane Society (lifesaving) movement did by encouraging people to save lives, and the Sunday school movement did by exposing children to a beneficial moral environment.[37] The second was to *end* the *promotion* of *im*moral conduct. Curbing the 'bad example' the dissolute 'higher orders' had on the lower sorts and reforming the poor law so that the poor no longer squandered 'industry' or money, both promised to eliminate *sources* of depravity.[38] The third and most direct method was to *stop* or *penalise* immoral behaviour. The abolition movement, with its mission to ban the slave trade, and the Proclamation Society, with its prosecution of people who broke laws prohibiting immoral activities such as Sunday trading, favoured this approach.

Activists pursued those strategies using a broad range of tactics. Least intrusive were methods of moral suasion. Reformers lobbied each other. After one London philanthropist

[32] Lee Davison, 'Introduction', in *Stilling the Grumbling Hive*, ed. Davison, Hitchcock, Keim and Shoemaker, xl Slack, *From Reformation to Improvement*, 133; Hitchcock, 'Paupers and Preachers'.

[33] Hitchcock, 'Paupers and Preachers', 153–4.

[34] Davison, 'Experiments in the Social Regulation of Industry', 29, 42, 43; see also Innes, *Inferior Politics*, 43–4

[35] Peter Clark, *British Clubs and Societies*.

[36] Roberts, *Making English Morals*, ch. 3.

[37] On the Humane Society, see Luke Davidson. 'Raising Up Humanity: A Cultural History of Resuscitation and the Royal Humane Society of London, 1774–1808', University of York PhD, 2001; on the Sunday school movement, see Thomas Walter Laqueur, *Religion and Respectability: Sunday Schools and Working Class Culture 1780–1850* (New Haven, CT, 1976).

[38] *The Reports of the Society for Bettering the Condition and Increasing the Comforts of the Poor*, ii (4th edn, 1805) 13; William Wallace Currie, *Memoir of the Life, Writings, and Correspondence of James Currie, M.D. F.R.S. of Liverpool* (1831), ii, 377: James Currie to the earl of Galloway, 25 Dec. 1802.

received a graphic representation of the evils of intemperance – in the form of a 'moral thermometer' showing how increasing consumption of spirits raised the level of danger to the drinker until death occurred – from an American friend, he printed up stationery with the graphic and used it in his letter writing to spread the message.[39] Similarly, concerned men and women, from devoted activists to the occasional commentator, wrote books, pamphlets, periodical essays, and poetry, or created visual art, to sway others' views and behaviour. Supporters of slave trade abolition produced masses of material meant to evoke the horrors of the traffic in humans and thereby heighten moral sensitivity to it. Women and people of African descent, generally excluded from governance of voluntary organisations until they began to set up their own groups in the late 18th and 19th centuries, took advantage of this method to play roles in the effort to reform British manners. Likewise, the most famous author of moral literature in the late 18th and early 19th centuries was Hannah More, who penned stories designed to inculcate pious and deferential behaviour among the poor. Reformers churned out especially large amounts of writing on the slave trade and religion, but they addressed themselves to all sorts of topics from sympathy for the poor to support for vaccination.[40]

A step more interventionist was activists' circulation of practical knowledge about morally salutary projects combined with hortatory appeals to move others to voluntary action. Reformers pursued this method both in their individual capacities and through voluntary organisations. In his books, the prison reformer, John Howard, catalogued detailed information about jails around the British Isles and Europe based on his travels in the 1770s and 1780s, offered suggestions for improvements, and urged his readers to fulfil their duties to relieve human suffering. He then distributed his books to men in positions to act on his ideas, such as county leaders and movers and shakers in philanthropic circles.[41] Likewise, humane societies – charities devoted to promoting the rescue and resuscitation of drowning victims – and the Society for the Bettering the Condition and Improving the Comforts of the Poor disseminated information on resuscitation techniques and plans of soup kitchens and other ventures, respectively, and they pitched their programmes to readers and listeners by invoking both moral obligations and moral benefits. Activists in these and other causes all held out a variety of advantages to those who followed their thorough blueprints for action, such as boosting national population and preventing disorder, but they also insisted across causes that their efforts would improve the nation's manners by checking sources of debauchery and spurring virtuous sentiments and good conduct.[42] One reason that they

[39]Library Company of Philadelphia [hereafter cited as LCP], Rush Manuscripts, xxviii: John Coakley Lettsom to Benjamin Rush, 31 July 1793.

[40]On British women's voluntary activism, see F.K. Prochaska, *Women and Philanthropy in Nineteenth-Century England* (Oxford, 1980), and Clare Midgley, *Women against Slavery: The British Campaigns, 1780–1870* (1992). On Hannah More, see Anne Stott, *Hannah More: The First Victorian* (Oxford, 2003). For literature about slavery and the slave trade, see James G. Basker, *Amazing Grace: An Anthology of Poems about Slavery, 1660–1810* (New Haven, CT, 2002). The most famous writer of African descent in the 18th century was Ouladah Equiano; see Ouladah Equiano, *Interesting Narrative of Oulaudah Equiano and Other Writings*, ed. Vincent Carretta (rev. edn, New York, 2003).

[41]On Howard, see Amanda Bowie Moniz, '"Labours in the Cause of Humanity in Every Part of the Globe": Transatlantic Philanthropic Collaboration and the Cosmopolitan Ideal, 1760–1815', University of Michigan PhD, 2008, ch. 3.

[42]See, for instance, *Society for the Recovery of Persons Apparently Drowned: Instituted M.D.CC.L.XX.IV* (1774); *The Reports of the Society for Bettering the Condition and Increasing the Comforts of the Poor* (6 vols, 1798), i.

believed their efforts would have such thoroughgoing effects was that reformers understood moral (and likewise immoral) behaviour to be very powerful. The good examples of some should encourage all – the high-born, middling people, and the lower classes – to live more righteously.

The most direct voluntary approach in pursuit of those ends was the establishment of institutions that promised moral benefits. The Proclamation Society and later the Vice Society focused exclusively on suppressing impious behaviour. Scores of philanthropic associations Britons founded in this era, however, had the reformation of manners as one of their aims. The moral components of charities for the reclamation of prostitutes or the religious schooling of poor children are straightforward. But, in addition, activists invested – or savvily stressed as part of fundraising tactics – such purpose in charities that at first glance might not seem to have much to do with moral reform, such as humane societies, dispensaries, and other medical charities. Besides fostering benevolence and social bonds, these philanthropies, proponents explained, preserved the fragile economies of poor folks and thus stopped them from descending into immoral behaviour or relying on industry-sapping public relief to make ends meet.[43]

Late-18th-century activists found voluntary means the most effective and acceptable way to wage their campaigns. Yet after the American revolution they increasingly envisioned parliamentary components to moral reform programmes and also relied more and more on publicity to sway the legislature. The imperial crisis had been a conflict over parliament. For 20 years, Britons and Americans debated whether parliament was sovereign. This sustained focus on its role, combined with the growing importance of parliament in running the empire and waging war and other factors, including broader European developments, led the growing ranks of reformers in the great era of voluntary associations to look to the legislature to advance their agendas.[44]

Some causes, most notably abolition of the slave trade, demanded legislative intervention, and their leaders naturally focused their energies on the legislature. Yet backers of goals that did not necessarily require legislative action but could have been pursued through moral suasion or voluntary means, too, looked to parliament or, leaving options open, to crown or parliament. Convinced that dueling was a 'great disgrace [to] reason, religion, morality, and good government', the Society of Universal Good-will, a Norwich charity that provided poor relief to foreigners in England, sought in 1789 either crown action or the passage of a law 'abolish[ing] the … destructive practice'.[45] Similarly, James Currie, the Manchester doctor and reformer, believed spirits harmed 'the human race morally, physically and of course politically' and thought an excise tax might be an effective way 'to annihilate the use of this poison'.[46] And philanthropist, Thomas Bernard, perturbed at the supposedly bad

[43] On the Proclamation and Vice Societies, see Joanna Innes, 'Politics and Morals: The Reformation of Manners Movement in Later Eighteenth-Century England', in *The Transformation of Politics: England and Germany in the Late Eighteenth Century*, ed. Eckhart Hellmuth (Oxford, 1990). On medical charities invoking their moral purposes, see for instance, *An Account of the General Dispensary for the Relief of the Poor* (1772), 5; *Society for the Recovery of Persons Apparently Drowned*, 6.

[44] On the various factors, including the loss of the American colonies, that led to the expansion of parliamentary activity, see Joanna Innes, 'Forms of Government "Growth", 1780–1830', in *Structures and Transformations in Modern British History*, ed. David Feldman and Jon Lawrence (Cambridge, 2011), 91–9.

[45] *Gentleman's Magazine*, xlix (1789), 715.

[46] LCP, Rush Manuscripts, iii: James Currie to Benjamin Rush, 16 May 1796.

morals of the poor, offered fellow activists various ideas for improving the lower sorts but also looked to parliament to repeal the salt duties that he – and others – believed encouraged theft, smuggling, and fraud. Taxation, in Bernard's view, had a role to play in moral policy. For his part, Bernard's friend, the London-based, Scots-born, Patrick Colquhoun, advocated a national education system modelled on the system long established by statute in Scotland.[47]

Perhaps surprisingly, medical philanthropists in this age noted for robust development of voluntary medical charities also sought legislative assistance for their programmes. An early call for parliamentary action came from William Hawes, a founder and the most active member of the London Humane Society, established in 1774.[48] In 1782, Hawes urged parliament to further the Society's efforts to save lives by setting up receiving houses – places where half-dead bodies could be brought for treatment – throughout the kingdom. This was no modest plan. Hawes 'proposed … that there be appointed, by AUTHORITY OF PARLIAMENT, in every Parish, A GENERAL RECEIVING HOUSE, or more if [the parish] be very extensive, the Expence to be defrayed by a General, County, or Parish Rate, which might be easily raised'. Besides being stocked with all the appropriate equipment as determined by a medical committee of parliament, each receiving house was to be staffed continually by 'one or two Intelligent persons' trained in resuscitation and preferably also a newly minted medical man whose studies had focused on the topic of animation. Needless to say, Hawes's plan went nowhere, but the Society reminded the public of its desire for parliamentary help time and again.[49] A decade later and several years before Edward Jenner's discovery, John Haygarth, a Chester doctor and philanthropist – and member of the humane society movement, proposed a public institution to eradicate smallpox. His unsuccessful plan called for parliamentary support for a nationwide system of personnel to undertake a general inoculation campaign and to pursue measures to prevent the spread of the disease.[50] Different from the vast institutions imagined by Hawes and Haygarth, but sharing their expectation of parliamentary intervention, smallpox vaccination proponents in the early 19th century asked the legislature to ban the older smallpox inoculation procedure: in their mind, allowing smallpox inoculation after Jenner's discovery of vaccination with the much safer cowpox virus was tantamount to sanctioning murder, since use of the live smallpox virus could spread the disease.[51] Advocates of these proposals touted various benefits they would bring the nation, such as strengthening its population and saving money. Fundamental to their causes, however, were moral goals. As Hawes saw it, reacting quickly to save the life of a drowning person might prevent a murderer or suicide from achieving his goal. Thus, 'Innocence might be preserved, and Guilt brought to Penitence without the Horror of capital Punishment.' More generally, these reformers understood their movements to further the 'Cause of Humanity' – the broad effort to lessen suffering

---

[47] Thomas Bernard was the main writer of the reports of the Society for Bettering the Condition and Increasing the Comforts of the Poor. See, e.g., *The First Report of the Society for Bettering the Condition and Increasing the Comforts of the Poor* (1797); Patrick Colquhoun, *A New and Appropriate Education for the Labouring People* (1806).

[48] On the Humane Society, see Davidson, 'Raising Up Humanity'.

[49] W[illiam] Hawes, *An Address to the King and Parliament of Great Britain, on the Important Subject of Preserving the Lives of the Inhabitants* (1782), 12.

[50] Francis Lobo, 'John Haygarth, Smallpox and Religious Dissent in Eighteenth-Century England', in *The Medical Enlightenment of the Eighteenth Century*, ed. Andrew Cunningham and Roger French (Cambridge, 2006).

[51] Charles Murray, *An Answer to Mr. Highmore's Objections to the Bill before Parliament to Prevent the Spreading of the Infection of the Smallpox* (1808), 3.

and increase order in the world – and they increasingly expected the government to abet their endeavours.[52]

To try to move parliament to act, reformers used an array of methods common in the voluntary arena. The Society of Universal Good-will opted for a cautious tactic to advance its anti-duelling agenda. It 'offer[ed] an honorary or pecuniary reward, or both' to the person who came up with 'a rational, practical, constitutional, and effectual plan' to end dueling, that the crown carried out or parliament passed into law. Other improving organisations, such as agricultural societies and humane societies, used prizes or premiums as incentives to foster study of a topic or to shape behaviour, and so the Society of Universal Good-will's proffered reward, publicised in the *Gentleman's Magazine*, was a familiar way to forward programmes. But there may have been another reason that the leaders took such a careful step to try to raise parliament's interest in the problem of duelling. The Society of Universal Good-will had begun as an ethnic aid society for Scots in the Norwich area and become a charity providing aid on a cosmopolitan basis to those not covered by the English poor law who met certain criteria. In response to the change in mission, the Society had dropped the rule that made only Scots eligible for membership and Englishmen, including the dean of Norwich, had joined. Nevertheless, the patron and long-time president were Scots, who had long suffered prejudice from the English. Moreover, the Society's very mission implicitly criticized the English law of settlement, although the Society took pains to insist it meant no such thing. Perhaps it favoured an indirect method out of concern that a less modest method could expose these outsiders who dared to reproach their host nation to censure.[53] Whatever the reason, the Society had shifted from a primarily social mission of aiding people in need to a more expansive moral agenda.

Others were more direct, although still deferential. Hawes, Haygarth, and Colquhoun authored works (with Hawes receiving the king's permission to dedicate the address to him) setting forth their proposals. By publishing pamphlets or books that explained their visions for legislative intervention, they respectfully brought – or tried to bring – issues to parliament's attention. But they also sought this way to build public approval for their initiatives. As these men well knew from their voluntary activities, the key to taking action effectively was to find a core of people very committed to a project, who would undertake it *and* to create a broader constituency that would support it. Publishing their proposals reflected that knowledge. They set forth their hopes for parliamentary action and encouraged others to back them. By doing so, these activists, although their proposals were not adopted, helped make it possible to imagine more vigorous activity by the legislature in moral supervision. Parliament, their advocacy said, had a leading role to play in the nation's moral life.

Working through members of parliament was another approach and one necessary if the goal was a legal reform. The well-connected Thomas Bernard appealed directly to Nicholas Vansittart, a member of parliament, and, though Bernard's document is undated, presumably at the time chancellor of the exchequer, with his suggestion that the salt duties be repealed to prevent their 'immoral effects' on the poor.[54] The movement best known for working through insiders is the abolition movement. Although abolitionists outside

---

[52] Hawes, *An Address to the King and Parliament of Great Britain*, 5; Lobo, 'John Haygarth, Smallpox and Religious Dissent', 243.

[53] On the Society of Universal Good-will, see Moniz, '"Labours in the Cause of Humanity"', 160–86.

[54] BL, Warren Hastings Papers, f. 62: Thomas Bernard's thoughts on the repeal of the salt duties, nd.

the legislature brought public pressure to bear on MPs, most notably through the use of petitions, they did so in co-ordination with William Wilberforce and other parliamentary supporters of the cause. The abolition movement thus presaged and helped make possible the closer relationship between the state and moral reformers that would become common in the 19th century. A comment by a humane society supporter in 1789, however, reveals another perception of the relationship between moral reformers and parliament. This man credited the 'present ardour in the cause of humanity', evinced in parliament's nascent efforts to abolish the slave trade, 'to the unremitted exertions of the [Royal Humane] Society', which had helped sow 'the spark of Philanthropy' – love of mankind – on which efforts to end the slave trade rested. As he saw it, benevolent societies influenced parliament simply by pursuing their mission, that is, by example. (He, however, also used his observation, expressed to the London Humane Society and printed in its annual report, as a way to urge parliamentary support for the lifesaving movement.)[55]

Reformers drew on tools familiar from the thriving arena of voluntary activity to appeal for legislative support for their programmes. It was, however, the expanding reach of parliament as a result of the century's repeated wars and the growth and reform of the empire, and the transatlantic crisis over whether sovereignty lay with parliament or not, that inspired activists to approach parliament on moral issues. Perhaps the best example of the link can be found in the case of John Murray, the president and leading force of the Society of Universal Good-will – the Norwich group with an anti-duelling effort. In 1771, Murray, a doctor and retired navy surgeon, had proposed a plan to the ministry for the 'better government' of the American colonies. In 1789, the same year as the Society offered its prize for an efficacious scheme against duelling, he put forth 'a Plan for the Gradual, Reasonable, & Secure Emancipation of Slaves', prompted, he explained, by the fact that the topic of slavery '[was] undergoing a strict examination before the British Parliament'. Murray thought in terms of the legislature's increasing intervention, from colonial administration to new oversight of the economic institution that was the basis of Britain's Atlantic colonies. Based on his naval years and also family ties, Murray had first-hand experiences with the American colonies and with slavery, and he believed that knowledge gave him the ability to put forward his ideas for reforms in those realms. But, in addition, his earlier expectation that he could offer ideas to parliament on colonial governance made it possible for him to later imagine that he, an ordinary subject, could address the legislature on a moral problem.[56]

More generally, reformers made moral claims with reference to the demands on the nation from the era's recurrent wars, although in no source examined did they make this point directly to parliament. In publicity materials for philanthropic causes, however, they explained that their endeavours were superior to killing. Supporters of a statue in honour of prison reformer John Howard, for instance, used the idea of a monument to him to criticize the existing order in which shedding blood brought men glory.[57] Likewise, a poem delivered at the 1808 anniversary festival of a smallpox vaccination charity contrasted 'Ambition's

[55]John Oldfield, *Popular Politics and British Anti-Slavery: The Mobilisation of Public Opinion against the Slave Trade* (Manchester, 1995); *Reports of the Royal Humane Society . . . For the Years MDCCLXXXVII, MDCCLLXXXVIII and MDCCLXXIX* (1790), 445: Henry Corbin to the Royal Humane Society, 31 Nov. 1789.

[56]Moniz, ' "Labours in the Cause of Humanity" ', 167–71.

[57]Anglus letter to the *Gentleman's Magazine*, 20 May 1786, reprinted in John Coakley Lettsom, *Hints Designed to Promote Beneficence, Temperance, and Medical Science* (3 vols, 1801), iii, 153; Seymour Drescher, 'Whose Abolition? Popular Pressure and the Ending of the British Slave Trade', *Past & Present*, No. 143 (1994), 136–66.

desolating car' that 'Impel[led] myriads to the grave' in war to the peaceful blessings that Jenner's discovery spread around the world.[58] The suffering of ordinary soldiers and sailors gave them moral claims on the public, as proponents of charities to relieve the demobilised men explained.[59] Similarly, being 'benefactors of mankind' – a favourite phrase of the day – gave philanthropists the moral authority to expect help with their goals from parliament and to approach the legislature with their new expectations.[60]

4. *The Global Phase: Legislating Moral Reform*

A new Atlantic emphasis in moral reform began with the Glorious Revolution, then a global phase emerged out of it during another revolutionary age. Both cause and effect of the American revolution, the first of the new era's revolutions, was Britain's increased attention to its other colonies, most notably the East Indies.[61] In the global phase, British reformers reflected and furthered that trend with moral improvement projects aimed at peoples throughout Britain's now more heterogeneous empire. Yet British historians' focus on moral regulation within either an imperial or an Atlantic context overlooks the links between the transatlantic and global dimensions to moral initiatives. Building on the precedents of the Atlantic phase, British and American activists drew on each other's work in anti-slavery, temperance, Sunday schools, settlement houses, vice control, and other causes.[62] Most notably in terms of parliament's role in moral regulation, in the global phase reformers from different countries sought to influence each other's legislative efforts.

Activists' Atlantic imagination gave way to a global frame of mind over the course of the age of revolution. In the 1780s, reformers, in response to a widespread sense of moral decline following the American war, launched the movement to abolish the Atlantic slave trade. Over the next decades, the geographic focus of their work expanded across the globe.[63] By 1825, Britons could boast of having distributed bibles in 140 languages through the British and Foreign Bible Society, founded in 1804.[64] Missionary efforts were a bedrock of reformers' overseas work, but over the 19th and early 20th centuries their goals ranged from

---

[58] John Dawes Worgan, *An Address to the Royal Jennerian Society, for the Extermination of the Smallpox, by Vaccine Inoculation: Delivered on their Anniversary Festival, May 17th, 1808* ([1808]), 8.

[59] 'An Address to the Public in Favour of Disbanded Soldiers', *Gentleman's Magazine*, xxxiii (1763), 119–21.

[60] Lettsom, *Hints Designed to Promote Beneficence, Temperance, and Medical Science*, i, p. vii.

[61] P.J. Marshall, *The Making and Unmaking of Empires: Britain, India, and America c. 1750–1783* (Oxford, 2005).

[62] In addition to other works cited, works exploring transatlantic co-operation and influence in moral reform and related areas include the following: Thomas Adam, *Buying Respectability: Philanthropy and Urban Society in Transnational Perspective, 1840s to 1930s* (Bloomington and Indianapolis, IN, 2009); Leslie Butler, *Critical Americans: Victorian Intellectuals and Transatlantic Liberal Reform* (Chapel Hill, NC, 2007); David Brion Davis, *The Problem of Slavery in the Age of Revolution, 1770–1823* (Ithaca, NY, 1975); Clifford S. Griffin, *Their Brothers' Keepers: Moral Stewardship in the United States, 1800–1865* (New Brunswick, NJ, 1960); Robert Kelley, *The Transatlantic Persuasion The Liberal-Democratic Mind in the Age of Gladstone* (New York, 1969); Daniel T. Rodgers, *Atlantic Crossings: Social Politics in a Progressive Age* (Cambridge, MA, 1998).

[63] On the personal connections that fostered this process, see David Lambert and Alan Lester, 'Geographies of Colonial Philanthropy', *Progress in Human Geography*, xxviii (2004), 320–41.

[64] Christopher Leslie Brown, *Moral Capital: Foundations of British Abolitionism* (Chapel Hill, NC, 2006); Boyd Hilton, *A Mad, Bad, & Dangerous People? England 1783–1846* (Oxford, 2006), 181.

seeking to abolish the Indian practice of *sati*, or widow-burning, to regulating prostitution from Malta to Hong Kong and beyond, to banning the sale of liquor in the New Hebrides.[65]

Not all moral reform efforts in the 19th and early 20th centuries aimed overseas. Many, even most, focused on domestic audiences. British moral activists sought to tamp down the profane behaviour of the lower classes with the Vice Society, to curb excessive drinking with the temperance movement, and to check aggression and violence in society by promoting tenderness toward animals through the Society for the Prevention of Cruelty to Animals.[66] Later in the century, activists tried to keep obscene materials out of Britain and even pursued moral reform through cultural engagement with urban slum-dwellers through home-visiting and by living in settlement houses.[67]

As the effort to prevent obscene materials from entering Britain suggests, many of these domestic undertakings were not confined within the nation but connected activists to places well beyond its borders. The empire was of paramount importance to British reform endeavours. The imperial frame of reference shaped activists' understanding of problems, as with missionary attitudes to benighted natives shaping perceptions about working-class Britons.[68] Much as anxiety about national sinfulness had inspired the movement to abolish the slave trade in the 1780s, the imperial mission in the 19th and early 20th centuries fostered concern about British moral legitimacy and moral strength that led activists to pursue moral reform at home. Concern, for instance, about the exposure of public schoolboys – the future rulers of the empire – to obscenity, and about imperial influences, including obscene print culture, undermining Englishness, prompted efforts to purify Britain by controlling such offensive materials. Likewise, criticism of Britain's moral flaws by peoples in the empire, including Indians, Malays, Ugandans, and Australians, prodded activists to make Britons worthy of imperial rule.[69]

Recent historians of Britain have stressed how the empire shaped British reformers' imaginations and projects. Yet transnational ties outside the empire and especially to Americans remained central too; historians of the United States have focused on the transatlantic links more than historians of Britain have. Common trends across the Atlantic undergirded those links. Besides, the larger commonalties, such as economic ties and industrial growth, Britain and the United States both saw similar developments in the reform and philanthropic sphere in the 19th century. The rise of evangelical religion influenced public culture and spurred moral activism in both countries.[70] Likewise, British and American women moved into

[65] Clare Midgley, *Feminism and Empire: Women Activists in Imperial Britain, 1790–1865* (2007); Deana Heath, *Purifying Empire: Obscenity and the Politics of Moral Regulation in Britain, India and Australia* (New York, 2010); Philip Howell, *Geographies of Regulation: Policing Prostitution in Nineteenth-Century Britain and the Empire* (Cambridge, 2009); Ian Tyrrell, *Reforming the World: The Creation of America's Moral Empire* (Princeton, NJ, 2010), 132.

[66] Ford K. Brown, *Fathers of the Victorians: The Age of Wilberforce* (Cambridge, 1967), 84; Roberts, *Making English Morals*, 116–17, 150–2, 165–8; Thomas, *Man and the Natural World*, 149–50.

[67] Heath, *Purifying Empire*, esp. ch. 3; Mary Poovey, *Making a Social Body: British Cultural Formation, 1830–1864* (Chicago, IL, 1995), 35; Seth Koven, *Slumming: Sexual and Social Politics in Victorian London* (Oxford, 2004), 237–9.

[68] Lambert and Lester, 'Geographies of Colonial Philanthropy', 320–41; Koven, *Slumming*, 237.

[69] Heath, *Purifying Empire*, 70–4, 22, 95.

[70] Brown, *Fathers of the Victorians*; for a more nuanced view, see Boyd Hilton, *The Age of Atonement: The Influence of Evangelicalism on Social and Economic Thought, 1795–1865* (Oxford, 1988); Charles I. Foster, *An Errand of Mercy: The Evangelical United Front, 1790–1837* (Chapel Hill, NC, 1960).

organised charitable and reform ventures at about the same time.[71] In addition, on both sides of the Atlantic reform and benevolent undertakings became increasingly professionalised from the mid 19th century, with activists drawing on their experiences visiting or living among the poor to forge the field of social work.[72] They also focused more on causes of immorality.[73] A final similarity is that voluntary associational activity with political dimensions became acceptable, although still contentious, in, first, the United States and then, slightly later, Britain.[74]

Transatlantic currents and long-standing ties combined to bolster and renew networks of activists that, in turn, shaped both common understandings of problems and reform agendas. Transoceanic ties in the global age built on connections forged in the Atlantic era, with older reformers introducing sons and, increasingly, daughters or protégés to faraway associates. Just as co-operation and exchange among far-flung activists, such as Dr Bray and his early modern colleagues or abolitionists a century later, had been fundamental to moral reform undertakings in earlier eras, so, too, it was in the global age. In earlier eras, activists had encountered and disseminated new ideas in moral reform through journeys usually undertaken for reasons unrelated to reform agendas. In the 19th century, however, reformers now travelled explicitly to advance moral reform causes. Travels went in all directions. American abolitionists – both black and white – toured Britain and Europe, as did temperance reformers and others.[75] German reformers visited Britain to learn about prisons, while British activists, like Josephine Butler, headed to Europe to further the anti-prostitution cause.[76] Meanwhile, many a British activist visited the United States, from abolitionist John Joseph Gurney in the 1830s to the social purity activists Henry J. Wilson and W.P. Gledstone in the 1870s. Even opponents of reform found travel useful, in their case to report on failures of foreign efforts.[77]

Activists' international travels were a key pressure tactic in the global age. Foreign interest in their work stimulated men and women on both sides of the Atlantic. Activists' travels thus often led to the growth of movements across seas or to the adoption of new models of reform. Americans, for instance, established an anti-vice organisation following the visit of Wilson and Gledstone to the northern United States.[78] In spite, or perhaps because of, how common ties to foreign activists were, international interactions could be fraught. Even while at home, reformers found themselves embroiled in foreign controversies thanks to their collaboration with distant colleagues. Anti-slavery, in particular, was a source of

[71] Prochaska, *Women and Philanthropy in Nineteenth-Century England*; Midgley, *Women against Slavery*; Anne M. Boylan, *The Origins of Women's Activism: New York and Boston, 1797–1840* (Chapel Hill, NC, 2002).

[72] Roberts, *Making English Morals*, 106, 139, 225; Carroll Smith Rosenberg, *Religion and the Rise of the American City: The New York City Mission Movement* (Ithaca, NY, 1971), 272.

[73] Roberts, *Making English Morals*, 119; Smith Rosenberg, *Religion and the Rise of the American City*, 262–3.

[74] Johann N. Neem, *Creating a Nation of Joiners: Democracy and Civil Society in Early National Massachusetts* (Cambridge, MA, 2008); Roberts, *Making English Morals*, 198.

[75] Betty Fladeland, *Men and Brothers: Anglo-American Antislavery Cooperation* (Urbana, IL, 1972), 300–1; W. Caleb McDaniel, *The Problem of Democracy in the Age of Slavery: Garrisonian Abolitionists and the Age of Reform* (Baton Rouge LA, 2013); Brian Harrison, *Drink and the Victorians: The Temperance Question in England, 1815–1872* (Pittsburgh PA, 1971), 196.

[76] Adam, *Buying Respectability*, 49; Judith Walkowitz, *Prostitution and Victorian Society* (Cambridge, 1980), 96.

[77] Fladeland, *Men and Brothers*, 235–6; Tyrrell, *Reforming the World*, 22, 140; Harrison, *Drink and the Victorians*, 197.

[78] Tyrrell, *Reforming the World*, 140.

tension, fomenting dispute from the famous feud over women's participation at the 1840 World Antislavery Convention, to a conflict over accepting donations from slaveholders for Irish famine relief.[79] Reformers, none the less, remained committed to global outreach in part because they aimed to have influence far and wide, but, in addition, because their international activities increased their impact at home.[80]

A defining aspect of British moral reform in the global age was that activists sought, often successfully, to promote their agendas through legislative approaches and state enforcement. Although that trend built on the enhanced expectations for parliamentary action that had developed in the Atlantic age, it was paradoxical because the era was characterised by a liberal ethos and an emphasis on self-help. The French revolutionary wars, however, had left Britons less tolerant of public disorder and more willing to accept robust government supervision of people – namely, the lower classes and radicals – understood to threaten societal order. In addition, public moralists – opinion-shapers – believed that the role of government was to nurture people's character. The ruling classes, therefore, increasingly accepted state supervision of morals.[81] As a result, reformers pushed for legislation, often using the leading pressure tactics of mass petitioning and 'lurid' reporting, in causes from regulating mines in the 1840s – to protect women's and children's morals – to prohibiting vivisection in the 1870s, to banning the local sale of drink in the 1880s.[82]

This parliamentary and state-focused approach to moral reform might seem to be at odds with reformers' international outlook. Yet the opposite is the case and, indeed, it underscores the global nature of moral reform in this era. Activists' legislative efforts connected them to peoples and places beyond the nation. Parliamentary leaders at the 1840s World Antislavery Convention aimed to spread their emancipation agenda.[83] In the next decade, one branch of British temperance reformers advocated the prohibitionist 'Maine Law,' after visiting American temperance activists familiarised British counterparts with that idea.[84] Similarly, the British reformers who supported the deeply controversial Contagious Diseases Acts drew on precedents in various imperial outposts. Their opponent, Josephine Butler, for her part, visited Europe to promote the abolition of state regulation – and thus condoning – of prostitution there. Later in the century, reformers, meeting in international conferences, crafted international agreements – such as to control liquor and drugs – that required legislative support.[85]

The international conventions and treaties favoured by moral reformers in the global age were often not successful. That activists pursued them, however, is significant. In the 18th century, reformers had had reservations about the appropriateness of trying to influence

[79] Fladeland, *Men and Brothers*, 264–8; Margaret Abruzzo, *Polemical Pain: Slavery, Cruelty, and the Rise of Humanitarianism* (Baltimore, MD, 2011), 165.

[80] Tyrrell, *Reforming the World*, 17, 170.

[81] Roberts, *Making English Morals*, 97, 197; Stefan Collini, *Public Moralists: Political Thought and Intellectual Life in Britain 1850–1930* (Oxford, 1991).

[82] Koven, *Slumming*, 42; Roberts, *Making English Morals*, 220; Harrison, *Drink and the Victorians*, ch. 9.

[83] Sam W. Haynes, *Unfinished Revolution: The Early American Republic in a British World* (Charlottesville, VA, 2010), 203.

[84] Harrison, *Drink and the Victorians*, 196.

[85] Howell, *Geographies of Regulation*, 63–4, 236–9; Tyrrell, *Reforming the World*.

foreign legislatures.[86] Later generations were not only willing to do so but saw such an approach as intrinsic to their efforts. As that shift suggests, interactions with foreign colleagues helped drive the development of English and British moral reformers' expectations about pressure on parliament.

[86]Thomas Clarkson, *The Rise, Progress, & Accomplishment of the Abolition of the African Slave-Trade: By the British Parliament* (2 vols, 1808), ii, 101–3.

'The *Too Clever by Half* People' and Parliament[*]

WILLIAM WHYTE

The role of intellectuals in shaping pressure on parliament has often been neglected and still more frequently downplayed. Even intellectuals themselves have doubted their own political importance; hence Walter Bagehot's observation that 'the *too clever by half* people, who live in *Bohemia*, ought to have no more influence in parliament, than they have in England, and they can scarcely have less'. This article considers what it is to be an intellectual in politics – and what political role intellectuals played in Victorian Britain. It concludes that intellectuals were crucial in helping to define the nature of parliament and of the political process, articulating an ideology which shaped the ways in which other groups put pressure on parliament.

Keywords: A.V. Dicey; Benthamism; British constitution; Comteian positivists; Erskine May; intellectuals; Jeremy Bentham; parliament; pressure groups; royal commissions; Social Science Association (SSA); universities; Walter Bagehot

1

In 1668, Thomas Hobbes completed *Behemoth*, his account of the causes of the civil war. A key factor, he argued, was the role of the universities; indeed, he went on: 'The Universities have been to the nation, as the wooden horse was to the Trojans.' It was in the universities that sectaries, presbyterians, and other malcontents had drawn up their programme of treason. It was from the universities that the rebels had fomented rebellion. It was at the universities that he addressed his strongest condemnation, for 'The core of rebellion', he contended, 'are the Universities.'[1] Three hundred years later, in 1968, Perry Anderson came to a completely contradictory conclusion. He attributed the weakness of contemporary radicalism to the failure of the universities to foster dissent. 'Only where revolutionary ideas are freely and widely available – forming part of their daily environment – will large numbers of students begin to revolt.' The English universities, with their stolid studies and their self-satisfied lecturers, had, he concluded, signally failed to create such an environment.[2] Both Hobbes and Anderson may have been mistaken – although it was once suggested that Hobbes was more acute in his analysis than even he could have imagined.[3]

[*]I am grateful to all the participants in the Pressures on Parliament Conference for their questions and comments, but for subsequent help and advice I must especially thank Richard Huzzey, Robert Saunders, and Zoë Waxman.

[1]Thomas Hobbes, *Behemoth*, in *The Collected English Works of Thomas Hobbes*, ed. Sir William Molesworth (12 vols, 1840), vi, 213, 236.

[2]Perry Anderson, 'Components of the National Culture', *New Left Review*, 1.50 (July–August 1968), available at *http://www.newleftreview.org/A67* (accessed 23 Nov. 2009).

[3]Mark H. Curtis, 'The Alienated Intellectuals of Early Stuart England', *Past & Present*, No. 23 (1962), 25–43.

But focusing on whether they were right or wrong in many ways misses the point. More interesting is the question of why they and their contemporaries believed that the universities – and, in particular, university teachers – exercised such a huge influence on British politics.

It seems particularly important to address this question because British universities – and British intellectuals more generally – have on the whole been seen by historians as insignificant political actors In place of Hobbes's subversive thinkers or Anderson's reactionary elite, most writers have tended to depict Britain's thinking classes as constitutionally inert or politically incapable. Indeed, so ingrained is this assumption that it is even shared by the intellectuals themselves, who tend, like the politician and academic, Shirley Williams – the daughter of an intellectual, twice married to intellectuals, and herself a university teacher – to write off other British thinkers as people who live 'comfortably in their ivory towers, blissfully disregarding the world outside'.[4] Nor was this attitude confined to the late 20th century. Victorian thinkers also shared it, with Walter Bagehot – himself a successful public intellectual – content to observe that 'the *too clever by half* people, who live in *Bohemia*, ought to have no more influence in parliament, than they have in England, and they can scarcely have less'.[5]

Such a perception has proved especially true when British intellectuals are considered in comparative terms.[6] The significance of the French universities in generating both a class of mandarins and a group of alienated intellectuals is now widely understood.[7] The role of German academics in legitimating state power and of German higher education in creating highly educated opponents to that power is also generally accepted.[8] The very term 'intelligentsia' is, of course, a Russian one and speaks of the political as well as cultural importance of Russian writers and thinkers,[9] whilst Spanish intellectuals – and especially the 'Generation of 1898' – have been the subject of a significant literature, which again points to their centrality within political debates.[10]

As a consequence of this widely held assumption, British intellectuals have tended to be studied by cultural and intellectual historians, rather than by writers on more political themes.[11] Those historians who have explored the relationship between thinkers and politicians have tended to focus on particular moments and discrete movements – examining the short-lived role of the Philosophic Radicals or the Comteian positivists as groupings within the house of commons.[12] Moreover, even these few studies have generally concluded that intellectuals have only a limited impact on politics. Indeed, they have, in general, been little

---

[4] Shirley Williams, *Climbing the Bookshelves* (2009), 239.

[5] Walter Bagehot, *The English Constitution* (1963), 179.

[6] See Christophe Charle, *Les Intellectuels en Europe au XIXe Siècle: Essai d'histoire comparée* (Paris, 2001).

[7] Christophe Charle, *Naissance des 'Intellectuels', 1880–1900* (Paris, 1990).

[8] Fritz K. Ringer, *The Decline of the German Mandarins: The German Academic Community, 1890–1933* (Cambridge, MA, 1969).

[9] *The Russian Intelligentsia*, ed. Richard Pipes (New York, 1961).

[10] Donald Leslie Shaw, *The Generation of 1898 in Spain* (1975).

[11] A key exception to this is Julia Stapleton, *Political Intellectuals and Public Identities in Britain since 1850* (Manchester, 2001).

[12] Joseph Hamburger, *Intellectuals in Politics: John Stuart Mill and the Philosophic Radicals* (New Haven, CT, 1965) William Thomas, *The Philosophic Radicals: Nine Studies in Theory and Practice, 1817–1841* (Oxford, 1979); Christopher Kent, *Brains and Numbers: Elitism, Comtism, and Democracy in Mid-Victorian Britain* (Toronto, ON, 1978).

more than accounts of failure and disillusionment.[13] This is all a long way away from the political impact of the intellectuals in the Dreyfus affair or the 'State Nobility' of modern France.[14]

This analysis is closely related to a couple of perennial problems within modern British historiography. In the first place, there is the question of whether Britain ever produced anything that could be described as an intelligentsia or anyone who could be called an intellectual.[15] For some writers, it is clear: 'Britain did not have an intelligentsia'.[16] For other writers, by contrast, Britain not only possessed a class of intellectuals, but granted them greater respect and cultural – though not necessarily political – influence than some continental European countries.[17] As Stefan Collini has argued, this debate is in many ways unhelpful. 'Dreyfus-envy' (as he calls it) has led many to overstate the differences between the British experience and that of other countries – especially France.[18] Yet it is also clear, even if one accepts that there was something like an intellectual class in Britain, that its role and relationship to politics was different from that of its continental equivalents.[19]

The second key theme is about the process of policy making within British government. A generation ago, administrative and political historians were convulsed by arguments over this issue. Some claimed that the 19th century's 'revolution in government' was the result of pure pragmatism: the product of civil servants and politicians responding to self-evident social evils.[20] Some argued quite the reverse, pointing to the importance of thinkers and ideas in shaping policy.[21] Yet others attempted to recast the question completely.[22] As time went on, the heat went out of the dispute, and historians' interest was refocused on identifying the institutions and structures that mediated influence: the pressure groups and public doctrines that informed and agitated for change.[23] In recent years, as a result, we have come to understand much more clearly how specific organisations and particular experts helped

[13] Christopher Harvie, *The Lights of Liberalism: University Liberals and the Challenge of Democracy, 1860–86* (1976); John Roach, 'Liberalism and the Victorian Intelligentsia', *Cambridge Historical Journal*, xiii (1957), 58–81.

[14] Pierre Bourdieu, *The State Nobility: Elite Schools in the Field of Power*, trans. Lauretta C. Clough (Oxford and Cambridge, 1998).

[15] M.S. Hickox, 'Has There Been a British Intelligentsia?', *British Journal of Sociology*, xxxvii (1986), 260–8.

[16] Ross McKibbin, *The Ideologies of Class* (Oxford, 1990), 33. The problems of definition are illustrated even here, for the evidence he adduces for this is Tom Nairn, *The Break-Up of Britain: Crisis and Neo-Nationalism* (1977), 33–8. This section is headed 'The Intelligentsia', and instead of arguing that that there was no intellectual class it rather maintains that Britain's intellectuals developed differently from the continental alienated intelligentsia.

[17] R. Hinton Thomas, 'German and English Intellectuals – Contrasts and Comparisons', in *Upheaval and Continuity: A Century of German History*, ed. E.J. Feuchtwangler (1973), 83–100.

[18] Stefan Collini, *Absent Minds: Intellectuals in Britain* (Oxford, 2006), 5.

[19] R.D. Anderson, *European Universities from the Enlightenment to 1914* (Oxford, 2004), 149.

[20] Oliver MacDonagh, 'The Nineteenth-Century Revolution in Government: A Reappraisal', *Historical Journal*, i (1958), 52–67.

[21] Henry Parris, 'The Nineteenth-Century Revolution in Government: A Reappraisal Reappraised', *Historical Journal*, iii (1960), 17–37; Jennifer Hart, 'Nineteenth-Century Social Reform: A Tory Interpretation of History', *Past & Present*, No. 31 (1965), 39–61.

[22] Valerie Cromwell, 'Interpretations of Nineteenth-Century Administration: An Analysis', *Victorian Studies*, ix (1966), 245–55; Harold Perkin, '"Individualism versus Collectivism" in Nineteenth-Century Britain: A False Antithesis', *Journal of British Studies*, xvii (1977), 105–18.

[23] *High and Low Politics in Modern Britain*, ed. Michael Bentley and John Stevenson (Oxford, 1983); S.E. Finer, 'The Transmission of Benthamite Ideas 1820–50', in *Studies in the Growth of Nineteenth-Century Government*, ed. Gillian Sutherland (1972), 11–32; *Pressure from Without in Early Victorian England*, ed. Patricia Hollis (1974).

shaped government action.[24] It remains the case, none the less, that we have little sense of how particular thinkers and strands of thought shaped parliamentary, rather than governmental, policy. To that extent, at least, the question raised by the administrative historians of the 1950s and 1960s remains to be answered.

They took their inspiration from an even older debate, one sparked by A.V. Dicey's 1905 *Lectures on the Relation Between Law and Public Opinion in England during the Nineteenth Century*. Here Dicey argued that 'doctrines' – often 'doctrines which were current, either generally or in the society to which the law-givers belonged, in the days of their early manhood' – undeniably shaped legislation. But Dicey was less than clear about how this process happened and often rowed back from this unsubstantiated claim, arguing – rather like Bagehot – that 'extreme and logically coherent theories have, during the 19th century, exercised no material effect on the law of England', but also, even more confusingly, maintaining that 'men's beliefs are in the main the result of circumstances rather than arguments'.[25] It is evident that there is work still to be done on this issue.

Exploring the impact of intellectuals on parliament thus forces together a number of previously self-contained debates. It requires us to explore the issue of how policy is turned from theory into action. It refocuses attention on the nature of British intellectual life and the existence (or non-existence) of a British intelligentsia. And it does much more besides. In this essay, I will argue that British intellectuals can be understood as a coherent social group – just like those that existed in Europe. I will also suggest that they were a significant influence on parliament and – more importantly – on how parliament was understood by other social groups. Indeed, they were crucial to the process of explaining and legitimating the parliamentary constitution. But this does not mean that the intellectuals formed a coherent pressure group or were effective in directing legislation – far from it. For although the intellectuals took their role very seriously – as Hobbes's and Anderson's and even Bagehot's comments suggest – their impact was always indirect and almost never conclusive. They were also constrained in important ways by the very beliefs they helped to engender. This tells us something about parliament. It also reveals much about British intellectual life and the lives of British intellectuals.

2. *Intellectuals*

A key part of any such project is to establish a robust definition of an intellectual. This is a genuinely difficult thing to do.[26] Indeed, it has even been argued that no convincing classification of intellectuals can ever be made.[27] For historians, the problem is especially intractable. On the one hand, intellectuals can exist within any society.[28] That is why, after all

[24] Of central importance in this is Lawrence Goldman, *Science, Reform, and Politics in Victorian Britain: The Social Science Association 1857–1886* (Cambridge, 2002).

[25] A.V. Dicey, *Lectures on the Relation between Law and Public Opinion in England during the Nineteenth Century* (2nd edn, 1962), 18, 34, 111.

[26] José Harris, *Private Lives, Public Spirit: Britain 1870–1914* (1994), 222.

[27] Zygmunt Bauman, *Legislators and Interpreters: On Modernity, Post-Modernity and Intellectuals* (Cambridge, 1987) 2, 18–19.

[28] Edward Shils, *The Intellectuals and the Powers and Other Essays* (Chicago, IL, 1972), 21.

historians of medieval Europe are able to write accounts of what they call 'intellectuals'.[29] Although the word would mean nothing to contemporaries, it is argued, it, none the less, can have a heuristic value for scholars.[30] On the other hand, however, the notion of a group of intellectuals – and especially of an intelligentsia – is one intrinsically bound up with modernity and with the creation of a Habermasian public sphere.[31] It is the evolution of public opinion, Habermas argues, that generates a 'stratum of "intellectuals"'; a stratum that is separate 'from the highly educated bourgeois strata'.[32] Even here, however, there is a lack of clarity. Sometimes Habermas refers to intellectuals as '"*Intelligenz*"' – and, in a self-conscious echo of Alfred Weber, to a '"*frieschwebende Intelligenz*"' (or free-floating intelligentsia). But he also refers to them as '*Intellektuellen*' (intellectuals) or '*Litersten*' (men of letters).[33] The distinctions are surely important – after all, whilst '*Intelligenz*' is always placed within inverted commas, '*Intellektuellen*' is not. But, as this suggests, a certain fuzziness tends to characterise even the most central texts on the nature and place of the intellectuals.

Within the last decade, Stefan Collini has offered three definitions of the word intellectual. First, there is the intellectual as sociological category. Then there is what he calls the 'subjective sense', which captures an individual's own commitment to serious-minded and sustained thought. Finally, there is the 'cultural sense': the idea of the intellectual as an authority speaking to a wider public, making pronouncements on matters of cultural importance. For Collini, only the third – cultural – definition is of any real analytical value.[34] This offers us some clarity and a partial solution to the problem – but it does not go far enough. By disregarding the social structures that make such 'authority' possible and the material basis of the 'wider public' to whom the intellectuals speak, this risks producing a partial account. It is, in fact, necessary to engage with all these definitions – and, especially, with the sociological and cultural approaches.

As Habermas suggests, the rise of the intellectual and rise of the public – especially of the notion of public opinion – go hand in hand. The 18th century, as Samuel Johnson claimed, was '*The Age of Authors*'. To some extent, this was an exaggeration: very few writers received Johnson's rewards or achieved his cultural authority. But the sense that this was an age that established the idea of an author is certainly true – and it was true in sociological, cultural, and subjective terms.[35] It was the age of authors because, for the first time, there was a celebration of men, like Johnson, who made a career from scholarship and a life of writing free from institutional or courtly support.[36] This itself was only possible because the literary market had expanded enough to support such a vocation. It was in that sense a material as

[29]Jacques Le Goff, *Les Intellectuels au Moyen Age* (Paris, 1985).

[30]Mariateresa Fumagalli Beonio Brocchieri, 'The Intellectual', in *Medieval Callings*, ed. Jacques Le Goff, trans. Lydia G. Cochrane (Chicago, IL, 1987), 181–210; Jean-Philip Genet, 'The Intellectuals: A Prehistory', in *Anglo-French Attitudes: Comparisons and Transfers between English and French Intellectuals since the Eighteenth Century*, ed. Christophe Charle, Julien Vincent and Jay Winter (Manchester, 2007), 25–44.

[31]T.B. Bottomore, *Elites and Society* (1976), 70.

[32]Jürgen Habermas, *The Structural Transformation of the Public Sphere: An Inquiry into a Category of Bourgeois Society*, trans. Thomas Burger (Cambridge and Oxford, 1989), 174.

[33]Jürgen Habermas, *Strukturwandel der Öffentlichkeit* (Nieuwand, 1962), 45, 46, 47, 192.

[34]Collini, *Absent Minds*, 46–8.

[35]James Van Horn Melton, *The Rise of the Public in Enlightenment Europe* (Cambridge, 2001), 123.

[36]Steven Shapin, '"A Scholar and a Gentleman": The Problematic Identity of the Scientific Practitioner in Early Modern England', *History of Science*, xxix (1991), 279–327, 282.

well as a cultural reality.[37] By the same token, it is possible to see the 19th century as the age of the intellectual. It was then that the term was coined, and – more significantly – it was then that a discrete culture of intellectuals emerged in Britain.[38] It was not until the Victorian era, indeed, that the sociological and cultural conditions were right to produce what one might call an 'intellectual' subjectivity.[39]

The underlying causes for this development were threefold. In the first place, the Victorian era witnessed an unprecedented and dramatic transformation in the literary marketplace. Rising literacy and the advent of new technology suddenly created a massively enlarged and profitable field of production. Whilst the 18th century was the age of a few highly paid authors, the 19th century saw authorship become a career for thousands. More people were writing for more money than ever before. In 1847, G.H. Lewes declared that 'Literature has become a profession.' 'In the present state of things', he went on, 'a man who has health, courage, and ability can earn by literature the income of a gentleman.'[40] The result was immediate and impressive. The 1841 census enumerated 167 authors. The 1881 census counted 6,111. By 1901, there were 11,060 of them.[41] Nor did this exaggerate the numbers involved. All told, more than 24,000 people wrote for Victorian periodicals.[42] This mass production of both literature and of litterateurs had simply never been seen before. In the second place, the growing complexity of modern life and the growing size of the professional middle classes produced an expansion of the public schools and of the universities. In 1801 there were 1,128 students in England. A hundred years later, there were nearly 20,000.[43] Such a dramatic rise in the quantity of students produced a similar increase in the numbers of those paid to teach them. In the 13 years between 1845 and 1858 Oxford saw a 40% increase in the number of college fellows.[44] By 1900, something like 2,000 lecturers and professors were employed by the universities.[45]

The gap between academics and journalists was not a great one – indeed, many were both.[46] The division between university teachers and those who taught in the public schools was also narrow – and people frequently moved from the academy to the school and back again.[47] There was a whole series of institutions – formal clubs, dining societies, discussion

[37] John Brewer, *The Pleasures of the Imagination: English Culture in the Eighteenth Century* (1997), 151.

[38] Peter Allen, 'The Meanings of "An Intellectual" in Nineteenth- and Twentieth-Century English Usage', *University of Toronto Quarterly*, lv (1986), 342–58; T.W. Heyck, *The Transformation of Intellectual Life in Victorian England* (1982). For a recent restatement of this argument, see William C. Lubenow, *'Only Connect': Learned Societies in Nineteenth-Century Britain* (Woodbridge, 2015), though cf. Collini, *Absent Minds*, ch. 1.

[39] I have explored this theme further in William Whyte, 'The Intellectual Aristocracy Revisited', *Journal of Victorian Culture*, x (2005), 15–45, and William Whyte, 'The Antinomies of Sage Culture', in *The Victorian World* ed. Martin Hewitt (2012), 519–34. These paragraphs draw heavily on both essays.

[40] [G.H. Lewes], 'The Condition of Authors in England, Germany, and France', *Fraser's Magazine*, xxxv (1847) 285–6.

[41] Richard D. Altick, 'The Sociology of Authorship', *Bulletin of the New York Public Library*, lxvi (1962), 400.

[42] K. Theodore Hoppen, *The Mid-Victorian Generation: 1846–1886* (Oxford, 1998), 376.

[43] Harold Perkin, *Key Profession: The History of the Association of University Teachers* (1969), 23; T.W. Heyck, 'The Idea of a University in Britain, 1870–1970', *History of European Ideas*, viii (1987), 205–19.

[44] A.J. Engel, *From Clergyman to Don: The Rise of the Academic Profession in Nineteenth-Century Oxford* (Oxford 1983), 87.

[45] A.H. Halsey and M.A. Trow, *The British Academics* (1971), 140.

[46] Christopher Kent, 'Higher Journalism and the Mid-Victorian Clerisy', *Victorian Studies*, xiii (1969), 181–98.

[47] Whyte, 'Intellectual Aristocracy', and 'Sage Culture'.

groups, even walking parties – that drew thinkers from all parts of the country together.[48] But these individuals were conscious of great differences between themselves and other groups within society. This was the third factor in creating an intellectual elite in the 19th century: the sense felt by an ever-increasing number of writers and thinkers that they had created and now inhabited a separate and superior culture.

The intellectuals self-consciously distinguished themselves from the other members of the professional middle classes and from the economic and social elites of their age. It was a process captured in Matthew Arnold's *Culture and Anarchy*, where he condemned the aristocratic 'barbarians' and the bourgeois 'philistines' and celebrated the 'aliens' – people who transcend the limitations of 19th-century society to pursue culture and lead lives of 'sweetness and light'.[49] But Arnold was far from alone. From Coleridge's clerisy to Wells's samurai, the ideal of a cultivated, disinterested and learned caste was celebrated again and again.[50] Clergymen like Frederick Temple,[51] scientists like John Tyndall,[52] conservatives and radicals alike: all of them agreed on the need for a 'voluntary nobility',[53] an 'aristocracy of talent',[54] a 'real aristocracy of character and intellect'.[55] This all spoke of a new consciousness, a new culture, a new identity: the construction of a self-conscious elite of intellectuals.

Not all academics were intellectuals, of course; much less all teachers or all writers.[56] Many were avowedly anti-intellectual. The fellows of St John's College, Oxford, greeted the earnest Arthur Stanley's lecture on the Holy Land in the 1860s with the immortal phrase 'Jerusalem be damned. Give us wine, women and horses.'[57] Others were less philistine, but no less suspicious of abstraction. Montagu James, the distinguished and learned provost of King's College, Cambridge, used to adjure his students: 'No thinking, gentlemen, please!'[58] Moreover, many academics were content to address a limited audience or to focus on only a few specialised areas of thought.[59] What distinguished the intellectuals from the others

---

[48] Alan Willard Brown, *The Metaphysical Society: Victorian Minds in Crisis, 1869–80* (New York, 1947); W.C. Lubenow, *The Cambridge Apostles: Liberalism, Imagination, and Friendship in British Intellectual and Professional Life* (Cambridge, 1998); Gerald Monsman, *Oxford University's Old Mortality Society: A Study in Victorian Romanticism* (Lewiston, New York, 1998); William Whyte, 'Sunday Tramps (act. 1879–1895)', *ODNB;* online edn [http://www.oxforddnb.com/view/theme/96363, accessed 26 Nov. 2009].

[49] Matthew Arnold, *Culture and Anarchy* (Oxford, 2006), 75–82.

[50] Ben Knights, *The Idea of the Clerisy in the Nineteenth Century* (Cambridge, 1978); Kent, *Brains and Numbers*.

[51] Simon Green, 'Archbishop Frederick Temple on Meritocracy: Liberal Education and the Idea of a Clerisy', in *Public and Private Doctrine,* ed. Michael Bentley (Cambridge, 1993), 149–67.

[52] Ursula De Young, *A Vision of Modern Science: John Tyndall and the Role of the Scientist in Victorian Culture* (Basingstoke, 2011).

[53] H.G. Wells, *A Modern Utopia* (1905), 259.

[54] H.R. Haweis, *The Art of Beauty* (1878), 211.

[55] *The Dairy of Beatrice Webb*, ed. Norman and Jeanne MacKenzie (4 vols, 1982–5), ii, 108.

[56] See Christoph Charle, 'Academics or Intellectuals? The Professors of the University of Paris and Political Debate in France from the Dreyfus Affair to the Algerian War', in *Intellectuals in Twentieth-Century France*, ed. Jeremy Jennings (Basingstoke, 1993), 94–116.

[57] V.H.H. Green, *Oxford Common Room* (1957), 129.

[58] Quoted in S.J.D. Green, 'A Land Unfit for Ideas? British Intellectual History, 1750–1950', *History of European Ideas*, xxvi (2000), 240.

[59] See Stefan Collini, '"My Roles and their Duties": Sidgwick as Philosopher, Professor, and Public Moralist', in *Henry Sidgwick,* ed. Ross Harrison (Oxford, 2001), 9–50.

was their public role, their willingness to discuss wider questions, and their authority in debate. Intellectuals did not just address one another, they spoke to a wider audience and they were, to adopt Collini's term, always 'public moralists'.[60]

Now there were many publics in 19th-century Britain. Some were well known, and some – as Wilkie Collins pointed out in 1858 – were unknown.[61] The periodical press was segmented by subject, religion, and politics.[62] As the century progressed, so these divisions grew greater and the publishing world grew ever more specialised. But intellectuals' role was to transcend these differences – at least to some extent. They used the cultural capital they had amassed in one field to underwrite their comments in other, broader debates.[63] Just as Matthew Arnold wrote on 'Literature and Science' (1882), so the biologist T.H. Huxley wrote on 'Science and Culture' (1880). Both men wrote on politics and on ethics, too, and in that way they were archetypal intellectuals. Whether it was A.V. Dicey trading on his legal knowledge to intervene in the debate over home rule, Sir John Seeley using history to agitate for an active imperial policy, or even Charles Darwin drawing on his scientific knowledge to oppose racial inequality, what distinguished the intellectuals was this capacity to reach out to a public and make their voice heard.[64]

In all three of Collini's definitions, then, the 19th century can be seen as an age that produced a significant group of intellectuals. These were not like the ideal-type alienated intelligentsia of the sociologists, it is true.[65] But they formed a distinct and coherent social fraction, none the less – what Noel Annan famously identified as an 'intellectual aristocracy'.[66] They owed their existence to real changes in the literary and educational marketplace. They were also self-conscious about this: sharing a subjective sense of being intellectuals; a sense that was captured in Thomas Carlyle's lecture, 'The Hero as Man of Letters' (1840). The Man of Letters, he declared, was a product of the modern world, and served for contemporaries the function of 'Prophet, Priest, Divinity'. Moreover, Carlyle claimed, 'Of all Priesthoods, Aristocracies, Governing Classes at present in the world, there is no class comparable for importance to that priesthood of the Writers of Books.'[67] Even allowing for his remarkable rodomontade, the fact that he felt able to make such a claim is revealing. And it points to the third way in which the Victorian era produced what can be regarded as a recognizable cultural role for intellectuals. These men of letters were seen more than just writers or teachers: they were prophetic figures, often adopting a quasi-biblical register to make their arguments tell. It was this that led George Eliot to 'venerate

[60] Stefan Collini, *Public Moralists: Political Thought and Intellectual Life in Britain 1850–1930* (Oxford, 1991).

[61] [Wilkie Collins], 'The Unknown Public', *Household Words*, xviii (1858), 217–22.

[62] Matthew Arnold, 'The Function of Criticism at the Present Time [1864]', in *Essays in Criticism* (1900), 1–41 19–20.

[63] Pierre Bourdieu, *Homo Academicus*, trans. Peter Collier (Cambridge and Oxford, 1990).

[64] A.V. Dicey, *A Fool's Paradise: Being a Constitutionalist's Criticism of the Home Rule Bill of 1912* (1913); John Seeley, *The Expansion of England: Two Courses of Lectures* (1925); Adrian Desmond and James Moore, *Darwin's Sacred Cause: Race, Slavery and the Quest for Human Origins* (2009).

[65] Karl Mannheim, *Ideology and Utopia: An Introduction to the Sociology of Knowledge*, trans. Louis Wirth and Edward A. Shils (1991), esp. 138–9.

[66] N.G. Annan, 'The Intellectual Aristocracy', in *Studies in Social History*, ed. J.H. Plumb (1955), 241–87; see also Noel Annan, *The Dons* (1999), 304–41.

[67] Thomas Carlyle, *On Heroes and Hero Worship* (1896), 207, 209, 224.

Ruskin as a 'Hebrew prophet', Froude to compare Carlyle to Isaiah, and Arnold to be attacked as an 'elegant Jeremiah'.[68]

3. The Intellectuals and the Powers

It comes as little surprise, therefore, that the thinkers, writers, and teachers of the 19th century found themselves called upon to exercise their authority in the political, as well as the cultural, world. Indeed, by the late 1880s, the journalist, W.T. Stead, felt able to claim that 'The Press has become to the Commons what the Commons were to the Lords. The Press has become the Chamber of Initiative.'[69] He overstated his case, of course. But he was right to note the way in which journalists increasingly influenced public debate.[70] Intellectuals could also use the media. A letter to *The Times*, a public lecture, or controversial article could raise issues and prompt action. So familiar was this as a method, that when the influential author and architect, T.G. Jackson, encountered any criticism of his work, his first thought was to fire off a missive to the papers. He even did the same when his house was burgled.[71]

The intellectuals were not, however, limited to these public forums when they sought to make a case. Thinkers and writers were welcomed in the homes of the rich and the powerful. Indeed, as one Russian visitor observed, there was 'no other country where the ruling few mixed so easily with the literary and artistic world'.[72] For university teachers, too, personal connections could prove useful. The Oxford reformer and Master of Balliol, Benjamin Jowett, famously observed that: 'I should like to govern the world through my pupils', and – through the many students who went into parliament or administered the colonies of the empire – he arguably came very close to doing so.[73]

The expertise that the intellectuals possessed also made them valuable to an executive that was, throughout much of the 19th century, understaffed and ill-equipped for policy making.[74] Lawrence Goldman has shown how influential the Social Science Association (SSA) was in shaping policy in the 1850s and 1860s. Its meetings, publications, and the office it maintained in London to facilitate parliamentary lobbying, all contributed to its success. It shaped the Taunton Commission and Endowed Schools Act 1869; the Royal Sanitary Commission and the Public Heath Act 1875; the Married Women's Property Act 1870, the Habitual Criminals Act 1869, and the Prevention of Crimes Act 1871.[75]

The SSA was uniquely important – but it was not unique. The British Association for the Advancement of Science, the Charity Organisation Society, even – for a short while – the National Association for the Advancement of Art, were among those organisations

[68] George Eliot, *Letters*, ed. Gordon S. Haight (9 vols, Oxford, 1954–78), ii, 422–3; J.A. Froude, *Thomas Carlyle: A History of the First Forty Years of his Life* (1882), 8; Arnold, *Culture and Anarchy*, 32.

[69] W.T. Stead, 'Government by Journalism', *Contemporary Review*, xlix (1886), 656.

[70] Stephen Koss, *The Rise and Fall of the Political Press in Britain* (2 vols, 1981–4).

[71] William Whyte, *Oxford Jackson: Architecture, Education, Status and Style, 1835–1924* (Oxford, 2006), 27–30.

[72] Constantine Benckendorff, *Half a Life: The Reminiscences of a Russian Gentleman* (1954), 98.

[73] Richard Symonds, *Oxford and Empire: The Last Lost Cause?* (1986), 24.

[74] John Vincent, *The Formation of the Liberal Party* (1966), 239–40.

[75] Goldman, *Science, Reform, and Politics*, 3.

that lobbied and sought to influence government action.[76] These were explicitly public bodies, setting out their case in grand public meetings, using the pressure of public opinion to force change. Naturally, this was not always successful.[77] But the most effective groups backed this public presence with private influence. Politicians were invited to join them – with Salisbury becoming president of the British Association in 1894 and Gladstone invited to address the SSA on numerous occasions. Still more powerfully, smaller, informal groups of intellectuals grew up designed to press for particular policies. The 'X Club', for example, agitated for science – and for its members' careers – in both the Royal Society and the wider world.[78]

The intellectuals were thus able to operate within a network of personal contacts and public forums, helping to shape debate and direct specific policies. Although separate from the world of politics, and distanced by occupation, class, and, indeed, income from the landed elites who governed the country, the intellectuals, none the less, had an entrée to the corridors of Westminster. This was made clear by their role in the numerous royal commissions of the era. Frederic Harrison expressed intense surprise at having been drafted on to serve the royal commission on trades unions of 1867–9.[79] He was only 36 years old and had had little practical knowledge of the subject. But his articles in the *Fortnightly Review* had impressed the cognoscenti (he was even consulted on labour laws by George Eliot), and his minority report was to be influential on future legislation.[80] Less surprising was the involvement of public thinkers on those commissions charged with investigating education. The work of intellectuals in prompting the establishment of the schools inquiry commission in 1864 and in informing its conclusions, is especially noteworthy. In particular, the Oxford philosopher, T.H. Green, proved to be a significant figure as assistant commissioner, using his investigations of schools in the west midlands to shape the report as a whole.[81]

It is fair to say that the intellectuals did not have it all their own way. They were never more than a minority even on those commissions that dealt with educational matters. Their ideas were not always taken up or were subsequently watered down.[82] Yet, increasingly, they were seen as adding something to the debate; providing a contribution that no one else could. As experts, as commentators, as agitators, and as the providers of evidence, intellectuals consequently had a key role to play in shaping Victorian legislation.

---

[76] Jack Morrell and Arnold Thackeray, *Gentlemen of Science: Early Years of the British Association for the Advancement of Science* (Oxford, 1981); A.M. McBriar, *An Edwardian Mixed Doubles, the Bosanquets versus the Webbs: A Study in British Social Policy, 1890–1929* (Oxford, 1987); Whyte, *Oxford Jackson*, 63–4.

[77] For an example of this, see William Whyte, 'The 1910 Royal Institute of British Architects Conference 1910: A Focus for International Town Planning?', *Urban History*, xxxix (2012), 149–65; William Whyte, 'Octavia Hill: The Practice of Sympathy and the Art of Housing', in *'Nobler Imaginings and Mightier Struggles': Octavia Hill and the Remaking of British Society*, ed. Elizabeth Baigent and Ben Cowell (2016).

[78] Roy MacLeod, 'The X Club: A Social Network of Science in Late-Victorian England', *Notes and Records of the Royal Society of London*, xxiv (1970), 305–22; see also Ruth Barton, '"An Influential Set of Chaps": The X Club and Royal Society Politics', *British Journal for the History of Science*, xxiii (1990), 53–81.

[79] Frederic Harrison, *Autobiographic Memories* (2 vols, 1911), i, 315.

[80] Mark Curthoys, *Governments, Labour, and Mid-Victorian Britain: The Trade Union Legislation of the 1870s* (Oxford, 2002), 66.

[81] David Ian Allsobrook, *Schools for the Shires: The Reform of Middle-Class Education in Mid-Victorian England* (Manchester, 1986), ch. 8.

[82] See, e.g., Colin Shrosbree, *Public Schools and Private Education: The Clarendon Commission 1861–64 and the Public Schools Act* (Manchester, 1988); Ciaran Brady, *James Anthony Froude: An Intellectual Biography of a Victorian Prophet* (Oxford, 2013), 298–316.

As legislators, however, they proved to be much less successful. The political ineptitude of the Philosophic Radicals – that small group of highly educated and high-principled parliamentarians that gathered round John Stuart Mill in the 1830s – is now notorious. True enough, they did achieve some marginal victories. They were instrumental in the foundation of the Public Record Office; they were central to the establishment of the 1837 select committee on transportation.[83] But the reality was, as William Thomas puts it, that 'the Philosophic Radicals were a political failure'.[84] Inept at tactics, hopeless in strategy, ill-fitted for a parliament increasingly based on party lines, Mill, Molesworth, Grote, Roebuck, and the rest, proved to be incapable of forming the alliances or exploiting the opportunities that might have yielded them some measure of success. In Edward Bulwer's damning assessment, they were a 'small, conceited, and headstrong party … the sect of the Impracticables'.[85] Partly, of course, this was due to the personalities involved. But the subsequent experience of intellectuals in politics suggests that wider problems were also to blame.

A generation later, another, broader group of thinkers also became involved in parliamentary politics. Some were the academics and former academics christened the 'Lights of Liberalism' by Christopher Harvie.[86] They formed an oddly assorted group, including historians like Goldwin Smith and lawyers like A.V. Dicey; Cambridge men like Lesley Stephen and Oxonians like James Bryce.[87] Others were the Comteian positivists and intellectual journalists studied by Christopher Kent: men like Frederic Harrison and John Morley.[88] Both groups were part of the agitation for franchise reform in the mid 1860s – and in the sense that the Reform Act was passed in 1867, they can be said to have been successful. None the less, their experience of politics after this was universally disastrous. The 1868 election was a catastrophe.[89] The Gladstone ministry was a bitter disappointment.[90] And slowly but surely the intellectuals were driven out of the Liberal Party and out of parliament itself.[91]

This should not have been the case. The British parliament should have been a more conducive arena for the intellectuals. After all, these were people who were paid for their rhetorical and analytical skills. In an age in which speech-making was central to political success, they ought to have been uniquely well-qualified as politicians.[92] Moreover, university graduates had their own seats in the house of commons. Throughout the 19th century, the Universities of Oxford and Cambridge each elected two MPs. From 1832 onwards, the University of Dublin also elected two. From 1868, the Scottish universities elected two

[83]Hamburger, *Intellectuals in Politics*, 291.

[84]Thomas, *Philosophic Radicals*, 3.

[85]*Edinburgh Review*, lxxi (1840), 282–3.

[86]Harvie, *Lights of Liberalism*.

[87]To take only the authors of *Essays in Reform* (1967). The other writers were G.C. Brodrick, R.H. Hutton, Lord Houghton, John Boyd Kinnear, Bernard Cracroft, C.H. Pearson, A.O. Rutson, and Sir George Young.

[88]Kent, *Brains and Numbers*; see also *Questions for a Reformed Parliament* (1867).

[89]Kent, *Brains and Numbers*, 48–52.

[90]Harvie, *Lights of Liberalism*, 197.

[91]Tom Dunne, 'La trahison des clercs: British Intellectuals and the First Home Rule Crisis', *Irish Historical Studies*, xxiii (1982), 134–73; Roach, 'Liberalism and the Victorian Intelligentsia', 58–81.

[92]H.C.G. Matthew, 'Rhetoric and Politics in Britain, 1860–1950', in *Politics and Social Change in Modern Britain: Essays Presented to A.F. Thompson*, ed. P.J. Waller (Brighton, 1987), 59–90.

more MPs between them and the University of London was granted a single member of its own. These seven MPs never amounted to a large block of members, but it did mean that the interests of the universities, their teachers, and their graduates were – in theory, at least – directly represented in parliament.[93] The presence in the upper chamber of figures like Lord Salisbury, who was a notably assiduous chancellor of Oxford, meant that in the house of lords, too, the universities were not without their champions. Indeed, 'defending Oxford was the only reason, other than war or forming a government, for which he [Salisbury] would cut short a holiday'.[94]

Even so, when it came to university business, the intellectuals proved to be ineffectual at Westminster. The story of university reform in the 19th century is one of confusion, missed opportunities, and bungled legislation as a result. The reforms of the ancient English universities in the 1850s satisfied no one.[95] The further reforms of the 1880s were similarly flawed.[96] Oxbridge dons proved to be better at thwarting change than at dictating the terms of reform. Just as they managed to see off legislation in the 18th century,[97] so they were able to exercise a veto over much further investigation well into the 20th century.[98] Scottish universities were also able to defer decisions for decades, not least because of the problems of finding parliamentary time for any contested bill.[99] In any event, the universities' MPs often had little contact with academic opinion and figures like Salisbury eventually gave up any attempt to represent the interests of Oxford on the floor of the house of the lords.[100]

What Salisbury found within his own university was a general problem in all universities. There simply was not a single academic interest to represent. Not only did the electorate include graduates as well as active members of the university, there were also numerous competing groups which formed and reformed around different issues. Some of the greatest politicians of the day learned the difficulty of discerning university opinion. Relying on faulty advice and partial knowledge, for instance, Robert Peel underwent the humiliation of defeat in the Oxford by-election of 1829.[101] The difficulty was not that the university seats were especially volatile. They were rarely contested. There was a convention that candidates did not campaign and 'controversies were either of the symbolic sort ... or progressively inward-looking'.[102] But they did not behave like normal constituencies. As F.M. Cornford observed of Edwardian Cambridge: 'the academic democracy is superior in

[93] See Joseph S. Miesel, *Knowledge and Power: The Parliamentary Representation of Universities in Britain and the Empire* (Parliamentary History, Texts & Studies, 4, 2011).

[94] Andrew Roberts, *Salisbury: Victorian Titan* (1999), 120.

[95] W.R. Ward, 'From the Tractarians to the Executive Commission, 1845–1854', in *The History of the University of Oxford. Vol. vi: The Nineteenth Century, part i*, ed. M.G. Brock and M.C. Curthoys (Oxford, 1997), 306–38.

[96] Christopher Harvie, 'From the Cleveland Commission to the Statues of 1882', in *The History of the University of Oxford. Vol. vii: The Nineteenth Century, part ii*, ed. M.G. Brock and M.C. Curthoys (Oxford, 2000), 67–96.

[97] Paul Langford, 'Tories and Jacobites, 1714–1751', in *The History of the University of Oxford. Vol. v: The Eighteenth Century*, ed. L.S. Sutherland and L.G. Mitchell (Oxford, 1986), 99–127.

[98] Janet Howarth, 'The Edwardian Reform Movement', in *University of Oxford. Vol. vii*, ed. Brock and Curthoys 821–54.

[99] R.D. Anderson, *Education and Opportunity in Nineteenth Century Scotland* (Edinburgh, 1983), 260–8.

[100] Janet Howarth, 'The Self-Governing University', in *University of Oxford. Vol. vii*, ed. Brock and Curthoys 599–644.

[101] Norman Gash, 'Peel and the Oxford University Election of 1829', *Oxoniensia*, iv (1939), 162–73.

[102] H.C.G. Matthew, *Gladstone, 1809–1898* (Oxford, 1997), 102.

having no organised parties. We thus avoid all the responsibilities of party leadership (there are leaders, but no one follows them), and the degradations of party compromise.'[103]

Moreover, what was true in the specific case of the university seats can also be seen in the world of the intellectuals more generally. They were always too divided to provide any sort of coherent movement or to work as any sort of convincing pressure group. In the 19th century, claims Michael Bentley, British intellectuals were only completely united on two occasions: for Gladstone in the debate over the 'Bulgarian atrocities' in 1876; and against Gladstone over home rule a decade later. In neither case, he goes on, were they effective.[104] Even this, however, overestimates their unity. There was always a minority of thinkers, for example, who spoke up for some form of Irish self-government – not least the 75 Oxford academics who signed a home rule manifesto in 1888.[105]

The problem was the product of a dual difficulty. First, the very nature of intellectual life was predicated against the formation of cohesive political parties. Not only were there those, like Matthew Arnold, who argued that the true intellectual was one who could 'keep out of the region of immediate practice in the political, social humanitarian sphere'.[106] The fact was that a calling which depended upon originality, individualism, and independence – and which was defended by its advocates as a properly manly, as well as gentlemanly, vocation precisely because of this – was always going to find it hard to produce machine politicians.[107] Second, and more importantly, the intellectuals themselves did not form a coherent ideological bloc. Harold Perkin famously described the intellectuals as 'the forgotten middle class … because they forgot themselves'.[108] Again, this is only partially true. As we have seen, Victorian thinkers were, in reality, acutely conscious of their separate culture and identity. But it is right to say that they did not conceive of themselves as just another class with its own class interest. Indeed, they rejected such an analysis completely. Arnold's notion of 'aliens' – 'persons who are mainly led, not by their class spirit, but by a general *humane* spirit'– thus gives a good sense of what they saw their role as being.[109] The intellectuals staked their claims to political influence on the grounds that they transcended class, religion, nationality, and occupation. It meant, in other words, that they represented no real constituency and possessed no real unity.

The failure of the intellectuals to cohere around class interests or ideological positions came into sharp focus in the mid-Victorian controversy over Governor Edward John Eyre. In 1865, Eyre was responsible for putting down a rebellion in Jamaica. His supporters maintained that he had rescued the white population from disaster and saved the British empire from acute humiliation. His opponents pointed to the horrific violence that this had involved and argued that he had acted illegally in imposing martial law and in executing hundreds of supposed rebels. The battle over Governor Eyre was the closest Britain came

---

[103] F.M. Cornford, *Microcosmographica Academica*, in *University Politics: F.M. Cornford's Cambridge and his Advice to a Young Academic Politician*, ed. Gordon Johnson (Cambridge, 1994), 100.

[104] Michael Bentley 'Party, Doctrine and Thought', in *High and Low Politics*, ed. Bentley and Stevenson, 123–53, 140.

[105] Harvie, *Lights of Liberalism*, 232.

[106] Arnold, 'Function of Criticism', 26.

[107] On this issue, see Norma Clarke, 'Strenuous Idleness: Thomas Carlyle and the Man of Letters as Hero', in *Manful Assertions: Masculinities in Britain since 1800*, ed. Michael Roper and John Tosh (1991), 25–43.

[108] Harold Perkin, *The Origins of Modern English Society* (1969), 257.

[109] Arnold, *Culture and Anarchy*, 75–82.

to its own Dreyfus affair. There were arguments about the nature of the state, debates about vested interests and about establishment corruption. There was even – just like Dreyfus – a tragic case of suicide.[110]

Throughout it all, as Catherine Hall has noted, intellectuals played 'a crucial part in defining the agenda for debate'.[111] Yet, despite their importance, they were critically divided. On one side, there were the members of the Jamaica committee, like John Stuart Mill, Charles Darwin, T.H. Huxley, Goldwin Smith, A.V. Dicey, and T.H. Green, who were Eyre's sworn enemies. On the other side, there were those like Charles Kingsley, Charles Dickens, Lord Tennyson, John Tyndall, and – especially – Thomas Carlyle, who eulogised Eyre and established the Eyre Defence Fund. There were also divisions within each of these opposing camps. The Jamaica committee split over tactics and was constantly wracked by internal dissention. The Eyre Defence Fund was ostensibly more cohesive, but no less full of competing egos. If this was, as Huxley wrote to Tyndall, 'one of the most important constitutional battles in which Englishmen have for many years been engaged', then it is all the more striking that the intellectuals were so torn by it.[112] That the result of all this angst was a royal commission which suggested that Eyre had acted illegally, and a series of court cases which concluded that he had not, only makes the matter more remarkable. For all the time spent on it, and all the words written about it, the Eyre case came to no clear conclusion. It thus reveals the problems, rather than the power, of the intellectuals.

Apparently incapable of overcoming their differences, Victorian thinkers failed to form anything like a unified pressure group. Their impact on parliament was consequently diffuse rather than decisive, and indeterminate rather than direct. Some contemporaries even imagined that it was almost entirely negligible. They assumed that the intellectual was constitutionally incapable of acting effectively as a politician. And, as Bagehot's dismissal of the '*too clever by half* people' makes plain, this criticism was even shared by the intellectuals themselves. 'The man of culture is in politics one of the poorest mortals alive', observed Frederic Harrison in 1867:

> For simple pedantry, and want of good sense, no man is his equal. Any quantity of ingenious arguments, based on wholly fictitious premises, he will give you. No assumption is too unreal, no end is too unpractical for him. But the active exercise of politics requires common sense, sympathy, trust, resolution, and enthusiasm, qualities which your man of culture has carefully rooted up, lest they damage the delicacy of his critical olfactories.[113]

He went too far, of course, and he did so to rhetorical effect: criticizing in one sweep Matthew Arnold, Robert Lowe, and all those who opposed widening the franchise. Yet the utter failure of his own political career suggests that his analysis was – ironically enough – not entirely wrong.[114]

---

[110]Bernard Semmel, *Jamaican Blood and Victorian Conscience: The Governor Eyre Controversy* (Westport, CT, 1962). For more recent studies of the rebellion, see Gad Heuman, *Killing Time: The Morant Bay Rebellion in Jamaica* (Knoxville, TN, 1994), and, esp., Catherine Hall, *Civilising Subjects: Metropole and Colony in the English Imagination, 1830–1867* (Cambridge, 2002), 406–24.

[111]Catherine Hall, *White Male, and Middle-Class: Explorations in Feminism and History* (Cambridge and Oxford, 1992), 256.

[112]*The Life and Letters of Thomas Henry Huxley*, ed. Leonard Huxley (2 vols, 1900), ii, 283.

[113]Frederic Harrison, *Order and Progress* (1875), 150.

[114]Kent, *Brains and Numbers*, ch. 9.

4. *The Intellectuals and the Public*

Does this mean, however, that the intellectuals were, in fact, unimportant players in British political life? Does it mean that they exercised no influence on parliamentary debates or political discourse? Does it ultimately mean that they provided no pressure on parliament whatsoever? The answer is clearly, no. Although the intellectuals were more effective at directly influencing the executive than the legislature, and although they proved strikingly ineffective in directly shaping party policy or primary legislation, this did not mean that they were unimportant. Indeed, they played a crucial role within the wider world of British politics. For it was the intellectuals who established the ground rules for political life; who defined and determined the structures and processes of parliamentary practice; and who – above all – legitimated British politics and the British constitution. The key influence they exercised on parliament itself was thus positive: defending the institution and helping to articulate both the ways that pressure was applied by other groups and the means by which parliament itself responded to the demands of an ever-increasing electorate.

The centrality of the constitution to political discourse in the 19th century is now well established. It was the constant reference point for the political elite.[115] It was also a key element in the debates of the politically marginalised.[116] Indeed, with understandable hyperbole, James Vernon has claimed that the constitution 'was central to the way people imagined themselves as both individuals and members of a sex, a class, a political movement as well as, perhaps most forcefully of all, a nation'.[117]

None the less, at least at the turn of the 19th century, the nature of the constitution was highly debatable. As George Dyer put it in 1812: 'We have at present three predominant parties in the country … yet they all talk of rallying round the Constitution like different religious sects, who all appeal to the same code.'[118] In the first few decades of the century, indeed, politics hinged on these variant versions of the British constitution; there was no consensus over what it meant or how it worked.[119] For radicals, it was even possible to imagine that parliament itself was the problem; that reform would require an anti-parliament – a grand convention which would sweep away oligarchy and abolish the restricted assembly at Westminster.[120]

By the middle of the 19th century, however, such an idea was anathema even to the most advanced political thinkers within Britain. As Peter Mandler puts it, far from being supplanted or replaced, parliament 'became instead the national cynosure, the centre of a

---

[115]Jonathan Parry, *The Politics of Patriotism: English Liberalism, National Identity, and Europe, 1830–19886* (Cambridge, 2006), ch. 1.

[116]James Vernon, *Politics and the People: A Study in English Political Culture, c. 1815–1867* (Cambridge, 1993), ch. 8.

[117]James Vernon, 'Notes Towards an Introduction', in James Vernon, *Re-reading the Constitution: New Narratives in the Political History of England's Long Nineteenth Century* (Cambridge, 1996), 1–21, 2.

[118]Quoted in Robert Saunders, 'Parliament and People: The British Constitution in the Long Nineteenth Century', *Journal of Modern European History*, vi (2008), 75.

[119]Boyd Hilton, 'The Politics of Anatomy and an Anatomy of Politics, c. 1825–1850', in *History, Religion, and Culture: British Intellectual History, 1750–1950*, ed. Stefan Collini, Richard Whatmore and Brian Young (Cambridge, 2000), 179–97.

[120]T.M. Parssinen, 'Association, Convention, and Anti-Parliament in British Radical Politics, 1771–1848', *English Historical Review*, lxxxviii (1973), 504–33.

whirlpool of demands and pressures from without'.[121] The nature and function of the constitution had also become more firmly fixed, with a general agreement emerging between governed and governing that the sovereignty of parliament and the constitutional monarchy were the guarantors of Britain's greatness. It was an attitude satirised in Dickens's comic character, Mr Podsnap, the man who believed that the constitution had been bestowed by providence and that England was thus uniquely blessed.[122] Podsnap was a caricature – but he was funny because he was true.

In part, this constitutional consensus rested on not much more than economic growth. Social, economic, and political stability went hand in hand.[123] But there was also an ideology underpinning all this – an ideology made and shaped by Britain's intellectuals. They had a vested interest in defending the parliamentary system. Not only were they closely connected through ties of friendship and fellow feeling to the governing elite, they also had a personal – emotional, indeed, vocational – interest in defending a system based upon free expression and government by debate. Whatever his scepticism about Bohemian intellectuals, in 1872 Walter Bagehot celebrated the British political system as one that 'gives the premium to intelligence' because it was based on discussion. 'Nothing promotes intellect like discussion', he went on; 'and nothing promotes intellectual discussion as much as government by discussion.'[124]

This belief explains why even the most advanced intellectuals tended to defend this aspect of parliamentary practice, although they sought to reform the institution as a whole. Jeremy Bentham, for one, never wholly lost the conviction that:

> the rules that suggested themselves as necessary to every assembly turned out to be the very rules actually observed in both assemblies of the British Legislature. What theory would have pitched upon as a model of perfection, practice presented as having been successfully pursued: never was the accord more perfect between reason and experience.[125]

Such was his admiration, he even recommended that the French Estates General of 1789 should adopt the rules and debating practices of Westminster.[126] Likewise, despite John Stuart Mill's commitment to radicalism, his defence of free speech has rightly been seen as a highly elitist one. His emphasis on cultivated intelligence and dispassionate debate excluded the ill-educated and linguistically less-assured from public discourse.[127] His defence

[121] Peter Mandler, *Aristocratic Government in the Age of Reform: Whigs and Liberals, 1830–1852* (Oxford, 1990) 2.

[122] Charles Dickens, *Our Mutual Friend* (2 vols, 1880), i, 163–5.

[123] *An Age of Equipoise? Reassessing Mid-Victorian Britain*, ed. Martin Hewitt (Aldershot, 2000).

[124] Walter Bagehot, *Physics and Politics: Or Thoughts on the Application of the Principles of 'Natural Selection' and 'Inheritance' to Political Society* (1872), 162, 199.

[125] Jeremy Bentham, *Political Tactics*, ed. Michael James, Cyprian Blamires and Catherine Peace-Watkin (Oxford 1999), 1.

[126] Christopher Reid, *Imprisn'd Wranglers: The Rhetorical Culture of the House of Commons 1760–1900* (Oxford 2012), 34.

[127] John Michael Roberts, 'John Stuart Mill, Free Speech, and the Public Sphere: A Bakhtinian Critique', in *After Habermas: New Perspectives on the Public Sphere*, ed. Nick Crossley and John Michael Roberts (Oxford, 2004) 67–87.

of liberty was seen even by his contemporaries as 'one of the most aristocratic books ever written'.[128] And one of his chief contributions to the debates about parliamentary reform was his assertion that in any future extension of the franchise 'a member of every intellectual profession' should be granted as many as five or six votes.[129]

This belief in parliamentary government and in the intrinsic virtue of the constitution shaped intellectual work in Victorian Britain. Lawyers and historians devoted themselves to a justification of the British way of political life.[130] They defended and defined a constitution which they believed to be the guarantor of their own role within public life; a constitution which ensured that the voice of the mob was drowned out by the writings of the educated elite. 'Our country', rejoiced the historian E.S. Creasy, in his *Rise and Progress of the English Constitution*, was a place where thinkers were given their due. It was 'the peculiar domicile of mental authority'.[131] Nor was it just academics and writers who defended this political settlement. Across the country, artists and architects embodied the constitution in their work: from the houses of parliament to the smallest town hall, the whig interpretation of history – a vision of the national past that celebrated the constitution in the national present – was evoked in murals, sculptures, and the buildings themselves.[132]

Of course, the constitution remained open to reform. Even its admirers admitted that it was 'a somewhat rambling structure … convenient rather than symmetrical'.[133] Hence Carlyle's contempt for parliament as 'a poor self-cancelling "National Palaver"', for example.[134] Moreover, as the franchise was widened, as politics became more democratic and demotic, many intellectuals expressed their doubts in tones that grew ever more shrill.[135] But even at the end of our period, the constitution remained the touchstone for intellectual debate and the loadstone of the intellectuals' political world.[136]

The consequences of this relentless focus on parliament – on parliamentary practice and on the place of parliament within the constitution – were threefold. In the first place, the dominant notion of politics as a rational process shaped by informed debate helped to determine how the intellectuals engaged with the public sphere. They were encouraged to present themselves not as bold and provocative speculative thinkers, dealing with lofty philosophical concepts, but as practical, sensible, down-to-earth experts. When Bagehot, for instance, praised the 'sound stupidity' of the English, he was not just contrasting the empiricism and stability of his native land with the revolutionary anfractuosities of France, he was also, implicitly, defining himself against dangerous French thinkers. The same was true of even such an archetypal intellectual as John Stuart Mill, who likewise regretted 'as much

---

[128] [John Morley], 'Mr Mill's Doctrine of Liberty', *Fortnightly Review*, xx (1873), repr. in *Liberty: Contemporary Responses to John Stuart Mill*, ed. Andrew Pyle (Bristol, 1994), 285.

[129] John Stuart Mill, *Thoughts on Parliamentary Reform* (1859), 26.

[130] J.W. Burrow, *A Liberal Descent: Victorian Historians and the English Past* (Cambridge, 1981).

[131] E.S. Creasy, *The Rise and Progress of the English Constitution* (9th edn, 1867), 391.

[132] William Whyte, 'Building the Nation in the Town: Architecture and National Identity in Urban Britain, 1848–1914', in *Nationalism and the Reshaping of Urban Communities in Europe, 1848–1914*, ed. William Whyte and Oliver Zimmer (Basingstoke, 2012), 204–33.

[133] Sir William Anson, *The Law and Custom of the Constitution* (4th edn, 2 vols, Oxford, 1911), i, 1.

[134] Carlyle to C.G. Duffy, 29 Aug, 1846, available at *http://carlyleletters.dukejournals.org/cgi/content/long/21/1/lt-18460829-TC-CGD-01* (accessed 7 Jan. 2015).

[135] See Harvie, *Lights of Liberalism*, and Kent, *Brains and Numbers*.

[136] See, e.g., Dicey, *A Fool's Paradise*, for the old arguments in a new context.

as it is possible to do, the habit which still prevails in France, of founding political philosophy on … abstractions'.[137] What Noel Annan termed 'the curious strength of Positivism in English political thought' may owe something to this suspicion of abstract concepts in politics.[138] Certainly, this attitude underpinned modes of self-fashioning that would prove surprisingly long-lasting, helping to shape the British intelligentsia – and their rejection of terms like intelligentsia – for generations. 'I shouldn't like anyone to call me an intellectual: I don't think any Englishman would!', observed George Bernard Shaw in *Fanny's First Play* (1911).[139] In this he spoke for many thinkers who wished to distance themselves from an idea that was thought somehow intrinsically unpatriotic.

In the second place, and still more importantly, by legitimating the constitution in general, and parliamentary practice in particular, the intellectuals provided a template for political activity at all levels of society. Continental revolutionaries complained that the British were incapable of organising a revolution. Instead, they organised committees. 'Even the most serious persons are sometimes over-come by the fascination of mere forms and manage to convince themselves that they are in fact doing something if they hold meetings with a mass of documents', wrote Alexander Herzen. 'England teems with hundreds of associations of this kind: solemn meetings take place which dukes and peers of the realm, clergymen and secretaries attend: treasurers collect funds, journalists write articles, all are busily engaged in doing nothing at all.'[140] Little wonder; this was precisely how one might move a parliament which you had been taught was amenable to rational argument and the pressures of 'wise, thoughtful, and consistent' public opinion.[141]

At a more popular level, the impact was just as great. As Ross McKibbin has shown, amongst the working classes, 'Crown and … parliament possessed an ideological hegemony which, if anything, increased throughout the [19th] century.' Parliamentary procedure was widely imitated and parliamentary practice shaped innumerable debating societies up and down the land. It proved as significant to the 'St Pancras Parliament', where the young Ramsey MacDonald learnt his politics, as it was to the house of commons itself.[142] 'We were extravagantly delighted at the chance of calling each other the honourable or right honourable member', recalled the poet Edwin Muir of his time in the 'Faldside Parliament' and, although he later came to see the experience as a rather sterile one, it is clear that the imitation of parliament had consequences for many others.[143] 'It was here', observes John W. Davis, of the South Lambeth parliament, that working-class men and women 'were able to develop their intellect, their powers of argument and oratory', as well as serving a sort of political apprenticeship.[144] In that way the intellectuals' account of the constitution not only shaped the content but the form of extra-parliamentary pressure.

[137]Quoted in Robert Saunders, *Democracy and the Vote in British Politics, 1848–1867: The Making of the Second Reform Act* (Aldershot, 2011), 136. I am most grateful to Robert Saunders for helping me to elucidate this point

[138]Noel Annan, *The Curious Strength of Positivism in English Political Thought* (1959).

[139]G.B. Shaw, *The Shewing-Up of Blanco Posnet and Fanny's First Play*, ed. Dan H. Laurence (1987), 117–18.

[140]Quoted in Melvin Richter, *The Politics of Conscience: T.H. Green and his Age* (Cambridge, MA, 1964), 299.

[141]Frederic Harrison, *The Meaning of History* (1862), 22.

[142]Ross McKibbin, 'Why was there no Marxism in Great Britain?', in Ross McKibbin, *The Ideologies of Class: Social Relations in Britain 1880–1950* (Oxford, 1990), 17, 22–3.

[143]Edwin Muir, *An Autobiography* (Edinburgh, 2000), 133.

[144]John W. Davis, 'Working-Class Make Believe: The South Lambeth Parliament (1887–1890)', *Parliamentary History*, xii (1993), 258.

Third, the intellectuals' description of parliamentary practice shaped how the institution operated itself. At a basic level, parliamentarians found themselves bound by the rules and conventions that the intellectuals drew up. Self-evidently, these included such fundamental works as Erskine May's *Parliamentary Practice* (1844), a text that came to standardise Commons' procedure. But they also encompassed more contentious volumes like Bagehot's *English Constitution* (1867). The unwritten constitution was similarly shaped by the opinions of lawyers and historians – for as they pointed out, within this system, custom was just as significant as statute law.[145] More importantly still, when considering the impact of the intellectuals on parliament, it is clear that they helped establish the tone of parliamentary debate and the style of parliamentary practice. It was Bagehot who praised the 'general intellectual tone' of MPs' discussions;[146] Erskine May who claimed that 'One of the proud results of our free constitution has been the development of parliamentary oratory.'[147] This general presumption that political speeches would be 'long, serious, detailed, well-informed' was shaped by the ideas developed by the intellectuals.[148]

'The first principles of government are no longer in dispute', wrote Erskine May; 'the liberties of the people are safe: the oppression of the law is unknown. Accordingly the councils of the state encourage elevated reason, rather than impassioned oratory.'[149] This was a prescription as much as a description – a self-fulfilling prophecy. Inside, as well as outside, parliament the intellectuals thus helped shape the contours of debate.

5. *Conclusion*

Seeking to trace the influence of intellectuals on politics, one might look at the executive or the legislature, at legislation or at discourse. In each field, the evidence suggests a different conclusion. Personal connections and the policy-making vacuum of the Victorian state led thinkers to be prized by the government. True enough, they were not always directly influential and sometimes failed to convey their ideas. Many, like Bentham himself, proved to be politically naïve, acting 'as if men in power only wanted to know what was right that they might do it'.[150] But others proved to be more assured operators, shaping policy through their advice and their place on royal commissions or in the public eye. Expertise even opened the corridors of power to women, with the popular political economist, Harriet Martineau, and the poet, Amelia Opie, both called in to give guidance about specific issues.[151]

Within parliament, by contrast, the intellectuals had less influence and far less immediate impact. 'A strongly idiosyncratic mind, violently disposed to extremes of opinion is soon hounded out of political life', wrote Bagehot, 'and a bodiless thinker, an ineffectual scholar, cannot even live there for a day.'[152] Many intellectuals, who were ill-disposed to party

---

[145] F.W. Maitland, *The Constitutional History of England* (Cambridge, 1908), 341–2.

[146] Bagehot, *Physics and Politics*, ii, 194.

[147] Thomas Erskine May, *The Constitutional History of England* (2 vols, 1861), i, 480.

[148] Matthew, 'Rhetoric and Politics in Britain', 39.

[149] Erskine May, *Constitutional History*, 491.

[150] John Hill Burton, *Benthamia* (Philadelphia, PA, 1844), xix.

[151] Kathryn Gleadle, *Borderline Citizens: Women, Gender, and Political Culture in Britain, 1815–1867* (Oxford, 2009), 50–1.

[152] Bagehot, *Physics and Politics*, 203.

discipline and ill-equipped for the plotting and planning of practical politics found this to be true. Again, in part, this was a product of individual predilections. It was also, however, a predictable result of the ideology of the intellectuals. Rewarded for their idiosyncrasies as writers and teachers, they found it hard to adapt to life as legislators. Committed to the idea of disinterested decision making and highly resistant to the notion of class politics, they found it difficult to respond to the changing circumstances of the political world.

Nevertheless, at a discursive level the intellectuals did have a major part to play in shaping pressure on parliament. In this 'country and epoch of parliaments and eloquent palavers', the intellectuals were crucial intermediaries for MPs and those they claimed to represent.[153] They interpreted the workings of parliament and legitimated them, helping to establish the increasingly hegemonic interpretation of the constitution that emerged after the 1840s. They also disseminated knowledge about parliament, shaping practice within Westminster and among those who sought to influence it – and even informing those who wanted to reform the system altogether. They likewise provided guides for other intellectuals seeking to participate in the political process.

In 1896, W.H. Lecky reflected on impact of ideas on the workings of Westminster, and rather conventionally concluded: 'in England, speculative opinion has not usually much weight in practical politics, and English politicians are apt to treat it with complete disdain'. But he went on to defend the importance of thinkers despite this: 'no one who has any real knowledge of history can seriously doubt the influence over human affairs which has been exercised by the speculations of Locke, of Rousseau, of Montesquieu, of Adam Smith, or of Bentham'.[154] Nearly a decade later, A.V. Dicey made a similar point, stressing the significance of the 'known leaders of public opinion' such as Mill, Martineau, and Dickens, and especially emphasizing the importance of the Benthamites in moulding legislation.[155]

Both Lecky and Dicey were writing with an agenda in mind, of course; and neither was entirely clear about the means by which ideas influenced political decisions. Yet each was right to stress the difference between the direct and indirect impact of intellectuals on parliament – and right, too, to see the intellectuals as an important indirect influence on British politics. Not because any one doctrine or policy became dominant, much less because Benthamite principles can serve as an all-purpose explanation for government action. But because the intellectuals helped create the conditions in which political debate was undertaken and political decisions could be made. In other words, they provided the context – the language, the rhetoric, the rules, the discourse – with which pressure on parliament could be articulated by other groups.

[153] Thomas Carlyle, *The Life of John Sterling* (2nd edn, 1852), 41.

[154] W.H. Lecky, *Democracy and Liberty* (2 vols, 1896), i, 185.

[155] Dicey, *Lectures on the Relation between Law and Public Opinion*, 414.

Index